The Pottery Cottage Murders

The Pottery Cottage Murders:

The terrifying untold true story of an escaped prisoner and the family he held hostage in Derbyshire

Carol Ann Lee and Peter Howse

ROBINSON

ROBINSON

First published in Great Britain in 2020 by Robinson

1 3 5 7 9 10 8 6 4 2

A CIP catalogue record for this book
is available from the British Library.

ISBN: 978-1-47214-393-8

Typeset in Adobe Garamond Pro by Hewer Text UK Ltd, Edinburgh
Printed and bound in Great Britain by Clays Ltd, Elcograf S.p.A.

Papers used by Robinson are from well-managed forests and other responsible sources.

Robinson
An imprint of
Little, Brown Book Group
Carmelite House
50 Victoria Embankment
London EC4Y 0DZ

An Hachette UK Company
www.hachette.co.uk

www.littlebrown.co.uk

'It is a universal assumption, shared by custodians and their charges, that the condition of captivity necessarily gives rise to attempts to escape from it.'

G. R. Twiselton, Director of Psychological Services,

Home Office Research Study No. 41, 1977

Contents

Part Three: Day 2, Thursday 13 January, 1977

Part Four: Day 3, Friday 14 January, 1977

Part Five: Aftermath

Foreword

WHY WRITE A book about a case that happened more than
forty years ago?

I have been approached a number of times to do so, or to assist
in writing a screenplay based on the case, but I always declined for
two reasons: when I was a serving police officer it would not have
been appropriate and, more importantly, I was sensitive to the
feelings of Gill Moran, the sole survivor of events, who had undergone an unimaginable ordeal. However, I was given leave by the
Chief Constable to use the material available on the case as I saw
fit for lecturing at the Police College, Bramshill, and to law agencies and universities in Illinois, Chicago, and much later,
Michigan, where the case had been widely reported and there was
a lot of interest in hostage situations.

Two years ago, I was approached by writer Carol Ann Lee, who
has an excellent reputation for writing deeply researched books
on true events. She had always been interested in the case and
could not understand why no one had written a book about it.

There was so much coverage about it at the time – 1977 – and more recently, on the fortieth anniversary, it had again featured in the press. But many of those reports, both historical and more recent, were painfully inaccurate.

The events covered within these pages document the first time in the history of the Derbyshire Police that any member of our constabulary had shot anyone. It was also the first time an escaped prisoner had been shot dead by the police in the UK. My co-author and I decided to examine the case from the very beginning and have spent the last two years intensely researching all the available material and speaking to those who were involved. This is their story.

It is also the story of what can happen when a dangerous prisoner escapes from custody. Billy Hughes had been in and out of prison all his life. The purposes of prison are manifold but one of those is to protect the public from those who would do them harm. For that to work, however, it requires cooperation from all the criminal justice agencies and in this particular case there were obvious failings. The antecedents of Billy Hughes alone should have marked him out as a criminal who required close observation, giving him not the slightest of chances to arm himself either within or without prison.

His record showed that he had displayed disturbing psychological traits throughout his career. But statistics don't tell the whole story. For that, we have to consult those people who had no choice but to face him whenever he went 'off the rails'. His violent tendencies were mainly directed at strangers or authoritarian figures and almost always when he had been under the influence of either drink or drugs – or both. He often acted on uncontrollable impulses. There were times, as we shall see, when Hughes was not under the influence of drugs or drink and was instead capable of acting normally. But he was a very convincing liar, too. He certainly displayed the key psychopathic trait of never accepting responsibility for his actions. He was adept at inventing stories and excuses for his actions, usually placing the blame on his victims. The incident prior to Pottery Cottage was a good example of this: it was his word against that of his two victims. The striking of a young man with a brick was self-defence; the rape of a young woman on a riverbank was consensual sex. He was helped by his counsel and the ineptitude of Chesterfield magistrates, who failed to process the case for trial at a higher court.

The press referred to him as 'Mad Billy' and in a clinical sense he had all the traits to classify him as a psychopath. He certainly had no moral conscience. Most people who experience extreme anger hold back from harming someone because the part of their brain that determines moral consciousness tells them it would be wrong to do so. But it is evident from his actions, particularly at Pottery Cottage, that Billy Hughes's brain did not work that way. No one will ever know why he did what he did to the Morans and Mintons. The awful thing is that the killings were totally unnecessary for his purpose of remaining at liberty.

It would be some years later, after the inquiries into the Bradford fire and the Hillsborough Disaster, that Lord Chief Justice Taylor concluded: 'Complacency is the enemy of safety.' If ever there was a previous case where the same conclusion could have been reached, it was this one.

There was every reason to follow the advice on Form number 293, sent to the prison authorities by Derbyshire Police in respect of Billy Hughes:

He was an exceptional risk;

He was liable to escape;

He was violent;

He might try to take his own life.

Under those circumstances, a psychiatrist's declaration that he was extremely dangerous is superfluous; it was a basic matter of fact.

The purpose of the criminal justice system is to bring offenders to justice and punish them for their proven misdemeanours. Most importantly, it is for the safety of the public and in this case the system failed. Yet after the murders at Pottery Cottage, no one was questioned at government level and no one was held to account at the Home Office, which controls staffing levels of both the prison and the police services. Alarmingly, it seems that nothing has been learned by those in power over the years that have passed since the events of 1977. Excessive cuts by today's government in the staffing levels of prisons and within the police service have resulted in another Billy Hughes scenario remaining a strong possibility.

Rudyard Kipling recognised the value in asking such questions, referring to 'six honest serving-men', who taught him all he knew; their names were 'What and Why and When / And How and Where and Who'.

These remain the principal questions we should ask in any investigation.

I hope our book goes a long way to answering all of them.

Peter Howse
York, May 2019

Prologue: Caveat Emptor

M OST PEOPLE NO longer give the house a second glance.
They simply pass by on their way to the beauty spots of
the Peak District National Park or to the towns and cities at either
end of the main road where it stands on the tourist trail to nearby
Chatsworth. Owned by the same family for over thirty years,
Northend Farm has been sympathetically modernised to make
the most of its panoramic views across bracken-clad Beeley Moor
towards Hell Bank Plantation.

'A delightful farmhouse conversion surrounded by glorious
open countryside,' read the carefully worded advertisement when
it was offered for sale in the summer of 1977. Estate agents Henry
Spencer & Sons pointed out that its location was well served by
road and rail, close to local amenities: Chesterfield was only six
miles away, Bakewell seven, yet it remained charmingly rural.
Recent history apart, the house benefited from being skilfully
divided to provide secondary accommodation for a young adult
or dependent elder relative, and boasted a double garage, large

gardens and French windows on to a patio overlooking wide pastures where sheep cropped the grass.

But the house, locked up and empty, had a forlorn air. The iron fretwork sign had been deliberately removed, allowing the building to be sold under its original name of Northend Farm. Tall weeds pushed through the gravel in the driveway and the stone flags of the patio, while the unmown lawn was a mass of dandelions. Peering through the windows it was possible to see that furniture had been drawn into a puzzling clutter. Heaters, a large yellow armchair, pots, pans, a jug and cardboard boxes stacked high with records and books awaited removal by the owner. She would not be showing potential buyers around, leaving that responsibility to the estate agents who, despite billing themselves proudly as 'Henry Spencer & Sons, HSS 1840, Auctioneers, Valuers, Land and Estate Agents, Fine Art Auctioneers, of 48 Knifesmithgate, Chesterfield', never advertised the house in their otherwise extensive section of newspaper property pages. 'We wish to keep this entire transaction at a very low key,' said a spokesman for the company.[1]

Nonetheless, the sale attracted nationwide attention. Editorials mused over the ethics and implications of buying such a house, while another estate agent vocalised the opinion of many: 'That type of property would find a ready market, but for its unfortunate history. Because of the events that have taken place there, I would have thought a lot of people would *not* be interested in purchasing it. But I suppose there are certain people who might even like the notoriety.'[2]

It did sell, a few months later, to a couple and their two young daughters, who insisted that they were not troubled by its past Their view was distinctly at odds with one of the country's most well-known journalists, Lynda Lee-Potter, who, shortly before her death in 2004, described her visit to the house twenty-seven years earlier: 'I've absolutely no doubt that wickedness leaves its mark on bricks and mortar and seeps into the woodwork. The first time I walked into the cottage I felt terrified. It was empty and clean, but there was a tangible, all-pervasive feeling of malevolence and evil. I was in the area for a week, staying in a hotel, but slept every night with the lights on.'[3]

Lynda Lee-Potter did not disclose her reason for visiting the house, but she had spent that week in the company of its then owner Gill Moran, a woman in her thirties. She was there to document Gill's story as the sole survivor of events that took place at Northend Farm in January 1977, when the house was known by the slanting name on that demolished ironwork sign: Pottery Cottage.

Part One:

Antecedents

Chapter One:

Persistent Absconder

I**N LATE JANUARY** 1854, Charles Dickens arrived in the Lancashire town of Preston. Seeking a northern setting for his tenth novel, his visit coincided with a months-long strike by thousands of Preston cotton workers. Dickens knew at once that he had found the right place, a town of 'red brick, or brick that would have been red if the smoke and ashes had allowed it; but, as matters stood, it was a town of unnatural red and black like the painted face of a savage. It was a town of machinery and tall chimneys, out of which interminable serpents of smoke trailed themselves for ever and ever and never got uncoiled. It had a black canal in it and a river that ran purple with ill-smelling dye, and vast piles of buildings full of windows where there was a rattling and a trembling all day long, and where the piston of the steamengine worked monotonously up and down, like the head of an elephant in a state of melancholy madness.'[1]

Before the industrial revolution, Preston had been a genteel market town popular with polite society. Gas lighting was installed in 1816, making it the first town outside London to embrace the new apparatus, and inventions such as Richard Arkwright's water frame, created in Preston, transformed cotton mills across the north. In 1838, the North Union Railway extended into the town, connecting it to major cities, and soon the docks were teeming, a shipbreaking yard was in noisy operation, and all the while a permanent pall of smoke hung across the rooftops, testament to the remarkable productivity of its mills and factories.

But with prosperity came oppression, and in 1842 cotton workers staged a mass demonstration outside the Corn Exchange, protesting against poor pay and working conditions; four were shot dead by troops brought in by mill owners and magistrates. Visiting the town afterwards, Karl Marx declared his revulsion of the men in charge ('these little Napoleons of Lancashire'), predicting that workers would one day declare Preston 'our St Petersburg'.[2] Instead, it became the ubiquitous 'Coketown' in *Hard Times*, and inspired scenes in *North and South*, a novel about love and class war by Dickens's contemporary, Elizabeth Gaskell.

The Hughes family might have stepped directly from the pages of either book. Billy Hughes's nineteenth-century forebears worked as weavers in Preston's cotton mills while subsequent generations lived in the same terraced house on North Road. Staunch Roman Catholics, they worshipped at nearby St Ignatius Church, newly built and the first church in Preston to bear a spire. They were ambitious, too, with family-run enterprises established before the turn of the new century: successive Hughes women ran a herbalist shop while sons were apprenticed to fathers in a decorating business that carried out both residential and commercial work.

Billy's father, Thomas Edward Hughes, was born in May 1924 at 29 Pump Street on the north-east fringes of town. After the

Great War, Preston experienced more seismic change brought about by advances in engineering and manufacturing, with thousands of council houses built as part of Liberal Prime Minister Lloyd George's promise of 'homes fit for heroes'. The Hugheses lived in an older property; Pump Street was another narrow red-brick terrace among the rabbit warren of its kind. The Royal Infirmary stood to the north, vast, proud and efficient, while to the south lay the grey bulk of His Majesty's Prison, rebuilt and extended during Queen Victoria's reign. Dominating the entire district was the 'Yellow Factory', as Horrocks's sprawling cotton mill was colloquially known, where Thomas worked as a bobbin weaver after leaving school. His elder brother William followed their father into the decorating trade, while their mother worked as a charlady following the closure of the herbalist shop.

War broke out in 1939, when Thomas was fifteen. He joined the army at the first opportunity and served throughout the conflict. Demobbed, he returned to Preston, working alongside his father and brother as an apprentice painter. He met Dundee-born Mary (May) Middleton Coventry, two years his junior, who was employed as a jute spreader in a textile factory. They married on 18 May 1946 at St Ignatius Church, with both bride and groom's fathers as witnesses. May was then six months pregnant and living with Thomas at 29 Pump Street, where she gave birth on 8 August 1946.

The baby was baptised William Thomas Hughes, 'our Billy'.

Five siblings were born in quick succession: Barbara in 1948, Alan in 1950, David in 1951, Malcolm in 1952 and Brian in 1954. Money was scarce, with May working between pregnancies as a Woolworths cashier until Thomas rejoined the army. Life in the services meant higher wages, allowances and a comfortable home for the family – first in Germany, where Thomas was posted for three years, then in Shoeburyness, a garrison town on the Essex coast. One year later, Corporal Thomas Hughes was dispatched to Hong Kong. He went ahead while his wife arranged to travel with their daughter and sons.

May and the children left Southampton aboard the SS *Nevasa* on 28 January 1958. For the six Hughes siblings – Billy the eldest at eleven and Brian the youngest aged three – it was an adventure like no other. The voyage lasted an entire month, travelling over 11,000 miles through the Mediterranean and Middle East on a troop ship built to accommodate 500 British servicemen and their families. Children were schooled by Army Education Officers and ate well from their own menu, sleeping in bunks that swayed in rough seas and eyeing shark safety nets at port. In March, the Hughes children stood at the rail as the ship sailed into Hong Kong's amazing natural harbour, above which squatter huts clustered on the steep hillside where tigers were still said to roam.

Thomas's rank provided his family with a beautiful home in Hong Kong: a large bungalow in its own grounds where the children could play, attended by a live-in Chinese servant. Facing trial years later, Billy told a psychiatrist tasked with assessing his mental health that as a child he had enjoyed a loving relationship with his strict but caring father and warm-hearted mother. The Hugheses witnessed little of the famine sweeping down from China that year as Chairman Mao attempted to match American levels of development; they departed less than six months after their arrival for undisclosed reasons. Conflicting reports claim this was either due to Thomas's ill health or because he crashed an army vehicle while drunk. As a result, on 31 July 1958, May and the children boarded the SS *Oxfordshire* bound for Southampton. They settled in Blackpool for eighteen months where Thomas worked as a decorator and Billy briefly attended Secondary Modern, before returning permanently to Preston.

The town was not as they remembered it. Under the banner of 'slum clearance', urban planners had begun redeveloping English cities, flattening terraced streets and grand civic buildings in favour of housing estates, office blocks and flyovers. Preston gained a Ringway for easy access to Britain's first motorway; an enormous concrete bunker in brutalist design that served as a bus station; and the local takeaway dish of parched peas lost its attraction when the country's first Kentucky Fried Chicken opened in town. Preston's cotton mills were becoming defunct, replaced by modern production lines in factories that attracted many Asian and Caribbean Commonwealth immigrants who made their homes in the area.

Billy's birthplace on Pump Street had been razed to the ground during the regeneration process. The Hugheses rented a similar Victorian terraced house on Gerrard Street, close to the railway line and docks. Billy was then twelve years old, a small, slight boy with fair hair and deep-set blue eyes. He had no interest in academic subjects and received consistently poor marks across the board at school. Remonstrations from his teachers only had the effect of making him defiant and hostile, while being teased by his schoolmates about his height enraged him. He retaliated with his fists, often instigating fights in order to prove himself, and gained a reputation as someone who was almost pathologically incapable of backing down. Tony Williams, a schoolmate of Billy's at Fulwood County Secondary School, offers an example: 'When we were boys picking blackberries in a field near Blackpool we were charged by a wild horse. Billy picked up a plank of wood and beat it away. That's the kind of lad he was.'[3]

Matters were different at home, where Billy's parents left him in charge of the younger children while they worked long hours to provide the food that he would prepare before and after school. His frustration at being given that responsibility manifested itself in antisocial behaviour and petty crime. Tony Williams's brother Joe confirms: 'Billy was the eldest boy in a family of six kids living near my home. Even in those days he was always in trouble for stealing from shops.'[4]

On 15 February 1961, Billy entered the British legal system when he was brought before Preston Borough Juvenile Court on two charges of stealing from motorcycles. He was given a conditional discharge and ordered to pay 7/6d costs.[5] Three months later, he stood in the same court charged with shop-breaking and stealing, for which he received two years' probation. His criminal career had thus begun, emerging as a textbook example of one young man's trajectory from petty theft to murder. Coupled with a failure on the part of the authorities to intervene effectively, the consequences would prove devastating.

After leaving school at fifteen, Billy became an apprentice fitter in a factory, but was swiftly dismissed for failing to attend a Day Release Course. In an effort to stave off further trouble, his father took him on as a trainee decorator but that lasted only a week. A third job as a metal polisher came to an end when Billy was caught stealing from his employer. He received a £1 fine at Preston Juvenile Court on 23 August 1961, for an unrelated theft of a purse and its contents.

Despite finding work as a British Rail apprentice, Billy's criminal activities escalated one night before Christmas 1961. Together with a twelve-year-old friend, he broke into Bare Dry Cleaners in Fulwood, stealing Electricity Board stamps and Christmas stockings. Later that evening he committed another burglary with a younger acquaintance but was caught by police as he bolted from the hairdressing salon with cash and small display items on his person. Billy managed to give officers the slip and set off in a rage towards Dock Street sidings where he worked. He broke in a third time, finding a length of iron which he used to smash seventeen train windows. He was apprehended by British Railway Police, who asked him why he had vandalised the carriages. 'The other police had just caught me and I was mad,' he replied.[6]

Billy appeared before Preston Juvenile Panel on 28 December 1961, charged with housebreaking, theft of articles and money, and committing malicious damage amounting to £31 2s 1d. Convicted on all counts and fined £2 for breach of an earlier probation order, he was put on probation for two years, half of which was to be served in a probation hostel. The *Lancashire Evening Post* covered the case, but to the relief of his parents, Billy was too young to be publicly named. His friend Joe recalls that Billy's mother was so distressed at the shame he had brought upon their good name in Preston that she 'disowned him completely. After that he used to go out with us lads into Blackpool to do "screwing" jobs.'[7]

May Hughes was not the only one to have lost patience with Billy. When he was brought before Preston Borough Juvenile Court on 3 January 1962, charged with three counts of pickpocketing, magistrates committed him to a Home Office approved school. It was a normal recourse for children aged ten to seventeen who had been found guilty of crimes that were punishable by custodial sentences for adults. Around 120 approved schools existed in England and Wales at the time, sanctioned by the

Home Secretary, but run by private voluntary organisations instead of the state or local authorities. Following assessment, children were sent to the school most suited to their needs and religious orientation. The fundamental aim was that of social re-education through 'discipline, character training, sympathy and understanding' and primarily, 'an attempt to make the child confident of his own ability'.[8]

Billy's impoverished background was typical of most children brought before the courts, whose offences tended to reflect their difficult circumstances. Magistrates also viewed neglect, bad parenting, the absence of male role models for boys and latterly youth culture and consumerism as causes of crime, with juveniles increasingly referred to psychologists for tests. Even so, birching remained an acceptable means of 'character building' in boys for years to come, and a legal punishment until 1948.

Approved school did little to stem the rising tide of delinquency in Billy Hughes. He absconded on five occasions, a transgression which the authorities regarded a delinquent act in itself and evidence of 'the failure of treatment at an early age'.[9] Having regained his liberty, on 26 July 1963 Billy appeared at Blackpool Magistrates' Court on three counts of stealing. He was sentenced to another stint in approved school, where his record observes that being bullied about his height caused him to react in a 'confrontational and competitive' manner.[10]

Discharged again, he burgled a shop and was brought before magistrates in Liverpool on 12 May 1964. This time he was sentenced to Borstal, where around 6,000 repeat offenders aged fifteen to twenty-one were detained annually. The authorities stressed that 'Borstal is not a prison, not even an institution any longer; it is an establishment . . . to be sentenced to Borstal is not to be sentenced to imprisonment, or even detention, but to training', yet admitted that Borstal was 'the end of the line' for the criminal young, with adult prison the next stage.[11]

Superficially, Borstal was run on similar lines to boarding school, with each establishment divided into 'houses' where inmates slept in dormitories. Education and sports were obligatory, while discipline was strict: minor lapses resulted in the withdrawal of small privileges but more serious transgressions were punishable by a spell in solitary confinement ('chokey'). Vocational training in courses ranging from cookery to bricklaying were offered on a first come, first served basis, aimed at securing employment upon discharge. Throughout their stay, inmates were graded on three levels, with home leave granted before final grading and release.

Billy left Liverpool for Wormwood Scrubs in London to be assessed for a suitable Borstal. The prison social worker tasked with evaluating his character and finding the right place for him was deeply unimpressed by their meetings. 'An immature, thoughtless little chap whose voice is just about breaking,' he observed. 'Has been a nuisance to all who have tried to help him. Needs secure conditions and probably further education. Persistent absconder.'[12] He suggested sending Billy to Everthorpe Borstal, built five years earlier in the flat East Yorkshire countryside, and advised him to take advantage of a training course in welding there.

Initial reports from Everthorpe were bleak, describing Billy as 'immature and unable to control himself' before deteriorating further: 'No progress . . . needs to be kept on a tight rein; a troublemaker; irresponsible.'[13] He failed the Institution Board for training grade on three occasions and even his pugilistic peers were wary of him, including his cellmate. A tattooed youth from Wigan, nicknamed 'Scarface' due to a 'bottle top shape weal' on his left cheek, he recalled sharing a 'gritty camaraderie' with Billy, but was watchful of his 'dark frustrations and violent tendencies' and an emergent obsession with 'weapons, especially knives'.[14]

Billy's other fixation was welcomed by staff trained in the institutional concept of a healthy body equating to a healthy mind: after participating in sports and exercise, he poured his energies into weightlifting and working out, turning his small frame into one that was muscular and immensely strong. His behaviour improved and he showed promise on the course he had opted for instead of welding, leading to positive comments on his report: 'Mature, self-confident, doing well on painting and decorating vocational training course.'[15]

Billy's choice of classes indicated an affinity with his parents, which tied in again with the Borstal ethos: 'Of all the influences that can work towards rehabilitation of a Borstal boy, one of the most potent can be that of his own family.'[16] Young offenders were encouraged to maintain or seek contact with their parents. Billy accepted responsibility for the breakdown of his relationship with his mother and father, who welcomed him home when he was granted leave for a short time towards the end of his sentence. He returned to Everthorpe in disgrace, nonetheless, on a charge of drunk and disorderly behaviour, with a note on his file to that effect from Preston police.

Billy spent seventeen months in Borstal. He was released into the care of his parents on 7 October 1965, but was turned out to live with a friend after a month of heavy drinking. It may be that he was regarded as a bad influence on his siblings, since all the Hughes brothers would find themselves 'in trouble with the law' at some stage.[17] Billy blamed his own problems on excessive drinking, yet seemed incapable of abstaining unless alcohol was unavailable.

He was brought before Preston Magistrates' Court on 22 November 1965, charged with shop-breaking and stealing, and asked for two other offences to be taken into consideration. Questioned about motive, he replied, 'I needed the money.'[18] His punishment was a six-month sentence at Borstal Recall Centre in Portsmouth, where he refused to write to his parents, telling staff that he would never return to them because they had 'washed their hands' of him.[19] His record from Portsmouth is scant on detail, describing him repeatedly as 'immature and a nuisance'.[20]

Released on 4 May 1966, Billy caught a train north to Preston. He soon found work as a labourer and lodgings with a friend on Ribble Bank Street, a stone's throw from his family home, but had little intention of remaining out of trouble. One week after leaving Borstal he slipped out in the early hours to meet two local girls, Lorraine and Brenda, planning to commit robbery. They chose a private house in upmarket Fulwood Hall Lane, where the two girls kept watch while Billy unsuccessfully tried to prise open a window with a screwdriver. They then headed to the nearby Co-operative Sports and Social Club, intent on filching alcohol and to raid the one-armed bandit. A constable on his rounds spotted movement inside the darkened building and caught the two girls as they tried to flee. He marched them back to the club, switching on the lights to reveal Billy crouched under the stage. The screwdriver lay beside the fruit machine.

Billy was sent to await trial at Risley Remand Centre near Warrington. Only a few days before, Britain's most notorious killers, Ian Brady and Myra Hindley, had been held there prior to receiving life sentences for the 'Moors Murders'. Aware that he faced jail himself, Billy was still incapable of the appropriate behaviour and was the subject of eight misconduct reports, which included failing to attend work, using bad language, fighting and being involved in bullying. He forfeited thirteen days' remission as a result. He had managed to rebuild his relationship with his parents – his notes record that he was on 'good terms' with them – but sent the majority of his letters to a girlfriend and received as many from her. She was the only person to visit him. Staff regarded him as 'of above average intelligence' when he applied himself, but most of the observations on his report are negative: he was a 'constant nuisance', 'irresponsible' and there was 'little hope for him on release unless he changes'.[21]

On 12 July 1966, Billy, Lorraine and Brenda pleaded guilty at Preston County Sessions to stealing from the club and attempted housebreaking. James Booth, defending all three, told the court that seventeen-year-old Brenda was supporting herself and a baby on a pittance; she, like her friend Lorraine, had committed the offences out of financial desperation. As for Billy, Booth stated that he had spent the last four of his nineteen years in institutions and might benefit better from probation. Magistrates granted each girl three years' probation but were disinclined to clemency for Billy: he was sentenced to eighteen months in prison.

Billy's friends were unsurprised by the outcome. 'He lived off petty crime,' Joe Williams recalled. 'There were times when he seemed to live in a world apart. He had no other interests or conversation except crime and talking about his old chums in the nick [but] he never did a big job . . . He never had much fun out of life. He was never quite right in the head. Sometimes, he had a faraway look in his eyes when you talked to him. He was a loner.'[22]

Raymond Glass knew him as 'Little Billy', a small-time crook. Aware of the dichotomy between Billy's inability to remain law-abiding and his terror of confinement, he felt certain the disparity would lead to tragedy: 'Billy could be talked or goaded into any crime but he was scared stiff of prison. I'm sure that was why, in the end, he committed those terrible murders. He was desperate not to go back to jail again.'[23]

Chapter Two:

Battle in the Streets

B ILLY SERVED HIS first custodial sentence at HMP Walton in
Liverpool. Situated in the heart of the city, it was rebuilt
during the nineteenth century to replace an existing prison no
longer fit for purpose. Wings led out from a central castellated
block in line with the era's radial design, housing a thousand
inmates and gallows where sixty-two prisoners were put to death.
The last execution in Walton was the last in Britain: in August
1964, two years before Billy entered its walls, Peter Anthony Allen
was hanged for his part in the murder of a laundry-van driver. His
accomplice, Gwynne Owen Evans, was simultaneously executed
in Strangeways. Allen was three years older than Billy and Evans
six; their paths may have crossed in Preston where they lived
within a few streets of each other, and all had resorted to petty
theft during periods of unemployment.

Billy served his time in Walton as a Category B prisoner, one
'for whom the very highest conditions of security are not necessary but for whom escape must be made very difficult'.[1] His

behaviour was satisfactory throughout, although his relationship with his parents had broken down again and he intended to
live in lodgings upon release. Billy's year of good conduct came
to an end shortly after his discharge from Walton on 28 June
1967; charged with store-breaking and stealing scrap copper, he
returned to Risley eight weeks later, sentenced to two years'
imprisonment.

'A complete social non-conformist who associates with others
who follow a similar pattern,' reads Billy's progress report from
the Local Review Committee some months later.[2] There would be
no improvement in that evaluation; his notes indicate that he was
suffering from depression and low self-esteem, exacerbated by a
lack of contact from his parents, with whom he hoped to recon-
cile. He attended the Roman Catholic chapel occasionally, but
there was no sign of his previous above-average assessment. The
committee concluded that Billy Hughes was 'pathetic – he seems
ashamed of himself and there is hardly any self-respect or ambition after nearly six years. It is difficult to get any idea of his atti-
tudes, he is cooperative but makes little positive contribution to
an interview. His response to prison is only fair, and although his
stay may teach him how to improve his prison standards it is difficult to see how this will benefit him outside.'[3] Once again, 'the
prospects of successful rehabilitation are poor at this stage'.[4]

Matters deteriorated further. Within a year, Billy was the
subject of eight disciplinary reports for breaches including 'traf-
ficking, fighting, absenting himself from work and bad language'.[5]
He lost twelve days' remission and was excluded from association
periods (socialising with other inmates), leading him to petition
about victimisation. Otherwise, his conduct was 'indifferent' and
he was 'not prepared to give any guarantee that he will attempt to
desist from crime'.[6] His correspondence consisted of letters to and

from relatives who were also in custody and his application for home leave was refused.

Billy regained his freedom on 15 January 1969. Although he was on better terms with his parents, he moved in with his father's elder brother, William, who had always tried to help him. Three days later, Billy repaid his uncle's kindness by breaking into an empty building on Preston's Blackpool Road with intent to steal. He was spotted by a constable and apprehended, but escaped from a panda car bound for Fulwood Police Station. Recaptured by another officer in Moor Park, at first Billy said meekly, 'I surrender,' before headbutting the policeman, then punching him to the ground, kicking him repeatedly until he was dragged off by other officers.[7] The injured man was treated in hospital and remained off duty for several days.

Remanded in custody at Risley, Billy came before magistrates in Preston on 27 January charged with burglary and assaulting a police officer. His solicitor told the court that his client was 'sorry for the offences and intends to settle down with the help of his parents', but Billy's sullen appearance belied his purported contrition. He was sentenced to six months' imprisonment for each offence, to run concurrently at HMP Walton.[8]

His conduct in prison was subdued. Classified a lower Category C inmate (i.e., those who cannot be trusted in open conditions but who do not have the ability or resources to make a determined escape attempt), Billy corresponded regularly with one of his brothers who was in Pollington Borstal, but failed to reciprocate when his parents wrote to him. The only matter deemed worthy of note on his report concerned his obsession with a series of warts on one hand; when he was admitted to Walton Casualty Hospital with a fractured little finger, he pestered medics about getting rid of the warts. He was released from prison on 22 May 1969.

Billy remained at liberty for less than two months, but in that time, he met and moved in with a girl and her family. On 11 July 1969 he returned to Risley charged with burglary and theft but escaped, fleeing to Preston. Despite being on the run for three weeks, he found lodgings and employment. He was at the wheel of a pick-up truck one evening when PC Rex Waite saw him driving erratically along Aqueduct Street before turning on to St George's Road, where he collided with a stationary van. Waite collared Billy as he emerged from the vehicle and escorted him immediately to Preston Royal Infirmary for a check-up. Billy seemed dazed, claiming not to remember anything about the accident. He sustained no injuries but breath tests revealed 175mg of alcohol in his blood against the permitted 80mg. He told his solicitor, Hodgson, that he had been drinking double whiskies that night and wasn't used to it, nor was he driving at the time of the collision, although he intended to plead guilty. Hodgson suspected that Billy was covering for someone but his client refused to be drawn further.

'Escaper Jailed on Drink Charge', read the headline in the *Lancashire Evening Post* on 6 August 1969. Billy's solicitor told Preston Magistrates' Court that 'while he was unlawfully at liberty recently, Hughes did secure some work in Preston. There was no question of him wanting to leave the town.'⁹ Billy admitted all the charges against him: driving a motor pick-up with too much alcohol in his blood, driving without due care and attention, using the vehicle without a test certificate, failing to produce his insurance certificate and driving licence, and failing to report to the police following the results of the breathalyser test. He was sentenced to four months' imprisonment for driving while drunk and banned from driving for twelve months, but given an absolute discharge on the other offences.

Removed to HMP Walton, Billy returned to Preston on 13 August 1969 to face charges of burglary and theft. Standing in court following rejection by his girlfriend, Billy made a dramatic gesture: he pulled out a razor blade and drew it across his throat and wrist. He was rushed to hospital, where his wounds were sutured: five stitches in the neck and four in his left wrist. Billy insisted that he had wanted to die, but the Senior Medical Officer at HMP Walton deemed otherwise, describing the incident as 'hysterical behaviour', which, while 'premeditated', was 'not carried out with any great determination'.[10] Billy received no counselling either for the action itself or for the reasons behind it. Instead, he was temporarily placed on the Escape List (those inmates most likely to attempt escape).

His anger boiled over with a serious assault on another inmate, and on 5 September 1969, the Visiting Committee awarded him twenty-eight days' forfeiture of remission, seven days' cellular confinement, seven days' stoppage of earnings and seven days' forfeiture of privileges. Discovering his former girlfriend had moved hundreds of miles south to Portsmouth seems to have been the trigger; Billy refused to believe that their relationship was over and petitioned for a transfer to Winchester to be near her. The denial of his request brought a reluctant acceptance of the entire situation and his conduct was described as fair in another petition for transfer to HMP Preston.

This, too, was refused but Billy successfully appealed against the decisions of the Visiting Committee and saw his sentence reduced to a £25 fine on 26 September 1969. On the same date, he received a custodial sentence suspended for three years after being found guilty of handling stolen goods, with two other offences taken into consideration. He was released from court and headed straight for Portsmouth, where he convinced his girlfriend to take him back. A note on his file records that he had informed the authorities that he was living with his common-law wife in Portsmouth and had one child.

Billy appeared in court again on 25 November 1969, charged with drunk and disorderly behaviour, assaulting a police officer, theft of a copper cistern and handling stolen goods. He received separate custodial sentences of one month, six months and six months, to be served concurrently, plus two years for breaching his suspended sentence, making a total of three years' imprisonment. He asked the authorities to send him to HMP Winchester but found himself bound for HMP Walton, with a note attached to his records regarding his previous escape attempts.

At first, his conduct was fair and he wrote regularly to a girlfriend in Borstal (presumably not the mother of his child in Portsmouth). He was twice placed on report: once for absenting himself from work, losing two weeks' pay as a result, and for sequestering a transistor radio in his cell, forfeiting three days' remission. Otherwise there were no adverse comments about his work.

Staff regarded Billy as a surprisingly skilled bookmaker with a weakness for gambling on horses. When he unsuccessfully applied for 'dining out association' a wry note was made on his record that 'were he granted Mess facilities, it would present him with greater opportunities to expand'.[11] A full year passed before Billy was allowed to join other inmates at mealtimes, largely because his tutor confirmed that he had 'made good progress with his work and gives no trouble'.[12]

Whenever he was confined to his cell, Billy made use of the time to exercise for hours. He also began amassing tattoos, including the ubiquitous 'LOVE' on the fingers of his right hand and 'HATE' on his left. He already had a girlfriend's name inked across his chest – 'DIANNE' – and added a large eagle with protracted talons, while his back was covered by a single tattoo of a stylised snake with a forked tongue and tail, and fangs dripping blood. Over the years he supplemented these with numerous smaller inkings on his arms and hands, including a bluebird, an anchor, stars, hearts, crosses and compasses.

As summer 1970 came to an end, Billy was eligible for parole. In his submission, he stated that he would return to live with his parents in Preston, where he would work as a decorator, having made a determined effort in prison to learn new skills. He had long since accepted the end of his relationship with the young woman in Portsmouth (with whom he had no further contact, nor with his firstborn child) and intended to keep out of trouble by being more circumspect about the company he kept. His past offences were mainly carried out as a result of alcohol and being, in his own words, 'stupid'.[13] The Review Committee were quick to notice his lack of remorse, however, and observed: 'His offending in company, his drinking, gambling and his steady and consistent application to crime inspire no confidence in his chances of avoiding further trouble . . . We cannot see anything in his record or performance which shows he would benefit by a period on parole.'[14] Consequently, parole was refused.

Exactly one year later, on 27 October 1971, Billy walked out of prison a free man. In his pocket was a railway warrant to Preston but from there he travelled to Blackpool, having decided to make a fresh start. The following day, he met the woman who would become his wife.

Billy had never had any trouble attracting women; he was ferally good-looking and chatted easily to anyone, especially after a couple of drinks. He would then lavish a girl with attention and declare his undying love, all the while masking a piercingly possessive nature and an inability to let go until he himself had moved on. His jealousy was profound, yet all his relationships suffered due to his own infidelity. In time, he became both emotionally and physically abusive, threatening partners with his suicide – or with their murder at his hands. 'He liked the birds,' his old schoolfriend Joe Williams recalled laconically. 'He was in prison so much that when he got out he tried to catch up on what he had missed. One woman wasn't enough for him.'[15]

Blackpool-born Jean Nadin was the illegitimate daughter of an office cleaner. One year older than Billy, she had lived in Blackpool all her life and was frequently out of work, having served several prison sentences for money-related offences. She married a local man in 1966 and had a child the following year. By 1971 she was divorced, unemployed, and living with her five-year-old daughter Tracey Taylor in lodgings near Blackpool's seafront entertainment complex, the Golden Mile. Small and slight, with bleached-blonde hair and a delicate face, she was also extremely vulnerable.

Jean gave a handful of interviews to the press in 1977, then vanished from public view. Over 'non-stop tea and cigarettes', she told journalists in the aftermath of the Pottery Cottage murders: 'I will never forget the day that Billy came into my life. It was October 28th 1971. I was living in a boarding house when a friend of mine asked if I could make room for a man called Billy Hughes. She told me that he was coming out of prison after a sentence for burglary. That didn't worry me too much. Billy came round to my address and he looked good – he was a good-looking boy and I suppose I fell for him. We went out together that night for a drink to celebrate his release and I slept with him for the first time. I didn't see anything wrong in that – we got on and it seemed natural. Our first few weeks together were great, he was gentle and I began to fall in love with him.'[16] Six weeks later, Jean found out she was pregnant. Billy seemed elated, promising to be there for her and their child.

Probation officers secured work for Billy, but he was unable to hold down the job. His father was then employed by a large decorating firm and pleaded with his boss, Arthur Carter, to give his son a chance. Carter recalled that Billy's father was 'a very good man. And his uncle, William Hughes, was my foreman for twenty years. I had respect for the family, so I gave Billy a job. He'd been trained as a painter in Borstal. But it was useless. He was lazy, sullen and contemptuous. Whenever his father would remonstrate with him, the son would fly into a rage and threaten physical violence.'[17] Carter sacked Billy when he was caught stealing money from a drawer.

Billy's domestic situation was even more troubling. Despite Jean carrying his child and with her own young daughter often present, he became repeatedly violent in the home. Over the course of five years he fractured Jean's arm, broke her ribs and perforated her eardrums. 'It began one day when I cooked his dinner,' she recalled. 'Each time I put a plate in front of him, he threw it at me. I cooked him four different meals and each time he threw them at my face. We moved from flat to flat around Blackpool because he didn't like paying landlords rent. He was just screwing houses for money. For weeks, I wouldn't get a cent and then he would dump a pile of money in front of me. That's how we lived.'[18]

Billy's aggression extended to Jean's five-year-old daughter. 'He was very strong and fast,' she remembered. 'He was bad to Tracey because she just could not get on with him. He was too violent for her. She was terrified of him.'[19] On 8 May 1972, Billy was brought before Blackpool County Borough Magistrates' Court, charged with assault occasioning actual bodily harm to Tracey Taylor, who had only just begun attending primary school. Jean was absent from proceedings, but Billy laid the blame for his cruelty squarely on her shoulders, claiming that his partner was 'uncouth and swore all the time', and he had simply been trying to discipline her daughter because Jean was 'too lax'.[20] He claimed to have 'slapped Tracey with an open hand when she was hysterical' but the little girl had injuries that included fractured ribs.[21] As a result, he was sentenced to six months in prison.

Jean had always sought to shield and defend Billy's violence towards her and that extended to his attack on Tracey. She did, however, attempt to persuade him to speak to a psychiatrist but 'there was no help for him at all. He just refused help.'[22] Jean's physician, Dr Joseph Cox, later gave an account of his negligible contact with Billy, which began in May 1972 and continued after the birth of their daughter: 'I had cause to visit the children at frequent intervals, possibly every month and usually the father, that is William, was there and from time to time he visited the surgery at the above address with the children. At no time did he show any evidence of psychiatric illness and struck me as a quiet and reserved individual and surprisingly polite . . . From the time of his birth he had not undergone any psychiatric investigation or treatment.'[23]

In the short time he served for assaulting a child, Billy was granted field association (socialising with fellow inmates during out-of-work hours, including taking part in games) and gained a reputation as one of the best bookmakers in prison. He appealed against his sentence, appearing at Preston Crown Court on 7 July 1972 after convincing Jean to speak up for him. She made a compelling witness on his behalf, with her pregnancy almost at full term, and claimed that relatives of Tracey's father had 'threatened to cause trouble' at the Blackpool hearing if she had given evidence there.[24] She told the court that she and Billy hoped to marry after their child was born, and that Tracey wanted him home. As a result, Billy's sentence was suspended for two years.

Discharged from custody, Billy returned to rooms that Jean had rented for them at 72 Grasmere Avenue. Along with all but the last of Billy's Blackpool homes, the terraced house stood in the impoverished Revoe district behind the seafront. Most Revoe residents worked in the countless attractions of the pleasure beach; donkeys were stabled behind boarding houses that were packed beyond the legal limit with seasonal workers trying to earn a year's wage in three or four months. The Tower soared above the coastal end of Grasmere Avenue, but the rowdy neighbourhood pubs were the only draw for Billy, despite impending fatherhood.

His daughter was born on 6 August 1972 at Glenroyd Maternity Hospital. 'Billy said he would come and help me at the birth,' Jean recalled. 'He was with me all the time until near the end when he turned sick and nearly blacked out. He had to leave, he couldn't stand it.'[25] The couple named their daughter Nichola Jayne. She bore a marked resemblance to her father's side of the family and Billy 'fussed over her all the time' until the infant and her mother returned home.[26]

'Three days after I left hospital he beat me up as I was feeding the baby,' Jean confirmed. 'He wanted his breakfast but I said I couldn't make it until after I had fed Nicky. He just started bashing me about.'[27] She managed to lay the baby in her cot, then ran downstairs and out into the street: 'He screamed to me out of the window to come back. When I said I wouldn't, he disappeared from the window and then came back with a bundle in his hand.

It took me a couple of seconds to realise that it was Nichola. I started screaming: he was holding her by the neck and shaking her. He said that if I didn't go back he'd drop her. What could I do? I went back. Then he calmed down again and started apologising. It was often like that. One minute he was beating me or the kids, and the next begging for forgiveness.'[28] She did not report the incident because 'I still loved him and thought we should keep it between ourselves'.[29]

During the three weeks that followed his last court appearance, Billy worked sporadically as a property repairer. He spent most of his time in the company of his twenty-three-year-old brother Alan. An unemployed demolition worker who was on a twelve months' suspended prison sentence, Alan had recently begun an affair with Jean's married best friend, Alice Swan. The two brothers whiled away their days drinking and occasionally taking drugs until committing an offence that remains in the memories of those involved to this day.

Police Constable Robert Ashworth was on panda patrol in Blackpool during the early hours of 2 August 1972. His radio buzzed twice with alerts about a hit-and-run accident. Ashworth knew of a drug den on the Mereside council estate and decided to investigate a possible link. He had just turned on to the estate when he saw Billy and Alan Hughes walking down Langdale Road towards the house he intended to visit. Billy had blood on him.

Ashworth pulled over. 'I had a chat with Billy and he said he had left his car round the corner and was going to visit a nearby house,' he recalled. 'That was the house connected with the drugs.

By this time, another officer had arrived on the scene, so we went with the two brothers to find his car – only to discover that it was parked two streets away.'[30] Aware that both brothers were 'drugged up to the eyeballs', Ashworth opened the car boot.

'It was full of drugs – it looked as if they had knocked off a couple of chemist shops. By this time another officer had arrived in a transit van. We told the brothers that we were taking them in and that's when the trouble started,' Ashworth confirmed. 'I suppose trouble isn't really the word – it was all hell let loose.'

Alan refused to enter the police van. He threw a punch before dashing into a nearby garden, but was quickly detained and was in the process of being forced into the van when Billy made his own bid for freedom. One officer locked Alan inside the van, then joined his two colleagues in tackling Billy. During the struggle, Alan smashed the vehicle lock and scrambled out through a rear window, kicking the officer who tried to stop him.

'The whole world seemed to explode,' Ashworth remembered. 'It wasn't a fight, it was a battle in the streets . . . I've never in my life come across two people like that. They went berserk.'

At twenty-six years old, Ashworth was the same age as Billy but almost a foot taller at 6ft 4in and a keen rugby player. Even so, it took all three officers half an hour to get control of the situation. Detective Constable Phil Goodison was twenty-one years old and fourteen stone, but Billy almost succeeded in throttling him before attempting to gouge Goodison's eyes out with his fingers. As Goodison lay unconscious, Billy leapt at Ashworth, punching him in the forehead. A moment later, he sank his teeth deeply into Ashworth's left arm through the officer's jacket, causing severe bruising.

'We were kicking and punching and every time we knocked them down they just bounced right back up again,' Ashworth reflected years later. 'I kicked Billy in the head with my boot for all I was worth and it didn't make any difference. He just kept coming back for more.'

Eventually, the two brothers were locked inside a second van bound for South King Street Police Station. About a mile and a half into the journey, as the vehicle passed the Oxford Hotel, Ashworth heard 'a hell of a rumpus' in the back as Billy and Alan tore the steel bench inside the compartment off its hinges and used it to batter the rear doors. 'We were going at about 40mph when they finally got the door open,' Ashworth recalled. 'They just jumped on to the road. It was unbelievable. We looked back and the two were off and running.'

More officers were drafted in to search for the pair, who were discovered hiding behind a garage. Although finally detained at South King Street, both brothers remained frenzied and dealt six policemen further kicks, blows and bites. Ashworth required hospital treatment and was on sick leave for a week afterwards, suffering dizzy spells. Another officer was away from work for a fortnight after tests and X-rays revealed a damaged kidney.

The two brothers were brought before court later that day. Billy's solicitor told magistrates that his client was badly hurt during the 'scuffles' with police, adding that he and Alan had 'got as good as they had given'.[31] He cited medical evidence that showed 90 per cent of Billy's body to be bruised and 85 per cent in Alan's case but there was no question of the brothers being released. Nor was the violence over: that afternoon in his cell at South King Street, Billy suddenly 'went berserk', headbutting a constable before ripping out the central heating system and using a length of pipe to smash up the toilet, causing £135 of damage.[32] Billy's solicitor later told the court that his client had assaulted the officer only after being grabbed by the arm himself. The family physician, Dr Joseph Cox, visited Billy in his cell, confirming 'extensive lacerations and bruising to the skin but nothing of a major significance. The only treatment he required was an ATS injection.'[33] Billy was then dispatched to Risley, where a note was made of his appearance on admission, including 'multiple bruises' and a 'blackened' right eye.[34]

Billy faced other charges while on remand in Risley. On 5 October he was convicted of burglary but was awarded two years' probation at Preston Crown Court on 8 November and allowed to walk free. His liberty was short-lived, however: both he and Alan Hughes appeared at Preston Crown Court four days later, on 12 November 1972. Journalists from the *Lancashire Evening News* and the *West Lancashire Evening Gazette* were now familiar with the Hughes name in connection with crime, and anticipated that this latest hearing would be worthy of major headlines locally.

And so it was: all the details of the two brothers' frenetic attacks on several policemen over a twenty-four-hour period were examined in court. Billy's solicitor Daniel Brennan had the unenviable task of representing both his regular client and the younger brother. Billy admitted biting PC Ashworth, plus four other charges of assaulting police officers and causing actual bodily harm, and an offence of criminal damage. Alan pleaded guilty to three charges of causing actual bodily harm to police officers and a further charge of criminal damage. Brennan said in their defence that the brothers 'had not used any weapons to ward off the police though they had ample opportunity to arm themselves'.[35] Both denied a further offence of burglary and theft of drugs from a chemist's shop in Garstang Road, Fulwood, which was allowed to lie on file. Three of their acquaintances were also brought before the court on charges of handling offences and burglary from pharmacies in Blackpool and York.

Before passing sentence, Judge William Openshaw addressed the two brothers sternly: 'These are particularly serious offences in that the violence you used towards these police officers was of a kind that cannot be tolerated in this country. If violence is offered to police officers the consequences must be penal.'[36] He ordered Billy to serve three and a half years in prison, and Alan two and a half years.

Local Detective Inspector Harry Mailer took grim satisfaction in the outcome, having been called out to deal with Billy several times in the past: 'He could be normal and then something would click. He wasn't a clever thief. He just had animal cunning. He was a very, very dangerous man. I don't think there was anyone like him in Blackpool.'[37] Another senior officer agreed: 'He was regarded here as a schizophrenic and we were always wary of him. We always thought he'd kill somebody.'[38]

Chapter Three:

Massive Hunt for Vicious Rapist

O N 18 FEBRUARY 1974, a small wedding party gathered at
Liverpool Register Office: bride and groom, bride's best
friend, and groom's prison warder.

Jean recalled that Billy had proposed to her over the visitors'
table in Walton after months of exchanging letters and the lengthy
trips she made from Blackpool. Despite everything, there was no
hesitation in her response: 'I wanted to be his wife.'[1] Like so many
individuals caught up in abusive relationships, she clung to vain
hope – 'I thought he might change' – and in the meantime, 'paid
eight quid for the special licence and even bought the wedding
rings'.[2] In a photograph taken after the ceremony, the newly-weds
radiate happiness and normality: Billy grins broadly, hair slicked
back, looking sharp in his suit and tie, while Jean beams as she
leans against him, slim and pretty in a Nancy Sinatra-style white
mini-dress, hair back-combed in long blonde waves. 'It was a big
day for me,' she confirmed.[3] But there was no reception or honeymoon, since within an hour of taking his vows, Billy was heading

south in handcuffs to spend his first night as a married man staring at the ceiling in his cell.

Billy's schoolfriend Joe Williams believed the marriage was
born of desperation: 'In the few months [Billy] was out of prison
in recent years his one thought was to chase the birds. That's all
the lads in the nick want to do when they come out. He married
that Blackpool girl because I think he needed some affection and
someone to cling to while he was inside. This is the way we all feel
in jail. It gives us something to think and talk about, to have a
wife and kid waiting.'⁴ Marrying Jean and becoming a father did
nothing for Billy's equilibrium, however. Rather than giving him
a sense of purpose, it fuelled his rabid insecurity during the
enforced separation, leading to jealous outbursts and threats. A
note in his file reflects: 'The prisoner's domestic affairs were
extremely complicated from February 1974 onwards. A great deal
of assistance was given by the Welfare Department during this
period.'⁵ Further details are unavailable, but the authorities medi-
ated between husband and wife, and may also have provided
financial support.

Paradoxically, Billy's conduct otherwise was steady and accom-
modating. He made several applications to the prison governor
for field association, backed by reports describing him as 'a good
worker needing minimum supervision'.⁶ The one attached to his
successful application reads: 'A good "number one" who works
well and is polite and courteous to staff. He has settled well in the
last few months. At this stage I would recommend.'⁷ By then,
Billy was making a sustained effort to regain control of himself
through association and creative pursuits. He became an expert
chess player, revealing an instinctive gift for the game, while art
classes enabled him to explore a considerable talent for painting.
Several of his artworks were later reproduced in the press,

captioned: 'His subjects ranged from faithful portraits to peaceful pastoral scenes and bracing seascapes filled with movement and colour. Most of his work was given away to friends by his wife. Two of her favourites hang in a friend's home in Blackpool. One, in delicate oranges, greens and browns, is a pastoral scene painted from Hughes's memory of a favourite haunt, near Chorley, Lancashire. He painted it in Walton Prison . . . The second is a seascape showing sailing ships trapped in a storm. That too was completed in his cell at Walton, and was copied from a box of mint chocolates.'[8] His artistic flair extended to woodwork, providing his family with detailed miniatures of gypsy caravans and beautifully carved toys.

With these new skills to his credit and a raft of glowing work reports, Billy's first petition for parole in early 1975 included his confident assertion that there was 'little doubt' in his own mind that he could make 'a successful life' for himself, even at that 'late stage'.[9] His application was undermined by the fact that prior to Christmas, the Welfare Department had received notice of Billy's domestic situation being 'in turmoil . . . feelings ran high and special visits were arranged'.[10] As a result, and having examined his 'long record of crime and heavy drinking', the Parole Board decided 'he hasn't been taught a lesson during his life and parole should not be granted at this stage'.[11]

Billy protested the outcome on 8 May 1975, requesting an early review. The attached report was to his credit and concluded that his request should be supported 'on the grounds that at the present time he is thinking more about the future than he has ever done before in his life . . . Unless this is encouraged, the future for him is extremely bleak.'[12] The Parole Board deemed otherwise, informing him that his appeal had been rejected and he would have to wait the requisite two months before making a new submission. A few days later, on 9 June 1975, Billy was called into the governor's office to be given news that, according to prison records, left him genuinely upset: his father had died.

For the past two years, Thomas and May Hughes had been living with their only daughter, Barbara, in Derwent House, a block of council flats on Samuel Street in Preston. While May continued to work at Hall's Cash & Carry warehouse on Blackpool Road, Thomas had been forced to retire due to ill health. He was treated for a stomach ulcer at Preston Royal Infirmary but died at home following a rupture on 8 June 1975, aged fifty-one.

Four days later, Billy was escorted to Preston for the funeral. Reports attached to his July parole plea noted that his behaviour afterwards had remained amenable, but there were strong doubts about how he might respond to release. On 29 September, he was told that his review had been unsuccessful. The Home Leave Board recommended meeting to discuss his case one month later, based on the accumulation of encouraging reports, but a difficulty regarding accommodation, together with concerns about his 'volatile nature', led to another refusal.[13]

By then Billy had been charged with three disciplinary offences: two were dismissed but the third – taking another inmate's meal – was proven, and for that he forfeited three days' remission. As the Board continued to assess him, there were clear signs of increasing disturbance. Frank Bowes, a prisoner in his thirties from Manchester, confirmed: 'His only topic was that one day he would kill. Everybody, including prison staff, heard him say things like that.'[14]

On 4 December 1975, Billy was released from prison.

*

'I was living with my kids above a fruit shop in Blackpool,' Jean recalled of the period when her husband regained his freedom. 'Alice and her kids were with me as well. He was really good when he came out and told me he was going to go straight and never bother with the cops again. He put an advert in the local paper asking for house repair work and he was really busy. He seemed really different.'[15]

The flat, together with further living accommodation and the shop below, was owned by Margaret and Peter Blatch, a couple in their forties. 'Pambs Fruitique' stood on Central Drive, opposite the distinctive elongated brick curve of the King Edward VII pub. Margaret had agreed to let the flat to Jean and Alice because they seemed 'happy-go-lucky'; she understood that Jean's husband would be joining them once he had 'completed a contract on a building site'.[16] Billy turned on the charm from the moment he arrived, making himself indispensable to such an extent that he regularly accompanied Margaret to visit her ailing mother in Manchester.

'I never guessed he had been in prison,' she recalled. 'His hair was long and I thought he had been working away. I felt sorry for him so I gave him an extra room because there was about six kids living in the flat. I felt he deserved some peace and quiet. He was really nice to me and my husband in the first month . . . Peter lost both his legs a few years ago and Billy took him out in his wheel-chair for a drink at nights. The two of them got on really well.' Margaret, a keen chess player, was delighted to find that Billy shared her enthusiasm for the game: 'He used to come down at nights and we would spend hours playing together. He was really good at chess. He could take in the whole board at a glance and he beat me every time. That really impressed me.'

She was even more pleased when Billy offered to decorate Pambs Fruitique: 'He was working in the middle of the night, painting the shop and repairing the doors. I paid him for it, but he made a really good job. He told me he wanted to go into business on his own.' She helped him draft a regular advert for the local newspaper and gave him use of her van, while May Hughes gifted him the substantial sum of £300 to start his business. Margaret also regarded him 'like a son . . . We talked together a lot, played chess and cards, and he seemed to want to tell me everything.'

The relationship soured when Margaret began receiving demands for payment from the newspaper, followed by a visit from their debt collector, who explained that Billy had placed the advert in her name without paying any instalments. She then discovered that he had been driving her van without a valid licence and reluctantly agreed to let him borrow it one last time to visit his mother at Christmas, but found three boxes of fruit hidden in the back: 'That was when Billy seemed to change towards me. I'd caught him stealing from me and he didn't like that.'

Billy's inability to remain law-abiding seemed coupled with his propensity for violence. He attacked Jean on their doorstep one evening in January after they had been drinking heavily in the pub together. 'He broke a few of my ribs that night,' she remembered. 'He just turned on me out of the blue.'[17] Two days later, according to Jean, he almost killed her eight-year-old daughter Tracey when he pushed the little girl towards the open fire 'because she wouldn't talk to him. She was always scared of him and wouldn't leave my side and he didn't like that. Tracey was all right, but he had a real mean streak in him about her. She was terrified of him.'[18] He was normally affectionate towards his own daughter, three-year-old Nichola, but Jean recalled a horrific incident when 'he punched her in the face for waking him up to show him her new toy. A couple of days later, he went for me and started banging my head on the floorboards. He just didn't stop – he was mad about a meal I had cooked him. That was the way he was: a savage bastard when he was mad and then calm as you like and apologising to everybody.'[19] In her 1977 witness statement, Jean refers to the abuse she and her daughters suffered, and how she initially made excuses to Dr Cox about their injuries. When it came to light that Billy was responsible, psychiatric treatment was offered to him 'on several occasions . . . but each time he refused it'.[20]

Margaret Blatch was aware of the violence occurring in the apartment above her own. She and her husband frequently heard '[Jean's] head banging on the floor above and there would be screams and shouts in the middle of the night. It was a bit of a nightmare.' The Blatches refused to intervene in what they regarded as a domestic matter between husband and wife, particularly since Margaret believed that Jean 'was to blame a lot of the time, she used to get under his skin and he would just snap'. She cited an occasion where Billy threw most of his mother's £300 business loan out of the window 'in a rage' and Jean 'climbed across the roof to get it back'.

The rows escalated in February 1976, when Billy became infatuated with another woman. It was the latest in a long line of infidelities, Jean insisted: 'There has been a lot of trouble with girlfriends. At one time I used to be upset.'[21] Teresa O'Doherty was five years older than Billy, and worked as a domestic supervisor for one of his colleagues in Blackpool. Born in the Derbyshire town of Chesterfield, she married at seventeen and had three daughters before divorcing. A second marriage lasted only a few months and her attraction to Billy was immediate: 'The first time I saw him,' she confirmed. 'He was a nice, shy kind of guy. It took him a week before he even got round to asking me out.'[22] Billy was equally besotted by the worldly blonde Teresa; with her husky voice and measured way of speaking, she seemed more glamorous than the other women in his life. Keen to impress her, he evidently succeeded since she described him as 'a very powerful and strong man', who 'loved the countryside and open spaces. He didn't like being inside. He loved records about life in prison by that singer Johnny Cash. He loved kids and was very fond of my daughter Rosie. He liked a good laugh as well.'[23] Eighteen-year-old Rosie was dating one of Billy's drinking partners, Gary Evans, a British army corporal aged twenty-three, and the four of them began socialising together when Evans was on leave. '[Billy] never said a lot,' Evans recalled. 'He never drank very much, usually a few pints of lager, but sometimes I felt it could be getting to him and he became a little violent.'[24]

In early March 1976, Jean confronted Billy about his affair with Teresa. Refusing to end the relationship, he moved out of the flat on Central Drive and into a terraced house on Belmont Avenue with his new partner. Almost simultaneously, Alice Swan was informed that a three-bedroom council house had become available for her family and she invited Jean to share it. Margaret Blatch was relieved when all nine of her tenants left the flat above the fruit shop: 'No one can really put into words what it was like having them living upstairs. I was glad when they all moved out.'

Billy's fixation with Teresa did nothing to lessen his aggression towards his wife, whom he visited regularly at 45 Loftos Avenue, a corner property in a cramped council estate. 'He kept coming to the house and causing trouble,' Jean recalled. 'He only wanted to be with me when he was in trouble. He did not see much of his daughter but when he did, he idolised her.'[25] Over twenty years later, Nichola confirmed in a *Daily Mail* interview, 'I loved my dad. When I used to see him, I was all over him and he was all over me. He'd tell me I was his baby, his princess. He took me to town once and said I could pick anything I wanted. I chose a check dress and had my photo taken in it . . . He was a painter and decorator by trade and he decorated my room with teddy bear wallpaper.'[26] She spent her entire childhood believing that her father's criminality was a product of his desire to look after them: 'The seventies were hard times and he'd do anything to provide for his family, even if it meant stealing. When we moved into Loftos Road we didn't have any carpet on the stairs. So he picked up a roll that was standing outside a shop and walked home with it. I know it was wrong, but he loved his family and one way or another he would get us what we wanted.'[27]

On 10 March 1976, Billy made his first court appearance since leaving prison. Police Constable Robert Ashworth, who had previously encountered Billy and his brother during the 'battle in the streets' incident, arrested him on suspicion of burglary after finding Billy hiding in the garden shed of the house he shared with Teresa on Belmont Avenue: 'Billy was sitting like a kid on the floor. We had a chat and a smoke – he was as meek as a lamb. But that was Billy all over – one minute, total violence and the next minute calm as anything. He was a strangely compounded man. He had this sort of blank look in his eyes. He could be talking to you but you weren't there. It was like a shield came down. I've only seen that look once before and that was on the face of a man who shot dead an officer in this town. Billy could look right through you. There was something evil about his eyes.'[28]

Brought before Blackpool magistrates on charges of burglary, theft and chequebook forgery, Billy received a deferred sentence to 8 September 1976 and was released from Risley Remand Centre. He began plaguing his wife with abuse during unsolicited visits to the house on Loftos Avenue, culminating in a terrifying attack that April, when he broke in during the early hours of the morning. Jean was at home with Alice and their children, and another girl was also present, having moved in with them, Jean recalled, 'in the hope that the three of us together would have some sort of protection'.[29] Billy entered the house at three o'clock in the morning one night over the Easter weekend. 'He had an axe and had cut the phone wires outside,' Jean confirmed. 'He forced the third girl – I'm not going to name her – to have sex with him on the settee downstairs. Alice and I were upstairs with the kids. Suddenly he burst into our room swinging the axe.'[30]

Alice continued: 'I was sleeping with Jean when I felt something cold on my head. I woke up and saw Billy standing over me with an axe. I was in such a panic and then Jean woke up. Billy said to her, "You're going to see your best mate cut up" and then he hit me with the axe on my head. I felt the blood coming down my face . . .'[31] Jean watched in horror as her friend 'went down, spurting blood all over the place. We were screaming, the kids were crying – I just can't say how terrible it was. I thought he would kill us all, I really did. Then he calmed down and took Alice into the bathroom and bathed the cut on her head. I went downstairs, made a cup of tea and put on his favourite record, Johnny Cash's "Folsom Prison Blues". But he still wouldn't let us go to bed. He kept us hostage for two hours – all three of us terrified that he would go berserk again with the axe. Then he just walked out.'[32]

Alice received hospital treatment for her wounds and gave a full account of the attack to police. On 17 April, Billy appeared at Blackpool Magistrates' Court on a charge of wounding with intent to do grievous bodily harm; there was no mention of the third woman at the house that night. Remanded in custody, on 11 June Billy was committed on bail for trial at Preston Crown Court on his own surety of £200 and another surety of £200. The outcome on 19 July was incredible, given the severity of the attack: the charges were allowed to lie on file and could not proceed without leave of court. There were further charges of criminal damage to a glass pane plus two light bulbs and fitting, and theft of a carpet (as recalled by Billy's young daughter). He received nine months' imprisonment suspended for two years, plus one month's imprisonment consecutive, also suspended for two years.

Billy regarded his dismissal from court as yet another chance to make a fresh start. He and Teresa had already discussed moving elsewhere, agreeing that he needed to put some distance between himself and Jean, and a few of his associates in Blackpool. Teresa's brother lived in Chesterfield and was willing to put them up until they had a place of their own. In late July 1976, Jean discovered that her husband and his girlfriend had left Blackpool permanently; the relief she experienced was overwhelming and shared to some extent by the local police. One officer recalled: '[Billy] caused a lot of aggravation here and frankly we were glad to get rid of him from the area.'[33]

Billy's drinking partner Gary Evans confirmed: 'He came to Chesterfield dreaming of a new life. He knew he couldn't keep out of trouble in Blackpool and moved over to Derbyshire with the idea of beginning with a clean sheet.'[34] But the pattern of Billy's behaviour was already set, and within days of relocating his life would begin to unravel faster than ever before.

It was Britain's 'best ever summer'. Not simply because of the record-breaking heatwave, which saw temperatures reach in excess of 28°C for a twenty-two-day stretch; under James Callaghan's government the economy thrived with the average house price at £12,700, a pint of beer costing 32p and a loaf of bread 19p. The year 1976 also saw the launch of the Ford Fiesta, which quickly became the nation's highest selling car, while children were equally captivated by Raleigh Chopper bikes and orange Space Hoppers.

Throughout July and August, not a single drop of rain fell in parts of the south-west. The drought sparked an epidemic of ladybirds, swarming in their billions over beaches, parks and gardens. Tarmac melted and grass turned to tinder, sending audiences flocking to the cool darkness of their nearest cinema to watch *Taxi Driver* and *The Omen*, as American sci-fi series *The Bionic Woman* broke television records. Sporting fixtures included several classic matches: underdogs Southampton FC beat Manchester United in the FA Cup Final and Björn Borg and Chris Evert smashed their way to victory on Wimbledon's tennis courts. Music charts were dominated by British act The Brotherhood of Man, whose Eurovision winner 'Save Your Kisses For Me' became the best-selling single of the year, two places ahead of Elton John and Kiki Dee's jaunty duet 'Don't Go Breaking My Heart', which began a six-week stint at number one as Billy and Teresa arrived to share her brother's home in Chesterfield.

Scrap merchant Robert Millan lived with his wife Pat and young family at 6 Boythorpe Crescent, a quiet, tree-lined street in an elevated position within walking distance of town. The house was used as emergency accommodation by the local council; the Millans were waiting to move into a Victorian semi-detached villa on Rutland Road, which Billy renovated for them. 'He knew his job,' Pat recalled. 'He spent six weeks decorating my new house and I was alone with him for hours on end. He never touched me and my kids worshipped him.'[35] Teresa saw a change in her partner almost immediately, however: 'He was very tense. I knew something was wrong because he was very childish. He was a Jekyll and Hyde. He could change very quickly and get angry over a chance remark. He was definitely psychopathic. Although he was very shy he changed when he had a drink. Although I never saw him commit violence I knew he could be violent. After a drink he would be quite capable of hitting anyone who looked at him twice.'[36] She recognised the signs that indicated a shift in his mood: 'He had this kind of look in his eyes, you know. And if I got annoyed with him or anything, then I knew when to shut up. I would just turn round. He wouldn't raise his voice or anything, I'd just turn round and look into his eyes and I could tell.'[37] While Billy was capable of inflicting both relentless physical and emotional suffering on others, he told Teresa that as far as he was concerned, pain was all in the mind: 'He said that he didn't feel pain – he had become immune to it. He was a very strong bloke – even without a knife people were scared of him . . . I told him that he should go and see a doctor about his problem – and he later agreed.'[38]

But nothing came of his apparent willingness to seek professional help, leading to a brutal crime that long, hot summer with repercussions beyond anything that had gone before.

Chesterfield's crooked spire – twisted out of shape by the devil fleeing in agony after a Bolsover blacksmith drove a nail through his foot, so locals say – offers a bird's-eye view of Holywell Street. On the sultry evening of Saturday 21 August, 1976, the pavement before one of the town's many mock-Tudor buildings thronged with denim-clad, long-haired young men and women waiting for entry to Jingles discotheque. On the upper level of a former cinema and ballroom, Jingles featured a sprung wooden dance-floor below a huge glass dome. Rock music belted out, with recent hits by Thin Lizzy, Queen and Led Zeppelin drawing fans from the bar to hook thumbs in their jeans and jerk from side to side.

Billy had begun drinking early that night on a solitary pub crawl before ending up in Jingles where he latched on to a young couple standing at the bar. Fiona Y., aged twenty, worked as a shop assistant and lived near Billy in Boythorpe, although they had never met; her boyfriend (later husband) Steven T. was a twenty-one-year-old labourer from New Tupton. They had no desire to spend what remained of the night with Billy. Leaving Jingles at the first opportunity, Steven T. started walking Fiona Y. home past the vast shadowy recreation ground of Queen's Park at the foot of Boythorpe hill. The park offered privacy but was locked, leaving them no choice but to scale the wall.

Thunder rumbled as the couple headed towards the back of the swimming baths; that night was the last of the heatwave, which broke a few hours later with torrential rain falling on parched land and empty reservoirs. For Fiona Y. and Steven T., a far more terrifying storm was imminent, in the shape of Billy Hughes.

Afterwards, the psychiatrist tasked with assessing his suitability for standing trial observed that Billy felt no guilt about what transpired that night. Nor did he tell the truth, claiming to have spotted the couple from Jingles in the park as he walked home and that a fight broke out with Steven T. throwing the first punch, after which Fiona Y. agreed to sex in another part of the park, leaving her unconscious boyfriend behind the Sports Centre. 'I went home to bed and never told a soul what happened,' Billy recounted to the psychiatrist, insisting that he had 'used no force on her nor threats' yet admitted to being 'shocked and scared' by his actions.[39]

The reality was very different. Constable Chris McCarthy, then the duty officer at Beetwell Street Police Station, remembers that during the early hours of the morning, 'Mr K., a young, fair-haired, slim man, burst through the doors to the reception desk. He was completely crimson, his head and face completely covered in blood. He was dazed but very urgently reported to me that he had been attacked at the rear of Queen's Park leisure centre. Mr K. further reported that he had been kissing his girlfriend, Ms C., at the rear of the swimming baths at the centre when he had been attacked and hit on the head with a brick. He stated that he then blacked out and when he came round his girlfriend was missing. He had then made his way on foot directly to the police station. He had attended the Jingles nightclub earlier with Ms C., and was returning to her home at the time via the Sports Centre. Together with other officers we searched the area around Queen's Park leisure centre and found Ms C., in the toilets next to Queen's Park, Boythorpe Road. She was in a dishcvelled state and reported the fact that she had been raped on the riverbank area off Queen's Park and Markham Road. She was young, white, slim and in a state of shock. The above complaints led to the hunt for an unknown rapist . . .'[40]

Twenty-five detectives and uniformed police were involved in the investigation led by Superintendent Tommy Hoggart. Extensive house-to-house inquiries and interviews with local firms were conducted, while police appealed to anyone in the Boythorpe Road, Markham Road and Park Road area between 2.30 a.m. and 3.45 a.m. on 21 August to come forward. The press reproduced an artist's impression of the rapist, 'believed to be around 26 years old, 5ft 7in, of broad build, with short, dark brown hair and long sideburns, wearing a white or cream shirt, black or dark green trousers and black shoes with Cuban heels'.[41]

Pat Millan heard about the attack within hours, although she did not make the connection: 'The day after the rape [Billy] got up as though nothing had happened. I remember that around that time we had a babysitter in one night. When it was time to go home, I told her, "I don't fancy you going home alone with this maniac on the loose." Billy offered to take her.'[42] But Pat's sister-in-law immediately suspected that her boyfriend was involved. Teresa recalled: 'I was having a drink with some friends and we were talking about the rape. I said that the description issued by the police sounded just like Billy and I said, "I have a good mind to tell the police." But I didn't shop him.'[43]

The *Derbyshire Times* devoted their front page to the story on 27 August 1976. Under the headline, 'Massive Hunt for Vicious Rapist', Superintendent Tommy Hoggart issued a prophetic warning to readers: 'It's an unusual case. These are serious incidents – and if the offender is not caught, there could be a repetition.'[44] For the time being, however, the danger had passed: Billy was already in custody, renounced by someone extremely close to him.

Rumours abound regarding the manner of his arrest, most commonly that he tried to evade capture by hiding in an ottoman at the foot of a bed, or in a cupboard under the stairs. Reality was more prosaic, as Detective Constable John Field remembers, since he and burly Detective Constable Brian Bunting were tasked with following up the tip-off: 'We knocked on the door and it was answered by another fella [Teresa's brother, Robert Millan]. We told him we were there for Hughes and why. He called over his shoulder and Hughes came out straight away from another room. He was docile, no arguments, nothing. We took him to Beetwell Street and that was the last I saw of him.'[45]

One of the few women then in Chesterfield CID joined DC Bunting in an interviewing room at the police station. WDC Ann

Wain (née Pennycook) has fragmentary recall of Billy's arrest but required no prompting on one aspect: 'His eyes were weird. Cold and penetrating. He looked right through you. He was cooperative enough and very polite, but he refused to say it was rape.'[46] Under caution, Billy admitted that he had been in the park on the night in question, but swore he had injured Steven T. only in self-defence and that Fiona Y. had been 'responsive' to sex.[47]

Scene of Crime Officer John Slater was also at the station that evening, photographing suspects in the rape case for presentation to Fiona Y. At 8.30 p.m., his door flew open: 'It was Brian Bunting and he needed me to take a photo of this chap they had just brought in. Brian led Hughes into the room then went next door for a cuppa. I pointed to a chair and Hughes sat down. It was a funny thing: where I set up my camera was just behind a table, and on that evening the table was laden with Stanley knives and weapons of various descriptions. He could have picked up any of them but thank God he didn't.'

Slater pauses, remembering. 'I looked at him through the camera lens and I got a shock. He was staring straight back at me, unblinking. His gaze was so direct: cold, grey eyes. I never get spooked, but there was just something about him. Anyway, I took the photo and Hughes left with Brian. He never spoke once and I was on my own with him for several minutes. Now, that's unusual – every suspect says something. But he didn't. Just that cold, grey stare . . . it made the hairs on the back of my neck stand on end, even then. And that was before Pottery Cottage . . .'[48]

Chapter Four:

Those Bastards Stitched Me Up

CHESTERFIELD MAGISTRATES' COURT was a place that Billy would come to know well in the months preceding his escape from prison. A modernist block built in the early 1960s, it comprised several offices and cells on the ground floor, and court-rooms on the upper storey behind a series of concrete gables and louvred glass. On the morning after his arrest, Billy made a brief appearance in the dock to confirm that he understood the charges. He entered no plea and was remanded in custody until 3 September.

Billy's transfer to prison took him fifty-five miles south down the M1 to HMP Leicester, home to sentenced and remand inmates since 1828. The imposing façade with its battlements and portcullis dominated Welford Road on the fringes of the city centre, deceiving visitors into imagining it was in fact a medieval castle. Inside were two cell blocks consisting of four landings each, where prisoners slept in groups of three. Built to house 218 men, in late 1976 that number was exceeded by at least 100 souls.

Upon admission, Billy gave at least one false statement to the authorities. After asking for his estranged wife Jean to be documented as next of kin, he supplied another woman's name and address as his second contact, falsely claiming her to be his sister. He was then examined by Dr G. B. Grayling, the Prison Medical Officer, who recalled: '[Billy] was in good physical health but stated that he was liable to outbursts of aggression and violence. This matter was discussed with him at the time and I advised him to seek an interview with me rather than become involved in any confrontations with other inmates. I made a note in the reception register that he gave assurances that he would not harm any person in this prison and from that time on I had no cause to see him again with regard to his conduct or attitude.'[1] Billy was allocated to the Remand Wing, where in accordance of the regulations for remand prisoners, he was allowed to retain his own clothing.

Form 293 in respect of William Thomas Hughes ('no fixed abode') was received at the Discipline Office of HMP Leicester the following day. Completed by Derbyshire Police, this was a standard form for prisoners who presented special risks, with statements to be deleted as appropriate and a box for any additional information that might assist the governor in determining whether extra security measures should be taken. In Billy's case, Form 293 advised that he presented 'an exceptional risk' on three grounds: being 'likely to try to escape', 'of a violent nature' and possessing 'suicidal tendencies'. No further details were given but in line with normal procedure, the officer on cell duty at Chesterfield Police Station confirmed the information with a phone call to the Reception Department that day. However, neither an up-to-date list of Billy's convictions nor his previous custodial records from Prison Department Headquarters were received until after his escape in January 1977. Full details of his most recent offence were likewise delayed, prompting the Chief of the Prison Service to comment in his March 1977 inquiry into the case: 'This offence is, of course, synonymous with rape, a word which appears on later committal warrants but which does not, to the layman, convey the same impression of the use of force; nor at the time had Hughes been charged with grievous bodily harm with intent, which appeared on some of the subsequent committal warrants but not until after 10 December 1976.' As a result, Billy was never subject to the level of extra security needed to contain him.

He appeared at Chesterfield Magistrates' Court on 3 September, conveyed via minibus and handcuffed to a single prison officer with another as escort. Remanded in custody until 10 September, he was described by the two guards as 'run-of-the-mill'. On 8 September, he arrived in Blackpool to face charges of chequebook forgery and burglary, deferred from March. Two officers accompanied him in a hired car; one was handcuffed to Billy and sat with him in the back of the vehicle, while the other seated himself in front beside the driver. The journey took around three hours, including a stop for petrol at an M6 service station.

Billy was sentenced at Blackpool Magistrates' Court to six months' imprisonment for each offence, to run concurrently. Afterwards, he was startled to see his wife, who received a suspended prison sentence for theft and handling stolen goods. Jean was shaken by their encounter, having only received one visit from Billy since he moved to Chesterfield. Although neither of them knew it, the meeting in Blackpool would be their last.

Billy's behaviour following his appearance in Blackpool 'gave no cause for concern'. Although Teresa later claimed to have destroyed two letters in which Billy 'pleaded' with her to stand by him, official records state otherwise: 'During his time at Leicester Prison, Hughes attempted a reconciliation with his wife and did not write to his girlfriend at all.' The Welfare Department continued to mediate in 'domestic upsets' between Billy and Jean, but there was no real possibility of his marriage surviving and most of his friendships collapsed. Gary Evans, Billy's former drinking partner, confirmed, 'We all washed our hands of him after he had been arrested, but I knew he would be feeling like a caged animal in prison. I thought it would send him loopy.'[2]

In the wake of his conviction, Billy was interviewed by the prison's Observation and Classification Unit, who made no reference to the concerns raised by Form 293, designating him a Category B prisoner. He was then assigned to work in the kitchens, almost certainly after expressing an interest in that department. On 9 September he completed the first of many shifts and was later described as having 'worked well on a demanding job', often making 'light conversation' with the Senior Officer Caterer. There were no reports of misconduct in any area and his interaction with fellow inmates was good, especially during recreation periods when he participated in games.

On the morning of 10 September, a prison warder collected Billy from work in the kitchens for another appearance at Chesterfield Magistrates' Court. In reception, he changed out of his uniform into civilian clothing and was led to a hired car, where there were two escorts as before. After arriving in Chesterfield, Billy received a visit from his solicitor in the cells below the courtrooms. Long-established local law firm W&A Glossops were representing him on Legal Aid and had commissioned consultant psychiatrist Jonathan Stirland, then in his early fifties, to examine their client. Billy opened up to Stirland about his childhood and criminal career but became visibly upset when asked how his mother had responded to the Chesterfield charges, admitting he had yet to write to her. Stirland's report of their interview remains confidential, but he saw no evidence of psychosis or 'sub-normality' in Billy and thus found him fit to plead.[3]

Since he was already serving a prison sentence, Billy was remanded on bail until 5 November for a notional fee. On the journey back to prison, he spoke little and seemed 'subdued'. The senior escort sought out the Senior Officer Caterer on arrival, informing him that the charge was now identified legally as rape. He suggested removing Billy from association with other prisoners for his own protection, but Rule 43 was never implemented.

Billy duly appeared at Chesterfield Magistrates' Court on 5 November and was again remanded on bail in the sum of £50 until 3 December. His escorts described him on that occasion as 'quiet and not talkative'. Two weeks later papers were served on Billy's solicitors, who telephoned Chesterfield Police the day before committal proceedings were due to begin, on 25 November. His request for an adjournment was granted.

On the morning of 3 December 1976, Billy headed to the prison kitchens, aware that a guard would collect him before the end of his shift for the journey to court. He spent the time cutting meat and making sandwiches until the escort arrived. In what was now an established routine, he changed from his prison uniform into civilian clothing at Reception, where three remand prisoners were also waiting for the same minibus, two bound for Chesterfield and the other for Burton-on-Trent. The men were handcuffed in pairs, then took their seats on the vehicle.

After stopping briefly for the first handover, the minibus drove on to Chesterfield, where police took custody of the two remaining remands. All seemed normal, until a court official appeared with a message for Billy's escorts to telephone HMP Leicester: a boning knife was missing from the prison kitchens.

The discovery had been made shortly before 9 a.m. by a Catering Officer, who immediately informed the Security Department. Instructions were issued for a search of the kitchens and the prisoners who worked there, together with their cells, while two officers spent a fruitless hour trawling through the refuse skip. The Regulating Officer realised that Billy had been in the kitchens earlier but was no longer on the premises; he told the Principal Security Officer to 'intercept the escort' on its way to Chesterfield, but it was too late. Instead, the warders in charge of Billy had to search and question him in the cells below the courts. They found nothing and he denied all knowledge of the knife, described as 7½ inches long and sharpened to a point for boning meat. He was then ushered into court.

A charge of grievous bodily harm was added to the offence of rape, and magistrates remanded him in custody until 10 December. Handcuffed to one of the two escorts for the return journey to Leicester, Billy made 'normal' conversation with them and gave the impression of being 'a model prisoner'. In Reception, he changed his clothes and was led back to his cell, which had been searched in his absence. Thereafter, Billy 'melted into the background and was unobtrusive'.

But the remand prisoner who had been handcuffed to him on the outward journey to court subsequently claimed that Billy had shown him the knife as they were driven towards Chesterfield. His story proved 'inconsistent' under cross-examination months later, but could not be entirely discounted. Reflecting on the issue, the Chief Inspector of Prisons stated that 'the possibility of the knife being taken out of the prison and returned the same day must remain'.

The Catering Officer who had reported the knife missing twice rang his Senior at home on sick leave that day; he in turn contacted the prison and was uneasy to be told the following morning simply that 'Security have it in hand'.

Three months later, when the Chief Inspector of Prisons examined all the documentation at HMP Leicester in relation to the incident, he found only one record: an entry in the Security Officer's Daily Diary, which read: '3 December 1976: Knife reported missing in the kitchen. Extensive search made of kitchen and surrounding area but to no avail.' He was unable to discover any statements about the searches and 'most' of the forty-five members of prison staff whom he interviewed admitted to being unaware that a knife was missing until after Billy made the headlines.

In addition, the Chief Inspector of Prisons found no statements from the escort staff regarding their on-the-spot searches and questioning of Billy, leading him to observe: 'This vital piece of intelligence was not recorded. Nor were the staff as a whole alerted to the fact that the knife missing from the kitchen was associated with Hughes in any way. No entry was made in the prisoner's record, no strip search was ordered on his return to the prison and he was relocated in the same cell.' The search itself 'was not coordinated or pursued with sufficient vigour'.

Nonetheless, a senior prison officer later told a *Guardian* journalist: 'We became concerned because we knew Hughes was a dangerous man. An officer asked for a full-scale search, which is normal, and it would have meant every prisoner being locked up and then a thorough search made of every cell. The request was refused by an officer holding governor's rank.'[4]

Billy's employment in the prison kitchen continued until 5 January 1977. He made three further appearances at Chesterfield Magistrates' Court prior to that date. The first of these was on 10 December 1976 with both the outward and the return journey following the usual routine; his escorts described him as 'quite a pleasant prisoner'. In court, however, Billy refused a Section I Committal in which all the evidence would be presented in writing, choosing to exercise his right to request that the young woman whom he was accused of raping should give her evidence in person. He refused advice offered to him by all parties on the issue, and arrangements were made for an old-style committal to take place on 17 December.

As per Billy's request, when he arrived handcuffed to his escort in Chesterfield on that date, a special court had been reconvened with a magistrate standing by. Fiona Y. and her boyfriend Steven T. waited to be called as exhibits were produced. Suddenly, Billy turned to his solicitor: he had decided to accept the Section I Committal after all. The two visibly shaken witnesses were sent home, along with the special magistrate. But as Billy prepared to face committal proceedings under the swifter system, he changed his mind again. A court spokesman reflected: 'If we hadn't let the witnesses go home we could have started an old-style committal even then.'[5] Remanded for one week, Billy was described by his escorts as 'placid' throughout the journey back to prison.

The morning of Christmas Eve saw Billy return to Chesterfield. His solicitor, Allan Cobain, visited him in the cells below the courtroom to discuss bail. As Billy stood in the dock, Cobain explained to the magistrates that his client's sentence would end on 6 January 1977, when he hoped to be released on bail. Arrangements were made for Billy to appear on 5 January for the outcome of that decision. 'Quiet and subdued', he returned to spend Christmas and New Year in jail.

Billy was on kitchen shift when an officer collected him during the morning of 5 January 1977. He changed into his civilian clothes in Reception before being subjected to a requisite rub-down. The Chief Inspector of Prisons described these searches as 'variable in quality, but even if they had been of the greatest thoroughness one could not be confident that, were a knife to have been secreted on his person, it would necessarily have been found'.

A hired car was used to transport Billy to Chesterfield on an 'uneventful' journey. He sat handcuffed to an officer on the rear seat while the senior escort sat beside the driver. At the Magistrates' Court, Billy had another meeting with Allan Cobain about his committal for trial; his solicitor informed him that bail would not be granted. Remanded in custody until 12 January, Billy seemed 'unperturbed' by the outcome. There was an impromptu stop on the journey back to Leicester when the senior escort realised that he had forgotten to book Billy off the Centre roll before leaving prison that morning; he rectified this with a call to the prison from a telephone kiosk.

For the remainder of the journey, Billy 'made general conversation' with his escorts, commenting that he was 'looking forward to a lie-in the next morning' now that he no longer had to work in the kitchens. He then added that he hoped to get bail within a fortnight.

The following day, despite his seeming acceptance of the magistrates' decision to keep him behind bars, Billy asked to speak to the Senior Officer. He told him that he had been refused bail, then remarked bitterly, 'I think those bastards stitched me up.' It was unclear whom he meant.

On average, prisoners could expect around ten weeks to pass between first remand and committal. In Billy's case, partly as a result of the delays he himself had insisted upon, four months had elapsed. And although his solicitor insisted otherwise, in view of events that were about to unfold, there can be little doubt that Billy made full use of the extended time and repeated journeys by familiarising himself with the route and plotting his escape.

Billy's next departure from prison would be his last.

Part Two:

Day 1, Wednesday
12 January, 1977

Chapter Five:

Hijack

Prior to 1977, only one inmate had managed to escape from HMP Leicester. In 1953, 'safe blower' Albert Hattersley used webbing and a pipe from the toilets to scale the highest prison walls in England, but broke his ankle dropping to freedom and was apprehended the following day.

William Thomas Hughes developed a more strategic plan based on what he knew best: opportunity and violence. His sequestering of the boning knife and knowledge of both route and routine during his trips to Chesterfield Magistrates' Court were fundamental, but the morning of Wednesday 12 January 1977 presented him with a further element: appalling weather. Parts of the country had already seen hail and snow, but overnight it had spread and intensified, leading to severe disruption on the roads that Billy was due to travel.

At 7.45 a.m., the prison officers tasked with escorting Billy to his remand hearing reported for duty. Former lorry driver Ken Simmonds was a forty-one-year-old amateur boxer who lived with his wife and children in Leicester Forest East. Described as 'a reliable, responsible officer' by a fellow warder, Simmonds had worked at the prison for three years when he collected Billy from his cell that morning and escorted him to Reception.[1] Simmonds's colleague was already in the green-walled room, filling in forms. As the senior officer with fourteen years' experience at Leicester Prison, forty-six-year-old Don Sprintall was responsible for hand-cuffs, keys and paperwork. Stoic and stocky, he too lived locally with his wife and children.

Simmonds carried out a standard search of the prisoner in Reception, running his fingers around the collar of Billy's mauve shirt and across his waistcoat, then along the inside and outside of his legs before checking the pockets of his blue pinstripe suit. He stopped just short of Billy's black, prison-issue boots. Slipping the handcuffs on, he secured Billy's right wrist to his left and handed the keys to Sprintall, who fastened them on to a lock on his belt and tucked them inside his trouser pocket.

'We had no reason to suspect [Billy] was dangerous,' the senior officer recalled. 'As far as we knew, he was just a normal weekly remand prisoner to be handed over to the police for the magis-trates' court. The only thing we knew was that he was on a charge of rape. If we'd known that he was of a violent nature, he would have been searched more thoroughly. He would have been given a strip search and the powers that be would probably have decided he would go under a security escort. We took the normal precau-tions . . . which was virtually nothing.'[2]

Informed that their transport had arrived, Sprintall left to collect the route form granting authority for the journey while Simmonds led Billy out into the whirling snow. Highfield Taxis proprietor David Reynolds, a thirty-two-year-old married father of two, waited at the wheel of a Persian-blue Morris Leyland 1800 saloon. 'Steady money' was how Reynolds described his previous experience of driving inmates to court hearings, although Chesterfield was new to him.[3] Throughout the country as a whole, around 24,000 journeys a year were made transporting remand prisoners to court in hired cars; on a peak day, there might be in excess of 200 taxis operating from remand centres and jails.

Ken Simmonds directed Billy to the rear nearside passenger seat and slid in beside him, pulling the door shut. A thick blast of hot air surged from the car heater as Reynolds drove to the castellated gatehouse, where Don Sprintall climbed in beside the driver, clutching the obligatory route form. Neither warder knew David Reynolds, who switched on the car stereo as they edged out on to busy Welford Road. Guitar chords strummed from the eight-track cassette player, followed by Elvis Presley belting out 'Jailhouse Rock'. The irony was lost on none of them.

At 8.20 a.m., travel was sluggish through the blizzard-hit suburbs but eventually the taxi merged on to the northbound M1. 'Everything was all right on the journey to Chesterfield,' Don Sprintall recalled. 'There was a little bit of conversation about motor cars and fishing.'[4] Ridges of blackened slush lay between each motorway lane, slowing traffic to an occasional crawl. As they progressed through Nottinghamshire, Billy began to fidget and asked for a toilet stop.

Sprintall shook his head. 'No chance yet, we're not far from the Chesterfield turn-off.'[5]

After a few minutes, Billy insisted, 'I'll have to go, boss, I'm bursting.'[6] When Sprintall refused again, Billy threatened to defecate in the taxi.

Almost simultaneously, a sign appeared for Trowell Services, between junctions 25 and 26 of the M1. Sprintall instructed Reynolds to leave the motorway and pull into the heavy goods area, hoping to avoid members of the public. At first Reynolds missed the transport parking area and had to go back to it. He remained seated in the car while his passengers headed for the toilets some twenty yards away.

Simmonds and Sprintall were relieved no one else was inside the building. After checking security, Sprintall took the handcuffs from Billy, who slipped inside a cubicle. 'He just pushed the door to but he never attempted to lock it,' Simmonds recalled.[7] They heard Billy use the toilet, then paper rustling and the chain being pulled before he emerged. Sprintall fastened the handcuffs on the two men as before, retaining the keys on his chain. The three of them then returned to their previous seating positions inside the car.

Afterwards, the general consensus among the authorities was that Billy had used his time in the toilet cubicle to withdraw the boning knife from where it was hidden – either between his legs or in his boots – and slipped it into a more accessible position for the imminent attack. He was silent as they joined the motorway again, biding his time but ready to seize the moment.

He did not have long to wait. Junction 29 to Chesterfield loomed out from the slanting snow and Reynolds swerved in from the centre lane, passing the three marker posts for the exit. 'I was leaving the hard shoulder on to the slip road when I heard a thud,' he remembered. 'I turned and saw the prison officer in the front seat slumping forward . . .'[8]

Billy had pulled out the boning knife and lunged at Sprintall, drawing the blade deep across the back of his neck.

'My immediate reaction was that a lorry had hit us from behind,' the wounded prison officer recalled. 'It was such a violent blow. I remember slumping forward and putting my right hand on the back of my neck. I remember feeling a large, sticky mass and somebody shouting, "Keep going!"'[9]

Handcuffed to Billy, Simmonds had no time to register what had happened to his colleague before seeing the blade flash: 'He turned on me and struck at my throat. I went backwards and then went to struggle with Hughes and saw a knife in his hand. He chopped out at my right hand, cutting me across my thumb. He was shouting, "Get the keys!" and telling the taxi driver to carry on. I saw my hand was bleeding and then I noticed blood dripping on to the seat and floor [from] my neck.'[10]

Billy had plunged the knife into Simmonds's throat and palm, leaving him fighting for his life and Reynolds stunned by the speed of the attacks. 'I was still on the slip road when I heard the officer in the back seat say, "You've got me in my jugular, stop, you don't want me to die, do you?"' the taxi driver recalled. 'By this time, I was almost on the [traffic] island, but the prisoner said to me, "Keep going!"'[11]

Sprintall managed to pass the keys from the chain on his belt to Simmonds, who tried to get his own hand free until Billy jabbed the knife into his ribs, barking to be released first. Shoving Simmonds to the floor, he got up to change places with Sprintall, shouting, 'Get your arm over here!'[12] The senior officer bent his arm awkwardly: 'I could see Ken still handcuffed in the back and [Billy] then handcuffed my left wrist . . . I was holding my neck, trying to stop the bleeding, but without any success.'[13]

'Get in the back, get down!' Billy yelled at Sprintall, dragging him backwards. As the officer collapsed face down on the seat above his colleague on the floor, Billy climbed over them both to sit beside the driver. He dug the knife into Reynolds's side, instructing him to turn right and keep going until he reached the main road, then right again at some snow-covered roadworks before the start of a dual carriageway.

'I had a knife pointed at me all the time,' Reynolds recalled. 'I was told I'd be all right – if I did as I was told. I was really worried about the warder who was stabbed in the neck. There was a lot of blood everywhere. I couldn't hear a word from him. I was badly frightened. As far as I knew the warder could have been dead. The whole journey was a nightmare – it's something I can't really put into words.'[14]

Twice Billy brandished the knife over the two injured men, warning, 'Keep your heads down or you'll get it!'[15] Simmonds struggled to stay conscious: 'I was bleeding quite freely from my neck and I could see my thumb was badly gashed and bleeding heavily. I could also see Don was bleeding heavily from a wound on his neck. When Hughes first put me on the car floor I was having difficulty breathing and I really thought he'd done my jugular. I asked several times for him to stop but he refused, saying, "Get down."'[16]

Billy leaned backwards, nudging Sprintall: 'Let's have your wallet.'[17] Almost catatonic, the warder mumbled, 'I've only got loose change.'[18] Simmonds passed his own wallet to Billy, who withdrew its contents – a single £1 note – before throwing it back and jabbing Sprintall again.

'I can't reach mine,' the senior officer moaned.

'Where is it?'

'In my back left-hand trouser pocket.'[19]

Billy found it and removed three £1 notes, remarking in disgust, 'You screws don't carry much.'[20] Dropping the wallet to the floor, he turned to Reynolds. 'Have you got any money?'[21]

Painfully conscious of the knife at his side, the driver removed a £5 note and several £1 notes from his jacket pocket. Billy counted out a total of £17, then glanced at Reynolds. 'You've got more than them two – they must be poorly paid.'[22]

Sprintall's gaze slid towards his watch. It was only 9.15 a.m. – one hour since they had left Leicester Prison, but it felt like a lifetime. He touched his neck, recoiling as his fingers found a bloody cavity instead of flesh. From the floor, Simmonds grunted, 'He's got me in my throat.'[23] Sprintall tried to reassure him but was too weak and groggy to sound convincing.

The dual carriageway ended at a set of traffic lights. Beyond the red light and a plain concrete bridge, Chesterfield's twisted spire emerged from the white pall like a ship's mast.

Billy issued further directions when the lights changed, taking the Morris through the suburbs and up a hill into open country-side at Stonedge, some seventeen miles from the scene of the motorway attack. Snowy boughs hung over the road as it steepened to a plateau. On Billy's orders, Reynolds took a right-hand turn towards open moorland, where the substantial stone building of the Red Lion pub stood a few hundred yards away on the left.

Billy twisted in his seat to look at the wounded men. 'When we stop, get out and get out quick. And keep walking.'[24]

He turned back, telling Reynolds: 'Pull over. Put your hand-brake on and leave the engine running.'[25]

The Morris slid towards the verge, where a large shrub drooped under a thick blanket of snow. On the opposite side of the road a steel gate led to a small, wooded knoll.

Billy pressed the knife lightly into Reynolds's ribs, speaking loud and fast: 'Get out, climb that gate, and don't come back until I've gone, understand?'[26] Reynolds unlocked the door and stumbled out. Desperate to put some distance between himself and the madman in the Morris, he half-ran half-fell across the road to the gate, vaulting over it and dashing for the trees.

'You two next!' Billy shouted at the prison warders. He scrambled into the driver's seat, swiftly checking the controls. Simmonds and Sprintall helped each other across the road, leaving a bloody trail in the snow. Sprintall clutched the gate for support. He turned to see Billy's face contorted with fury and concentration as the Morris quickened into life with a series of loud revs, then set off at speed, tyres screeching on the ice until the car righted itself, disappearing over the white horizon. A deafening silence descended, broken only by the soft flurry of snow.

Reynolds edged down the knoll to join the two guards, shocked beyond words at the severity of their injuries. Sprintall, especially, had lost a lot of blood from the gaping hole in his neck, while Simmonds also bled copiously as he mutely handed his wallet to Reynolds for safekeeping.

All three men heard a sports car roaring up the hill, but only Reynolds was fit to sprint towards the vehicle as it turned in at the junction. The driver pulled up sharply and wound down his window, aghast at the explanation for the scene at the roadside. He sped off to call for an ambulance from the Red Lion, where he worked as manager. The publican was the first person to alert the authorities; Chesterfield Police logged his call at 9.56 a.m. and dispatched a traffic car to Stonedge.

A GPO Land Rover rounded the junction a few minutes later, driven by telephone engineer George McClymont and his young colleague Mark Fisher. Assuming the badly injured uniformed men were Securicor officers who had been robbed, Fisher searched out the first-aid kit while McClymont used bolt-cutters to remove the handcuffs. Fisher later described how Simmonds's wounds 'were still bleeding quite profusely' and Sprintall 'was holding a yellow rag to the right of his neck'. He added: 'I gave him a bandage and saw that there was a lot of blood there. Both men seemed shocked and to be suffering a lot through their injuries. The taxi driver was uninjured but appeared shocked and shaken up.'[27]

A third vehicle appeared as the group discussed a course of action. Reynolds approached the bronze Hillman Hunter, calling, 'There's been a stabbing accident – can you take these two men to hospital?' The driver agreed but needed Mark Fisher's help in directing him there. He recalled: 'On the way I was told what had happened. The only comment I made was to say, "Where did he get the knife from?" and one of the officers in the back said, "I don't know. He was searched." '[28]

The last vehicle to stop was a Severn Water Authority van. On Reynolds's urging, the driver used his radio to contact police at 10 a.m., informing them that a prisoner had escaped 'from Walton' (rather than Leicester, as was the case) and was 'heading towards Matlock' in a stolen Morris saloon.[29] Mobile units were sent to road junctions in the Matlock area to watch for the hijacked car, with observations at static points and patrols in the surrounding region.

While Reynolds left the scene with McClymont in the Land Rover, bound for Beetwell Street Police Station, Mark Fisher rang the station at 10.07 a.m. from Chesterfield Royal Hospital. Detectives arrived but were unable to speak to either prison officer, both of whom required emergency surgery. The medical report on Sprintall found that he had sustained 'a serious gaping and deep wound over 5 in. in length around the right side of the neck from just behind the right ear to the middle of the back of the neck. The deeper muscles very near the spine were lacerated.'[30] Surgeons considered a blood transfusion but Sprintall proved as resilient as his colleague Simmonds, who bore two knife wounds: 'One to the face and another to the right hand. He had an S-shaped laceration about 1½ in. long and nearly ½ an inch deep on the right side of the chin over the lower jaw bone and just into the neck below the chin. In the centre of the wound the jaw bone was exposed. There was also a deep wound nearly 3 in. long in the palm of the right hand around the base of the thumb. The muscles were cut through almost down to the bone.'[31]

At 10.23 a.m. a traffic officer located the Morris Leyland saloon, peering in at the blood-soaked upholstery. It had crashed into a wall on the moors two miles from the Red Lion, in the vicinity of Hell Bank Plantation.

The man in charge of the immediate search for Billy Hughes was thirty-nine-year-old Peter Howse, son of a Glossop millworker. He had joined the police in 1956, on his return from National Service in Iraq as a member of the RAF. For the first ten years he worked operationally in uniform, CID and Crime Squad, and became a qualified police training instructor. In 1975, he was promoted to Chief Inspector as Sub-Divisional Commander of Buxton South.

Howse was in his office at Bakewell Police Station when the call came through alerting him to the escape of Billy Hughes; Beeley Moor, where the crashed Morris had been found, was on the border of Bakewell's sub-division. Despite the inclement weather, he and Detective Constable John Burton drove straight to the scene.

Four police officers were already there: the traffic patrol officer, two dog handlers, and a police constable from Chesterfield, who strode up to Chief Inspector Howse and loudly informed him, 'The dogs are useless, sir. They just bounded on to the moor for a piss, then ran back to their handlers.'[32] The two men responsible for the Alsatians looked uncomfortable. Knowing from his own experience that Derbyshire's dog section was among the country's finest, Howse curtly dispatched the constable to a static point on the other side of the moor. He then conferred with the handlers, who explained that the predominant scent in the car belonged to the wounded prison officers, whose blood saturated the floor, seats and doors.

In the hour that had passed since the crash, that same strong, easterly cross wind had barrelled down from the moor, depositing snow on either side of the road under the drystone walls and obliterating any footprints or tyre tracks. Eyewitness reports of the Morris and its hijacker were also absent, given that anyone living in the vicinity who needed to travel was sticking to the roads in the valley below.

While the traffic patrol officer returned to his vehicle, Howse and Burton accompanied the dogs and their handlers over Hell Bank Plantation. The ground was treacherous, rising and falling with no discernible path and few distinguishing features. The dogs ran towards the spine of trees rising from the flatter land to the skyline but were unable to pick up any trace of the escapee. After numerous stumbles and muttered curses, the four men returned to the Morris and the traffic patrol officer, who sat inside his own vehicle, speaking to headquarters via the radio. Its distorted static crackle snapped in the air.

Chief Inspector Howse and Detective Constable Burton left the handlers to continue the search. Returning to Bakewell Police Station they found a series of Ordnance Survey maps had already been pinned to the walls alongside a blackboard and an easel showing a rough sketch of the area where Billy had crashed the car. Given its position, it seemed possible if not probable that he had been heading for Blackpool and still might aim to reach the A6, perhaps hiding out until he could obtain further transport. Working on the blackboard, Howse started from the last place their quarry was known to have been – the crash site on Beeley Moor – and drew two concentric circles: one of three-miles radius and a second of six miles. Then, using the Ordnance Survey maps, Howse and his team identified the most likely places where Billy might be.

'Isolated farms, houses and outbuildings were the most obvious choices, as were the nearest villages,' Howse explains. 'But to do the job properly we needed a lot more officers. By early afternoon I had managed to secure three dog handlers and enough manpower to form small search teams of three or four officers each to search farms and more isolated buildings and houses within the three-mile radius. At first, we didn't realise how long it would take to search a single farm and all the barns and outbuildings. It took on average four hours, which meant that a single team could only search two properties per shift and were exhausted when they had finished climbing into roof spaces and investigating other odd spots that were hard to access. Given the resources we had, it simply wasn't possible to visit every single property in the district, so we had to decide which were the most vulnerable.'[33] Nonetheless, 256 premises were searched during the first few hours by officers across the region, briefed to question farmers and home owners to ensure that the fugitive was not clandestinely present and 'threatening the inhabitants'.[34]

Reflecting on the early stages of the search, Howse states: 'It seemed unlikely Hughes would have run across the open moorland on either side of the road. But a man in fear of being caught might do anything. He could well have done what was least expected of him. He could even have doubled back but that seemed unlikely. It would be natural to run away from the crashed car in case of immediate pursuit. We didn't have a photograph of him then but one was on its way and a copy of his record had been received by tele-printer. I spoke to the CID at Preston and Blackpool and was left in no doubt that Hughes was a danger to the public and anyone who confronted him.'[35]

Three policing divisions were involved in the immediate search and resources were later drafted in from Derby Division in the south of the county. Buxton Division was divided into north and south sub-divisions. The one in the north was based at Buxton itself and the other – where Chief Inspector Howse was in charge – was based at Bakewell and covered a wide area of the Peak District National Park, from Ashbourne in the west to the Hope Valley in the east.

'Basically, we ran a three-shift system from our office,' Howse recalls. 'Most of the staff were long-serving and very experienced officers who had to cover wide areas while working alone, and they lived in the area too, of course, so they had a huge amount of local knowledge. An inspector and a sergeant were allocated to each shift and when one wasn't present, I covered for them, so it was very much team policing. We all knew each other very well.'[36]

The three divisions would carry out search procedures for their own area of responsibility while liaising closely with each other. After manual collation, these results were then to be fed via fax or phone into the incident room at Chesterfield, run by Superintendent Tommy Hoggart, who was familiar with Billy Hughes from his most recent offences in the town.

'Chesterfield had more resources and staff trained in incident-room procedures,' Howse explains. 'There were no computers in those days. It was mostly as a result of reservations about this case and, far more so, the then current Yorkshire Ripper investigation in nearby Yorkshire that would help bring about the changes that saw the introduction of the computerised HOLMES system in dealing with major incidents. HOLMES was developed by a specialised team of police and scientists at the Home Office and allowed us to feed everything we had learned about a case into the computer, which could then cross-reference any number of points. So, for instance, if one witness talked about a suspect in a red car, we could put that into the search engine and the computer would bring up every single previous mention of a red car. I played a small part in that when the system was trialled and tested following a murder at Cromford, Derbyshire, in 1979, where the bodies of two teenagers were found in woodland. But I think it's fair to say that even if HOLMES had been available during the search for Hughes, the results would have been the same. There was no information forthcoming from any source which we could have acted upon and the family he went on to take hostage went to great lengths to cover his tracks by convincing their workmates, relatives, friends and even callers to the house that all was well at Pottery Cottage.'[37]

Promised more men as and when they became available, in the meantime Chief Inspector Howse arranged for the morning shift to be kept on and brought forward those officers working the afternoon shift. Nevertheless, apart from those already engaged in the search, everyone seemed preoccupied by the snow storm forecast to hit later that day. 'Under the circumstances, the best tactic seemed to be to spread the word about the escape and seek help from the public,' Howse recalls. 'I had agreed to give a talk to the Rotary Club at the Rutland Arms Hotel that day – instead of cancelling by phone I did it in person, knowing there would be about thirty businessmen present who employed local people. I also spoke to the deputy headmaster of Lady Manners Comprehensive School, which had a wide catchment area, and called in at the British Legion Club to leave a message for the Colonel, asking him to notify everyone. Basically, we returned to the old "Hue and Cry" system, which had been a common way of mobilising and alerting the public to any potentially dangerous incident before the Derbyshire Police Force was founded in 1857. The principle being that one person passed the message on to another and that person did the same until the whole community was alert and on the lookout for the wanted man. In that respect, the "Hue and Cry" approach worked: we later found out that the house where Hughes was hiding out received calls from friends who had heard our announcements about his escape and who did as we asked, ringing to check that all was well. But the family at Pottery Cottage covered for him and they did it very well – because they thought that was their best chance of surviving. So under those circumstances, there was little else we could have done.'[38]

Area constables undertook similar tasks in all the surrounding villages. Officers arriving from outside the sub-division were directed to a briefing room in the market place at Bakewell while other facilities were organised at Chatsworth Institute and the Wheatsheaf Hotel in Baslow. With Chatsworth House and Haddon Hall both within range, police contacted the estate workers, asking them to be vigilant. Likewise, all the publicans and shopkeepers in the district were notified to spread the word among staff and customers.

'The media were my next port of call,' Howse continues. 'The *Star* was the first paper to contact us after receiving a tip-off about an escaped prisoner. We relayed information to the local press throughout the day and thereafter extended it to the nationals. I also rang Radio Sheffield, who sent someone out to interview me. As well as asking people to pass on any information about Hughes, I was keen to impart how dangerous he could be. In addition to his long history of violence, Hughes was carrying a knife with which he had viciously attacked two prison officers. Their wounds were of a very serious nature and could easily have resulted in the deaths of either officer. Under the circumstances, it was amazing they were still alive. Hughes's determination to escape was no doubt matched by his determination to remain at liberty, rendering him a risk to anyone with whom he came into contact. Prior to that morning, he was looking at seven to ten years in prison for rape and GBH, but his actions since meant he faced life imprisonment. He had nothing to lose by killing someone who tried to confront or detain him. We knew he had form for stealing cars and burglary so he may well have nicked a vehicle or broken in somewhere. But with no reports of either, we had to assume he was still with us.'[39]

The second edition of all local newspapers highlighted the story on every front page. 'Knifeman Prisoner Hijacks Taxi' read the headline in the *Lancashire Evening Post*, warning: 'A massive police hunt was launched this afternoon for a former Blackpool man who attacked his prison officer escorts with a knife and escaped while on his way to court ... Police who are searching the Chatsworth Park area with dogs appealed to members of the public not to approach him and they also advised motorists in the area not to pick up hitchhikers.'[40] The *West Lancashire Evening Gazette* declared: 'Blackpool Danger Alert for Fugitive: Blackpool and Fylde police were put on alert today to watch out for an escaped dangerous prisoner who used to live in Blackpool ... A Blackpool police spokesman said they had been alerted to look out for Hughes and a watch was being kept on his old addresses in the resort.'[41]

Detectives collected Jean Hughes and her children from home and placed them in a refuge. Billy's daughter packed a favourite rag doll and a toy hairdryer and rollers, gifts from her father:

'Because he wasn't in prison I thought we'd be together. I can remember feeling excited, happy.'[42] From the old sash window of the refuge, Nichola watched the snow falling and worried about her dad alone in the cold. Jean was out of her mind with worry, but not for herself or the children: 'I was sick for the warders. I thought he would come back to Blackpool but I didn't think he would come to do me any harm. He had no reason to.'[43] The police assured her that they would accompany her daughters to and from Revoe Infants School every day until their quarry had been found. A special watch was placed on the trains carrying thousands of Blackpool football supporters to Derby, where they were due to play the home side in an FA Cup replay; detectives believed it possible that Billy might head for the match and return home in the crowd. But as the day wore on and the weather worsened, the game was cancelled.

'All our efforts to gain public support in the hunt for Hughes fell on deaf ears,' Howse reflects. 'We received no feedback whatsoever. Despite the coverage in the press, the weather remained the top story on local news bulletins.'[44] Overnight, the Peak District would experience the heaviest snowfall in over half a century, sweeping north from the south. The Snake Pass connecting Sheffield to Glossop was the first major route to close, quickly followed by many others. In Macclesfield, more than one hundred people, including schoolchildren and pensioners, took refuge in a police station, served tea and toast from the canteen by local traffic wardens. A school bus in Leek became stranded and the children had to walk back to their classroom for the night. One man died in the blizzard and a woman making a call from a public phone box found herself trapped when the door froze. By early evening, Yorkshire was cut adrift from Lancashire due to roads being impassable, and Sheffield was a city of abandoned cars, along with Manchester, Leeds and Bradford. In Penrith, the temperature dropped to minus eighteen.

'The terrible weather affected us all, including my family,' Peter Howse remembers. 'My wife Beryl, who taught at Birdholm school in Chesterfield, had given lifts to other members of staff but left it too late to get home herself on the blocked roads. She had to spend the night at the packed Railway Station Hotel. I had to work so arranged for our children, David, twelve, and Julia, eleven, to be brought to the police station while I was out directing the search. I came back to find the two of them enjoying bowls of tomato soup in the station canteen, chatting excitedly. I took them home and asked a neighbour to keep an eye on them before returning to my office to concentrate on the search for Billy Hughes. But there was little I or anybody else could do.

'The blizzard had arrived with a vengeance and everything came to a standstill.'[45]

Chapter Six:

The Mintons and Morans

THE IMPACT OF the Morris against the drystone wall had damaged the car but not its driver. Billy emerged quickly in the bitter morning air, tucking the wooden-handled knife and court papers inside his jacket. Scrambling over the wall, he saw open land in every direction, save for the line of trees forming a spine towards the horizon. After a moment's deliberation, he chose an obviously difficult path with the aim of confusing any dogs sent after him, walking roughly north-east and keeping the trees to his left. Occasionally he sank into the bog beneath the snow and had to drag himself out, then crossed a stream that filled his boots with murky water. The knife and papers were lost after he had climbed a soaring rocky escarpment, but he was at least confident about not being seen; the whirling whiteness rendered everything indistinct. Spotting a radio relay mast, he headed towards it, following the land down into a shallow valley before it rose again in a patchwork of fields divided by low, primitive walls. A main road, grey and empty, unfurled like a ribbon at the foot of the fields.

Exhausted after walking over four miles in appalling conditions and mindful of exposure to passing traffic, he dropped into Wadshelf Brook.[1] Wading through the water, he saw a pair of stone entrance pillars on the opposite side of the road. Beyond them stood Dalebrook House, a substantial property with several outbuildings that offered the shelter he sought.

A van approached from the Chesterfield end of the A619. Billy watched and waited: to his frustration, the vehicle turned into the long drive. Forced to reconsider his options, he climbed out of the stream and walked through the field at a crouch in the shadow of a stone wall.

The house appeared suddenly, materialising out of the snowstorm as if summoned. A handsome, low building parallel to the main road but without any neighbouring properties, it seemed as fortuitous as the weather. Billy edged forward, stepping deftly over a small wall into a large garden and courtyard. There was a shed in one corner, its open door revealing well-kept tools, tins of paint and a tall woodpile where two axes lay with gleaming blades. He picked them up.

At the back of the house, evergreen shrubs filled the plant pots dotted about a side terrace and a child's pink bicycle stood propped against a wall. Lights glimmered in the white-framed windows, holding the dark afternoon at bay. Billy stole along the edge of the courtyard towards the back door.

Inside a well-appointed kitchen stood an elderly woman expertly preparing vegetables at a sink. Billy tried the door handle. It gave easily; the key had been left inside the lock.

The woman at the sink turned, expecting someone else. His eyes met hers, and she put a hand to her mouth, letting the potato peeler fall to the floor. Soaked to the skin, his dark hair plastered against his face and armed with the newly oiled axes, Billy looked threatening and he knew it.

Locking the door as he entered the kitchen, he said in a soft, urgent voice, 'I'm wanted by the police but I'm not going to hurt you.'

The woman stared at him, petrified. The fact that she neither screamed nor tried to get away gave him confidence.

'Tell me who lives here,' he said.[2]

'We come from good stock, Gill,' Amy Minton often reminded her younger daughter. 'We're strong.'

Born to an unmarried laundry worker in the affluent Midlands town of Solihull in July 1909, Amy Aubrey's earliest years were spent at her grandparents' home. She was twelve when her mother married and took her stepfather's surname until her own wedding in June 1931 to grocer Arthur Minton. Five years Amy's senior and the son of an umbrella maker, Arthur grew up in Solihull's fastest developing suburb, Acocks Green. As gregarious as his wife was reserved, Arthur suffered life-changing injuries in a motor accident six years after their marriage. Aged thirty-three, he had his right leg amputated but was 'tough in both body and spirit' and adapted well to using an artificial limb. He remained active in the shop that bore his name on School Road in Acocks Green, but Amy took over most of the heavier duties in the storeroom until her first pregnancy.

Barbara was born in 1936 and a second daughter, Gillian Ann, on 24 March 1938, at the Queen's Hospital in Birmingham city centre. Three years later, the hospital was damaged during Luftwaffe raids, when German bombers turned the streets into molten tar. The area where the Mintons lived was targeted due to the Rover factory in Acocks Green producing tanks and engines, but their shop thrived during the war and afterwards. Arthur and Amy worked hard to provide their daughters with the best of everything; Gill's favourite toy was an expensively exquisite German doll bought as a birthday present by her father, to whom she was especially close. Arthur worked six days a week but devoted Sundays to the girls, often indulging Gill's love of animals by making hutches for her rabbits or driving her with the family's dogs to shows in Birmingham; her ambition was to become a professional dog breeder.

Dark-haired and pretty, with a gentle, dreamy look, Gill later described herself as a 'happy, uncomplicated and content' teenager, but lacked confidence, leading her to seek approval from everyone, including her doting father and protective mother. 'She is rather shy but she has forced herself to meet people,' one acquaintance recalled. 'In fact, she was very popular and has made a lot of friends.'[3] Strong-willed, she was the envy of her school-mates due to an ability to see through any task, including the latest restrictive fad diet.

Gill's parents paid the course fees when she began attending secretarial college and she rewarded them by going straight into an office job. Arthur gave her driving lessons in his blue Singer when she reached seventeen and after passing her test she found better paid work as a typist and driver for a Birmingham company producing car parts. In June 1958 she made a delivery to a building firm; the clerk who took receipt of the components was Richard Moran, a handsome young Irishman with dark hair and an engaging grin. Normally garrulous, he was too nervous to ask Gill out on the spot but approached a mutual friend to do so on his behalf.

Their first date was a dance at Trentham Gardens, a landscape park in Stoke-on-Trent, where she learned something of his past.

Born to a single mother on 19 May 1935 in Kilmoganny, a village in south-east Ireland, as a baby Richard was fostered by a local Catholic family, the Hawes. Fussed over by the girls in the family, he remained close to them for the rest of his life and regarded them as sisters. He was a bright, popular pupil at school but started full-time employment at the age of fourteen as a labourer. Naturally gifted as a footballer, he helped Kilmoganny win the country championship before joining the Irish Army during his National Service. He followed his foster sister Margaret Hawe to Birmingham, where he found work in a factory while spending his evenings studying. The long hours paid off when a building firm took him on as a sales clerk and brought him into contact with Gill.

Charming and self-deprecatingly funny, Richard told Gill on their first evening together that she was too pretty to get 'left on the shelf', adding, 'If you're not married within a year, I'll marry you myself.' By autumn they were engaged and married a year later, on 21 September 1959, in a traditional ceremony at Christchurch, a small Victorian parish church scarcely a two-minute walk from Gill's home. Her sister Barbara flew in from Paris, where she lived with her French husband and children. Richard promised Gill that any children they had together would want for nothing; full of 'energy and ambition', he would do his best for them all.

Their income improved substantially when Richard became departmental manager for Hunter Plastics a few years later and they moved to Derbyshire to give him a more convenient base for travelling to builders' merchants north of the Midlands. Gill worried about her parents after the move, fearing that her father's disability would lead to him becoming housebound after retirement. The solution proved simple: Arthur and Amy sold their business and relocated to Derbyshire, sharing Gill and Richard's large, modern home in Old Tupton, a busy commuter village south of Chesterfield. Arthur kept himself active with a part-time job at Tupton Park's newly opened pitch-and-putt course, easing his daughter's concerns.

Gill's marriage to Richard was everything she had hoped for except in one respect: after seven years in which they had 'tried and hoped and prayed' for children, there was no possibility of parenthood other than through adoption or medical intervention. Following this intensely painful realisation, on 20 September 1966 the couple made an official application to adopt. The process could often be lengthy and difficult, but three months later they became parents to an infant born on the day of their application. The coincidence meant everything to Richard and Gill, who gave their daughter the name Sarah Jayne. The adoption order, dated 14 April 1967 at Chesterfield County Court, completed their lives.

The house in Old Tupton no longer suited them; the Morans wanted to raise Sarah in the countryside, where they could indulge her instinctive love of animals, and were keen to buy a property that needed work. One stood out from the rest: Northend Farm, an eighteenth-century gritstone pottery barn divided into four homes, set back from the A619 Chesterfield road in Eastmoor. Its location offered breathtaking views across the Peak District National Park, but it was not completely isolated; apart from a few properties scattered along the road, including the Highwayman Inn approximately 200 yards away, the far end of the building was occupied by a professional couple in their early fifties.

Gill's parents contributed towards the purchase price and conversion, which gave them their own quarters via a connecting door on the ground floor. The family of five moved into their new home in October 1969, having renamed it and displaying a sign in cast-iron script on the stone wall by the white wooden entrance gate: Pottery Cottage. Next to the sign and by the front door was a pair of lucky horseshoes.

Their neighbours at the far end of the building were both headteachers at Church of England primary schools in Nottinghamshire. Len and Joyce Newman had lived in 'Seconds' since the previous summer and owned the section next to it. The smaller property adjacent to Pottery Cottage had stood empty for two years but was in the process of being renovated by a young man who seemed in no hurry to move into it. Joyce later told detectives that Pottery Cottage had previously been divided into a house and cow shed, with an old dairy near the back door: 'Mr Moran bought what I could best describe as the shell of the building. Before they moved in, the building was modernised and built to its present form. The house [is] sub-divided into two parts, the dividing line being broadly speaking the wall separating the Mintons' lounge from the Morans' kitchen. Looking at the house from the road, the Morans would reside to the right and the Mintons in the smaller part on the left. Each unit had its own toilet and bathroom facilities but there were connecting doors via a hallway into each part . . . There are no connecting doors between the upstairs rooms. Again looking at the house from the road, from the right the first bedroom was occupied by Mr and Mrs Moran, the next smaller bedroom by Sarah and the last was a spare room. This is next to the Mintons' bathroom and the last room was the Mintons' bedroom.'[4] The conversion was such that from the front, little seemed changed, but at the side and rear of the property, large picture windows and French doors took advantage of the wonderful views and allowed light to flood in during summer and spring.

Pottery Cottage was large enough for the family to have several pets. Gill recalled that the four additions to their home immediately became Sarah's 'very best friends': Emma the basset hound, a black Labrador named William, Ginger the cat and Bobo the rabbit. At the age of five, Sarah began attending Wigley Primary School, where her granddad Arthur worked as a caretaker. Keen to find employment herself with Sarah in full-time education, Gill successfully applied for a position as secretary in a firm of Chesterfield accountants. Her boss, John Roberts, described her as 'first class' at her job: 'competent, efficient and always pleasant'.[5] Gill's mother Amy also earned 'pocket money' cleaning the Newmans' home every Monday and Friday while the couple were at work, and exercising their dog daily in the garden.

Richard's career went from strength to strength after moving to Pottery Cottage. In 1973, a friend in the building industry asked if he might be interested in joining a new firm specialising in plastic piping. It was the brainchild of young businessman David Brown and his friend Francis Hall, who had sold their previous company to set up offices and a factory on Speedwell Industrial Estate in Staveley, five miles north-east of Chesterfield. Brett Plastics was named after Francis Hall's black Labrador. 'It seemed as good a name as any,' David recalls with a smile.[6] He and Francis brought on board another friend, engineer Paul Goldthorpe, to work in production and sales but needed a designated salesperson.

Richard Moran thought over the proposal, wary of leaving his established position for a new company, but after discovering that another trusted friend of his, Irish businessman Billy Martin, had invested heavily in Brett Plastics, he decided to take a leap of faith, joining the Board as Sales Director. With David Brown and

Francis Hall as Managing Directors and Productive Director Paul
Goldthorpe, Richard played a major role in expanding the business into a thriving company employing seventy people.

'He was a superb guy,' Paul Goldthorpe remembers. 'We used
to call him Derbyshire's answer to Terry Wogan – Irish, with a
real twinkle in his eye and the gift of the gab. He was always
very smartly dressed and didn't smoke, which was quite unusual
then – Gill did. He never really spoke about family other than
Gill, Sarah and Gill's parents and sister. Her mother was an
unassuming woman but very warm and her father was an old-
fashioned gentleman in the best sense. Richard was very close to
them. We often used to have dinner with them at Pottery
Cottage – it was beautiful, with a huge stone fireplace in the
lounge. Gill and Richard were a lot of fun – genuinely a very
happy couple. Gill's dream was to become a dog breeder – she
really loved her dogs. Sarah was a livewire, a very forward, intelligent and affectionate little girl. When we had our first child –
Sally – we asked Richard and Gill and David and his wife Glynis
to be godparents.'[7]

Paul's wife Ann explains: 'We had been trying so long for a
baby and went through every treatment available. It was absolutely heartbreaking. Gill and Richard understood because they
had gone through it too before adopting Sarah. We decided to do
the same and were put on the adoption register. One day the
agency called: a baby had been born and would we still like to
adopt? That moment was so wonderful. Paul was at work – in
fact, he was in a meeting with David, Richard and Francis, and
when I asked to speak to him their secretary told me they had
asked not to be disturbed. But I knew they would all want to hear
the news. She put me through and I made the announcement and
they all cheered! It was very moving. We became parents to Sally,

a beautiful baby girl, and every Wednesday she and I would visit Gill at Pottery Cottage. Sarah absolutely loved Baby Sally, as we called her then. She knew that Richard and Gill had adopted her and clearly felt a real affinity with Sally because of it. Sarah was so sweet with her; as soon as we arrived, she would get out all her toys and sit and play with Sally until it was time for us to go. She was really like a big sister to her.'[8]

Ann agrees with her husband Paul that Richard's personality made him a natural salesperson: 'You know the saying about an Irish person who can charm the bird out of the trees – that they've kissed the Blarney Stone. Richard must have swallowed it! He was a great man: funny, talkative, kind and hard-working. He and Gill were ten years older than us and they took us under their wing. We often went out together as a foursome, and sometimes with David and Glynis Brown, too. Richard and Gill were sophisticated: they taught us about wine and so on. And Gill got me into eating rare steak. We went out one evening to the Berni Inn at Meadowhead and she said, "Oh, Ann, you should try it. You'll love it." We had the ultimate seventies meal that night: prawn cocktail as starters, rare steak and salad for the main dish and gateau for pudding! But they did educate us to some extent.'[9]

The Morans were on equally good terms with the Browns, whom Ann Goldthorpe had known since they were all in their teens, while the Browns were also near neighbours of Francis Hall and his wife in the pretty little Plague village of Eyam. On one occasion Glynis Brown stayed at Pottery Cottage with Gill while their husbands were away visiting a trade exhibition; the two families later holidayed together in the Lake District, where Sarah played happily with their two sons. Richard also introduced Paul and David to Chesterfield 33 Round Table, a charitable organisation for men aged twenty to forty, whose money-raising functions created opportunities for businessmen to form contacts. Gill joined the attendant Ladies Circle with Glynis Brown. When Richard reached the age limit for the Round Table he applied for membership of the Rotary Club and then the very similar 41 Club, while Gill was accepted on to the Ladies' Committee of the Round Table. Their social circle thus continued to expand; they were well-known and well-liked in the area.

Sarah was an equally gregarious child with many friends at Wigley Primary School; the mother of her friend Sharon Hall remembers Sarah turning perfect cartwheels in a burst of high spirits at her daughter's birthday party, to the delight of all the other children. Outspoken and creative, Sarah was also extremely bright – so much so that headmistress Mrs Margaret Goodall consulted Gill about moving her to senior school a year early when the time came.

There were many dinner parties at Pottery Cottage; the Morans entertained in style and were developing a wine cellar. They had their own interests, too: Richard liked motor sport and was an enthusiastic rally driver while Gill continued to give serious thought to turning her passion for dogs into a career. There was time to enjoy life, with Gill's parents comfortably ensconced next door, and Sarah proving a happy, well-adjusted child. The renovation of Pottery Cottage was long since complete: a perfect family home that was described afterwards in the press as being luxurious 'without being flashy or pretentious. Everything was spotlessly clean, the brass shone, the glass gleamed. The carpet was thick and soft. The drinks trolley displayed nearly full bottles of spirits and sherry. The bookcase was full of books, which were clearly there for reading. There were many books about President Kennedy, as well as popular, best-selling novels. The record rack was very thick, the first disc being an album of Sacha Distel. The colour TV in the corner of the big living room was 24 inches and new.'[10]

Life was everything the Mintons and Morans wanted it to be, until the snowstorm of January 1977 brought Billy Hughes through their door.

Chapter Seven:

Pottery Cottage

THE FOUR DAYS preceding the end of normality at Pottery Cottage were pleasantly mundane. On Saturday evening, Gill and Richard dined with their friends Linda and Grenville Browett, who lived in a beautiful cottage in the Derbyshire county town of Matlock. Over topside and gooseberry fool, and a couple of bottles of Lambrusco, the two couples listened to music and discussed plans for a holiday together in Brittany.

Following Richard's departure for work on Monday, Gill deposited Sarah at the Victorian gates of Wigley Primary before driving to the accountancy offices in Chesterfield. That evening, Gill invited her parents to share the meal she had cooked for herself and Sarah; Richard had a dinner meeting with fellow Brett Plastics director Francis Hall at the Chequers Inn in Froggatt Edge.

Overnight, temperatures across the region plummeted. On Tuesday morning, the iron latticework of the Pottery Cottage sign was draped with frosted spiders' webs as Richard patiently scraped the ice from the windscreens of both cars in the courtyard before leaving for Staveley. When Gill arrived home from work that afternoon, her mother complained of the cold, adding that she had called Len Newman earlier, at the Nottinghamshire school where he worked, to say that his gate was frozen solid and she had been unable to exercise the dog.

Their final hours of peace were upon them.

It was already snowing when Gill opened the doors on to the terrace on Wednesday morning to let Emma and William out for their first run. She and Richard sat down to breakfast together in the kitchen: coffee for her, tea for him, and starch-reduced crispbread for them both as part of their post-Christmas diet. Sarah never ate breakfast but Gill took the packed lunch she had made the previous night from the fridge and zipped it inside her daughter's school bag. Richard wondered aloud if the weather might affect his plans for the day; he had arranged to meet one of their sales representatives for a trip to Birmingham. He told Gill that his last appointment was at 4 p.m. and should take no more than an hour, after which he would drive straight home, rather than call in at the office.

At half past eight, Gill threw on her coat and collected her car keys and handbag, calling to Sarah. Richard drove out first but had to wait behind other vehicles as a lorry reversed into the driveway of Crossgates Farm nearby. Sarah waved frantically to her father as Gill turned the Hillman Avenger into Top Lane while Richard's car vanished down the hill into Chesterfield. It took no more than a couple of minutes to reach Sarah's school, where Gill kept the engine running as she kissed her daughter goodbye and reminded her not to run across the icy playground. Then she set off for town, where traffic was chaotic as a result of the snow, but still managed to arrive at her desk on time.

Gill's day at the Glumangate offices ended at three o'clock. The blizzard had swept in and people struggled against it on the pavements outside the shops and terraced houses of Chatsworth Road. The Hillman Avenger laboured up the long, winding hill towards home and Gill was relieved when the road levelled out just before the Highwayman Inn on her left. The lights within the old square building glowed softly against the snow, but the presence of three police cars gave her a moment's disquiet. She had neither listened to the radio while at work nor bought a newspaper.

On reaching Pottery Cottage, she forgot all about the police cars: the gate that was always kept locked to prevent the dogs running out on to the road was open wide. She left the car in the garage, wondering why her parents had failed to secure the gate.

She walked to the back door and pressed the handle, expecting it to give as usual. But the door was locked. 'I knocked,' Gill recalled. 'My mother came to the door and opened it. She seemed normal.'[1]

But Amy's first words were anything but ordinary. As Gill went through into the warm kitchen, asking about the gate, Amy stilled her: 'Don't panic, Gill, but there's a man here with a knife. He's hiding from the police. Keep calm – he won't hurt us.'

In her witness statement to the police four days later, Gill recounted what had occurred at Pottery Cottage before she arrived home, as told to her by her mother.

Arthur Minton had heard his wife talking to someone in the kitchen, after the fugitive's initial entry, and emerged from the annexe inquisitively only to be struck savagely to the floor. As he lay dazed on the lino, their uninvited guest crouched down beside him.

'The police want me,' the younger man said. 'I need to stay here until it's dark. If you do as I say, everything will be all right.' The inference was obvious. He reached out a hand. Arthur hesitated, then took it and got to his feet, the strain showing in the set of his jaw, coupled with anger and humiliation.

For Arthur's benefit, Billy gave his name again and repeated how he had escaped in transit from prison that morning. 'There's no need to be frightened,' he said, in the quiet voice they came to dread. 'Do as I say and it will be all right. How many people live here?'

Amy told him. He asked when she expected the rest of her family home and she was able to tell him the usual times for Gill and Sarah, but had no idea about Richard, given that he was on a business trip some eighty miles south and the weather was particularly foul.

Digesting this, Billy instructed the couple to show him around the house. Seeing Arthur's frown, he grasped one of the axes he had brought in, ensuring that the seventy-four-year-old retired grocer would harbour no ideas about challenging him. Amy led the way into the main lounge. Billy looked around the neat room with its huge stone fireplace, bellows and gleaming brass companion set; the comfortable chairs and sofa, smart colour television, and the dark beam studded with bright horse brasses. He went through a stone arch into the dining room, where his boots squelched on the parquet floor. Returning to the hall, he noticed a blue telephone on a small table and disconnected it. After a cursory glance at the cloakroom, he indicated that Amy and Arthur should head upstairs.

The tense couple showed him into their daughter and son-in-law's bedroom first, where teak fitted wardrobes helped keep the space tidy and two windows – one to the rear and another to the side – allowed the light to flood in on a clement day. Their unsolicited visitor removed his footwear there, together with the filthy wet socks he was keen to replace. He opened a chest of drawers and found a thick woollen pair belonging to Richard, wiping the dirt from his feet before pulling them on. Automatically, Amy Minton picked up the discarded socks; later, she washed them in the sink and left them to dry on a radiator.

Billy went out on to the landing, ignoring the bathroom to the left in favour of a door filled with images of its occupant's passions, including a trio of friendly looking horses and bespectacled Uncle Bulgaria from the popular children's TV show *The Wombles*. To quell any doubt, a floral ceramic sign declared it to be 'Sarah's Room'. Billy pushed open the door. Everything inside the room reflected the personality of the ten-year-old girl who slept there: lots of accomplished childish artwork, including a collage of wallpaper circles, and a school of vivid fish swimming towards the tightly packed bookcase of Blytons; soft toys, Christmas balloons, a Sunblest sticker on the busy bedside table, a proudly displayed National Cycling Proficiency certificate next to a cassette player, several pony posters, and a wooden headboard with a Sellotaped photo of a baby seal. On the soft pink candlewick bedspread lay a grey nylon elephant in a tasselled jacket.

Billy left the room without a word, peering around the door of the spare bedroom before Amy and Arthur led him downstairs and towards the door in the main kitchen that linked the two households. They passed through another, narrower kitchen and into the Mintons' sitting-room diner. Billy recognised the spiralled design on the carpet from the one in the main lounge and the stone archway into the Mintons' television room, together with the parquet floor, was also the same. Billy followed Amy out and up a second staircase that led directly to their bedroom and bathroom. Satisfied that he had grasped the layout of his fairly substantial hiding place, Billy prodded the couple downstairs again and into the Morans' kitchen.

Without a word, he put down the axe within reach and began opening drawers. He found the cutlery compartment in one and selected an item, holding it up to examine it properly and to demonstrate again to his hosts that he was as dangerous as they feared. Arthur exchanged a glance with his wife; Billy had pulled out a specialist knife used to bone sides of bacon in their old grocery store. Arthur kept it in pristine condition, as he did all his tools, resulting in a five-inch blade as mortally sharp as the day it came into his possession.

Billy slid the knife into his belt. He turned round and said to Amy, 'Let's have some tea.'

She did as he ordered, putting a pot of hot tea, cups, milk and sugar on a tray. He told her to take it into the lounge, locking the communicating door before joining Amy and Arthur.

'Tell me about your daughter Gill,' he said, sipping from a cup.

Amy glanced at Arthur, sitting rigid with anger and frustration. She began to talk, tentatively at first, then just saying whatever came into her mind about Gill and their lives at Pottery Cottage. Billy listened and she kept talking until a beige car travelled slowly past the front window and turned in at the drive. Amy got to her feet. 'Here she is now.'

Billy unbent from the chair and stood, stretching slightly. 'Answer the door,' he said. 'Tell her I'm here, but not until she gets indoors.'

A few minutes later, Gill came face to face with the man her mother called 'Billy' as if they had met under normal circumstances. She was in a state of shock, but soon became aware of the knife he had tucked in his waistband 'because every time he sat down, it fell out'. Nonetheless, to her own surprise, Gill was 'quite calm at first. I made a cup of coffee for all of us. We stood in the kitchen and drank it. He sat at the kitchen table and he talked about what he'd done. He said he'd taken over a taxi and taken money from people in the car. I had trouble catching what he said because of his accent and his quiet voice.' But she immediately heard Billy's remark about attacking the two prison officers: 'I did not kill them. I could have killed them. I know exactly how to kill.'

Gill's presence seemed to invigorate him. He said that the police would probably make house-to-house inquiries in the area and might call at Pottery Cottage: 'If they do come here, this is what we'll do. Gill, you'll come upstairs with me and run the water for a bath.'

He nodded at her mother: 'You'll go to the door and say she's having a bath and can't come down. They'll soon go away.'

Gill's sense of calm was starting to splinter. She prayed silently that Billy would do as he said and leave at nightfall. In the meantime, she could not countenance the thought of Sarah sensing danger. Her clever, sensitive daughter was due home from school at any moment and Gill's mind raced to summon a plausible reason for the stranger being there. A simple solution came to her: in order to pacify Sarah, they would say that Billy had asked to use their telephone after his car had broken down and he was waiting for assistance. Such an event had happened at least twice in the past and Sarah would remember how they offered tea or coffee to a stranded driver. Billy agreed willingly to the fiction, knowing it could only be in his favour.

Aware that Sarah would also be curious about the two axes lying on the stairs, Amy hid them under a pile of fresh ironing in the kitchen, just as the school bus pulled up on the road directly opposite. It was 3.40 p.m. as Sarah flew down the drive, a small figure in her blue uniform, kicking up snow exuberantly. Gill rose and went through to the kitchen to greet her as usual. Hyperactive and full of spirit, with her long blonde hair flicking from side to side in its ponytail, Sarah was full of chatter about a recent achievement: as gifted athletically as she was academically bright, she had won the school sports cup. When she paused for breath, Gill put an arm around her and said, 'Come into the lounge. We've got a visitor.'

Billy stood, smiling. Sarah reciprocated.

'His car has broken down,' Gill said, holding her daughter a little tighter. 'He's waiting for the recovery truck.'

'Hello,' said Billy easily. 'What's your name?'

'This is Sarah,' Gill responded. Sarah's smile widened. She looked up at her mother, asking if she could fetch her sewing box and went off to recover it from her room.

'More coffee,' said Billy, and Gill made it, bringing the mugs into the lounge on a tray again. Sarah sat cross-legged on the carpet, working on a patchwork cushion.

Gill held out a packet of Gold Leaf to Billy: 'Help yourself.'

He shook his head. 'No, I like my own brand.' He drew out a box of John Player Special from inside his jacket. 'These are the best.'

The four adults made small talk for a while. Then suddenly, Billy got up and walked across to Sarah.

Gill held her breath.

He crouched next to the young girl. 'Hey, Sarah,' he said softly, 'let me do that for you.'

While Gill and her parents had been too intent on watching Billy to notice anything else, he had spotted that Sarah was having trouble re-threading her needle. His deft fingers held the thread and slipped it effortlessly through the eye of the needle. Sarah thanked him as he gave it to her before returning to his seat.

That moment stayed with Gill ever after; at the time, it was such a calm and domesticated scene that she suddenly believed everything would be all right: 'It felt just like it did at other times when we have had motorists in the house. And suddenly, I didn't feel frightened at all.'

A few minutes later, Sarah laid her embroidery to one side and went to fetch herself a drink from the kitchen. 'What are these for?' she called.

Gill walked through to the kitchen where Sarah had found the axes. She responded with deliberate casualness, 'Oh, Granddad's been using them.' She guided her daughter back into the lounge and Sarah carried on with her sewing.

At that point, the tension in Pottery Cottage began to build. Billy got to his feet, moving through the house. Gill watched, exchanging glances with her parents. None of them said a word, waiting instead for the intruder to enlighten them. 'He wandered between the lounge and the kitchen and he also went upstairs alone,' Gill recalls in her witness statement. 'He also opened the communicating door and allowed the dogs to come through. He was very friendly with the dogs and they seemed to like him. He went upstairs and moved a chair from my bedroom into the bathroom. He made me partly fill the bath with water . . .' This last demand appeared to be part of the ruse he had devised in case the police called at the house.

Sarah noticed his restlessness, whispering to her mother, 'He's a nice man, but why does he go wandering all over the place?'

'He's worried about his car,' Gill replied quickly. 'He can't sit still.'

Sarah seemed satisfied with that. She turned on the television and then the standard lamp, but the bulb blew, sending the picture on the television screen haywire. '[Billy] offered to mend it,' Gill states. 'I found two fuses and he took the plug to pieces, trying to mend it but he couldn't. Dad was helping him . . . We were waiting for Richard to come home and for darkness to fall, because the man had said that he would go when it was dark. Up to this time, his manner was friendly.'

Sarah grew impatient with the flickering television. 'I'm going to Granddad's to watch it,' she announced. Arthur looked at Billy, who nodded almost imperceptibly. Easing himself up from the chair, Arthur took Sarah's hand and led her out into the hallway and through to the annexe.

Billy replaced the screws in the plug, asking Gill again, 'What time will your husband be home?'

For the second or third time, she answered, 'I don't know, he's gone to Birmingham today.'

Billy was on edge, plainly anticipating some sort of confrontation when Richard arrived. Hoping to pacify him, Gill said that Richard would do anything he was told. Her mother agreed that her son-in-law was not the type to react aggressively. But Billy seemed uncertain and queried whether Richard might ring Gill on his journey home. 'I'll reconnect the phone,' he said decisively. 'There's no need for it to be cut off. You'll answer it exactly as I say, Gill.'

He went through to the hall, where they heard him reconnect the line.

Almost instantly, a shrill sound filled the house.

'Answer it,' Billy said, jerking his head at Gill. 'And talk normally.' She lifted the receiver.

*

Ann Goldthorpe had spent the previous Wednesday afternoon at Pottery Cottage, taking Baby Sally to see Gill and Sarah as usual. 'But I didn't go on the day of the blizzard,' she remembers. 'I never missed a single Wednesday except that one, because of the weather. At lunchtime, I watched the local news and found out about the escaped prisoner. They said he was in the Chatsworth area and that really frightened me because we were living in Holymoorside at the time, which is only a few miles away. Then at four o'clock one of our neighbours stopped by to say that she had just collected her child from school and everyone had been warned about this man. So I rang Paul to ask him to come home as soon as he could because I was really starting to worry. After I'd spoken to him, I thought: I must ring Gill. It was about quarter past four then.'[2]

Keeping an eye on her daughter Sally, Ann called Pottery Cottage. After several rings, Gill answered: 'Chesterfield 68382.'

Ann asked her 'more or less straight away' if she had heard about the man on the run. 'She said she hadn't and I told her what I knew, which wasn't much,' Ann remembers. 'I asked if her mum and dad were there and if Sarah had arrived home safely. She said they were all fine, but Richard was in Birmingham on business, which I had just learned from speaking to Paul. We didn't really talk about anything else and I apologised for worrying her but explained I had just wanted to make sure that she was extra careful and would keep all the doors and windows locked, at least until Richard got back. She thanked me and put the phone down.'

Ann pauses, then reflects, 'What I didn't know was that Billy Hughes was already in the house and standing right next to her as she spoke to me. She sounded so normal and I had no suspicions that anything was wrong. There was absolutely nothing in her voice to hint at the fear she must have been feeling.'[3]

Gill replaced the receiver. She turned to face Billy, who walked through to the lounge, switching off the lights. He grabbed the swivel chair that always stood by the archway into the dining room and set it down near the window facing the road.

Amy joined her daughter in the kitchen. The two of them stood talking in hushed voices, but were frequently interrupted by Billy who could not sit still. 'He kept getting up and down and coming into the kitchen,' Gill recalls. 'He also went upstairs and looked out of the landing window. He asked me if we'd got any maps.' Richard kept one in his car, but she thought her father might have another in his Hillman Minx, parked in the garage. Billy told her to check and accompanied her to the vehicle, where she found an old AA route book. Then they returned to the house, where Amy was sitting stiffly on the sofa in the main lounge. Gill sat next to her and Billy once more took up a position seated slightly away from the front window. He watched and waited.

Through the open curtains, they could all see the snow falling in a thick, pale flurry against the black sky. The road was empty, save for one or two motorists speeding past to reach home before the blizzard put an end to everything. But at quarter past six, twin beams of orange light blurred by the spiralling snow lit up the gravel drive.

'Richard's home,' said Amy.

Chapter Eight:

Five Hostages

B ILLY LEAPT UP, drawing the knife from his belt. He pulled
Gill towards him, twisting her right arm up behind her back.
He stood behind her, putting his left arm around her neck and
holding the knife to her throat with his right hand. 'I could feel
the point of the knife,' she remembers.[1]

'Go outside to Richard,' Billy instructed Amy. 'I won't use the
knife if he does as I say. Go!'

Amy scuttled through the house to meet her son-in-law as he
climbed from his car, weary after a hectic day and a long journey
in appalling conditions, but looking forward to relaxing in front
of the television. Instead, he found himself standing stupefied at
the door into the lounge, where a stranger held a knife to his
wife's throat.

'Don't come near me or I'll kill her,' Billy said quietly.

No one moved, and in that moment, their fates were sealed.
'Richard was a man of peace,' the Morans' friend Grenville
Browett recalled a few days later. 'He detested violence. He was

the sort who would have tried to reason with this man.'[2] And Richard did precisely as was expected, calmly offering his car keys to the intruder, who kept his eyes locked on the older man's face.

'I'm not going to do anything,' Richard said steadily. 'Look, take my car – the tank is full of petrol – you can get away. We won't telephone anyone. We won't *tell* anyone.'

Billy relaxed, satisfied that the entire household was under his control. He loosened his hold on Gill and knelt down by the standard lamp, cutting the unplugged flex with Arthur's knife. He then walked into the kitchen and slashed at the flex on the iron and vacuum cleaner, before returning to the lounge and dropping the cable lengths on to a chair.

'I'm going to tie you up,' he said to Richard, seizing his arms backwards and binding his wrists.

Richard pleaded, 'Don't – there's no need, I won't do anything—'

But Billy forced him to the floor, face down and hands bound, pulling the flex tight around his ankles. Panting slightly, he asked Gill, 'I want rope, I need a clothesline. Where is it?'

Terror stilled her voice; she led him outside to the terrace, where all was darkness and silence. Her neighbour Joyce Newman was only a scream or shout away, having arrived home from work later than normal because of the blizzard. Joyce remembered putting her car in the garage at 6.30 p.m. and going into the kitchen of Seconds, 'which is lit by a time switch. I remember noticing that one of the outside lights was on at the Morans' but I can't say which one. But I do remember noticing that there were not as many lights on in their house as usual . . . I let my dog out for a run in the back garden, but I did not take him for a walk as is my usual practice. I did go into the garden, but I did not take any particular notice of the Morans' house.'[3]

Billy had found a length of plastic-coated wire which he used to secure Gill's ankles while she sat on a stool in the lounge. Amy Minton looked on in horror, exclaiming, 'What on earth are you doing? You can't tie them up – we aren't going to do anything!'

Hearing his wife's raised voice, Arthur threw open the connecting door. Sarah rushed in after him. Neither was prepared for the sight of Gill and Richard lying face down on the carpet with their limbs rigidly bound.

Arthur lurched towards Billy, shouting, 'What the hell do you think you're doing?' His granddaughter's scream was louder yet: 'Don't you hurt my mummy and daddy! Don't you dare! Get out – you hurt people!'

From the floor, Gill turned her head and tried to calm her father: 'Don't, Dad, he's not going to hurt us!'

Richard addressed his daughter equally awkwardly: 'Be quiet, Sarah, it's all right, everything's okay.'

Billy ignored them all, unravelling more lengths of flex.

'He started to tie Mum up,' Gill recalled. 'He tied her hands behind her back. He sat her on a chair and tied her ankles together. [Dad] said, "You're not tying me up." There was a bit of a commotion as we all pleaded with Dad to do as he asked . . . [Sarah] was very upset. She told the man not to harm any of us.' Arthur tried to resist, but was no match for the younger man's brute strength. Forced to lie down while Billy tied his wrists and ankles in the same manner as before, Arthur fought valiantly, but his breathing became painfully laboured and Billy was riled by it. 'He was obviously becoming very tense,' Gill confirms, 'but he didn't speak very much. He dragged Dad across the floor and sat him in an armchair.'

She begged him not to do the same to Sarah, who was now sitting so quietly that he left her alone and instead collected a bundle of tea towels, and ties belonging to Richard. He began tearing the material into strips, declaring, 'I'm going to gag you all so if anyone has false teeth, take them out.' He realised his mistake immediately and made an impatient sound. The Mintons wore dentures but had their hands tied, meaning it was up to Billy to remove them. He did it with an expression of disgust, throwing the dental plates to the floor. Gill turned her head away; she had never seen either of her parents without their teeth and felt physically sick at the indignity to which they were being subjected. She closed her eyes tightly, telling Billy, 'Please don't gag Mum, she's got sinusitis. She'll suffocate!'

He took no notice and gagged them one by one.

Gill watched him bend down to Richard again, heaving him on to his shoulder as if he were a bag of coal rather than a man weighing twelve stones or more. After depositing Richard in the spare room, he returned to lift Gill in the same way, placing her on the double bed in the room she shared with her husband. She heard him carrying her mother into Sarah's room and then the house fell eerily still.

'Don't be fooled, Mum!' From downstairs, Sarah's high voice broke the silence. 'He's being quiet – he hasn't gone yet!' They were the last words Gill heard her speak before Billy took her through to the annexe. She presumed Arthur was either through there already or remained in the lounge.

It went quiet again and Gill found herself trying to count the minutes until suddenly the telephone rang, bringing Billy into the room. He put her over his shoulder again and carried her downstairs. Through the glass doors into the lounge she caught a glimpse of her father, gagged and bound in the armchair, moving his head and shoulders as if in agony.

Billy set her down and removed her gag, warning her to act normally.

'Chesterfield 68382,' she said automatically.

A man's voice answered, 'Hello, Gill. Is Ritchie there?'[4]

It was Alan Buckley, the son of Richard's foster sister Margaret, who lived in Birmingham. Married with a young son and living with his parents, Alan had canvassed his uncle about the possibility of a job at Brett Plastics.

Gill responded, 'No, Richard hasn't come home from work yet.'[5]

Since it was half past eight in the evening, Alan asked if Richard could call him as soon as it was convenient and said goodbye. 'As far as I could tell, she appeared normal on the phone,' Alan recalled. 'Not distressed. I didn't hear any sounds or unusual noises in the background.'[6]

Billy replaced the receiver on its cradle and lifted the gag to cover Gill's mouth again before returning her to the bedroom. As he dropped her on the bed, she mumbled, 'Sarah?'

He replied, 'She's in your mum's, with the dogs. She's all right.'

She listened to his footsteps growing fainter on the staircase. In their wake she heard something else: a shuffling on the landing.

'Mum!' Gill's eyes widened as her mother edged past the door.

'I got free, Gill,' Amy whispered, approaching her daughter, who shook her head violently, mumbling but somehow managing to convey that Billy was still among them.

'I think then he must have found out that Mum had got free,' Gill recalls. 'He tied her up again, tighter than before. I knew he must have done this because I could hear her moaning. I heard her asking him to loosen the gag and the bonds. He must have done because I heard her thank him.'

Gill lay prone again, blinking rapidly, trying to listen to different parts of the house for some indication of how each member of her family was coping, and refusing to think about what might happen if Billy changed his mind about leaving, or if the police arrived. All the while, she felt as if her nerves had been set alight, the blood crackling like fire in her veins. And then, eventually, she heard something: a cry, and then a moan, followed by a sound she could not place but which she knew was the result of her father being savagely beaten by the intruder below.

Gill's mind raced, her thoughts tumbling over themselves: Dad has lots of spirit, he doesn't like giving into anyone, but he'll never stand up to the punishment, he'll die, no, he won't die, he's tough, he'll be all right, he'll be all right, he'll be all right . . . She kept repeating the last phrase like a mantra to help herself and her father, whose cries became fainter.

The house fell silent.

Time passed, but whether it was in minutes or hours, Gill had no idea. She heard Billy's footsteps on the stairs and cups rattling on a tray. He went in to her mother first, removing the gag to allow her to drink; Gill heard her croaking, 'Thank you, oh, thank you.' Then she heard his footsteps again and Richard's voice, but she could not make out any words.

The bedroom door creaked. She watched him place a single mug on the bedside table before he turned to her. He put his hands underneath her back, lifting her until she sat upright with her legs over the side of the bed. He worked the gag from her mouth and held the cup to her lips. She sipped the lukewarm tea and was grateful for it. When she had finished every drop, he took the cup and left it on the bedside table, then turned to look at her. Slowly, he removed the bonds on her wrists and ankles.

Gill knew what was about to happen but she still had to force herself not to scream or resist when his fingers reached out, tearing off her blouse and bra. He undressed himself, then told her to remove her skirt and pants. She did as he said but told him that she had her period and he could see this to be true. Forced to relieve him another way, she shut down her mind on the reality of it while telling herself that what she was made to do was happening because 'it made the difference between life and death, for all of them'. Afterwards, she would ask him about Sarah and she would not be afraid to ask, because of this thing she had been forced to do for him.

He got dressed. Gill lay shivering on the bed, her neck throbbing where he had bitten it. 'I was very cold and terrified,' she recalls. 'I put my dressing gown on and he tied me up again. This time my hands were in front of me and he didn't gag me. He put me into bed and covered me up with the blankets. He seemed concerned as to whether the bonds were too tight.' The shift in his behaviour astounded her. She found it unnerving, but was emboldened by it, asking, 'Where's Sarah? You wouldn't hurt her, would you, Billy?'

She used his name purposely, hoping to strengthen the bond she sensed he now imagined to exist between them. When he offered her a cigarette, she accepted: he lit one, held it to her mouth and let her inhale, then took it out and repeated the action.

She asked him again.

He replied that Sarah was well. Then with a small smile he revealed, 'I've got a little girl of my own.' Registering Gill's surprise, he told her about Nichola, finishing, 'So that's why I would never harm Sarah.' Gill fought back tears of relief, certain now that – whatever else he might do – this man would not hurt her daughter. Afterwards, when he left the room, she lay holding on to the memory of that exchange and drew strength from it.

Eventually, she realised that Billy had gone into the spare room and was talking to Richard as if he had met him in a pub, except that he was boasting about his criminal past. She heard him say that he had once strangled two police dogs with his bare hands and her stomach clenched, not knowing that it was fiction. He continued with the story of the Grange Park raid, when he and his brother had injured several police officers, and followed that with a careless remark about having broken into countless houses like Pottery Cottage, which their owners spent a fortune on without thinking of security.

Gill tried to block out Billy's voice. She strained to hear movement from the Newmans' house, Seconds, but there was nothing, just the wind funnelling the snow across the moors. Nonetheless, at 10.30 p.m. Len Newman stepped outside for a while to exercise his dog on the terrace and would have heard Gill, had she shouted.

'I cannot recall seeing anything unusual or hearing any unusual noises,' he told detectives three days later. 'Despite the twelve-foot cottage dividing my cottage from Pottery Cottage, I do hear noises . . . i.e., I've heard Mr Moran whistling and Sarah "playing up". On this night, however, I heard nothing.'[7] Len and his wife watched the midweek soccer match on the television in their bedroom and fell asleep shortly after 11 p.m.

Lying beneath the blankets in her bed, Gill felt the temperature drop as the night wore on. She had no sense of the hour, and heard nothing from her parents or Sarah, just Richard talking quietly to Billy, feigning an interest in his life in order to establish a rapport between them.

'They talked off and on all through the night,' Gill remembers, 'but I didn't sleep at all.'

1. Richard and Gill Moran: a happy, devoted couple who had worked hard to make good lives for themselves and their family.

2. Sarah Bridget Moran with her father. Adopted as a baby by Richard and Gill, Sarah was a bright, vivacious young girl.

3. Richard Moran's business colleagues at Brett Plastics became close family friends: *(left to right)* Richard Moran, Ann Goldthorpe, Gill Moran and Paul Goldthorpe, *c.*1976.

4. William Thomas Hughes, better known as Billy Hughes, was in trouble with the law from early adolescence and spent much of his life in Borstal and prison before making his final escape in January 1977.

5. Hughes the family man: with his daughter Nichola in Blackpool, 1972.

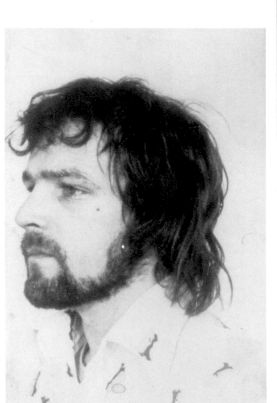

6. Hughes the criminal: almost unrecognisable after one of his many prison sentences.

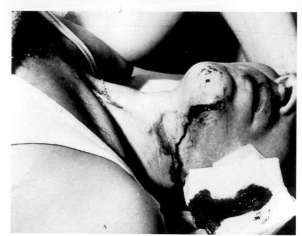

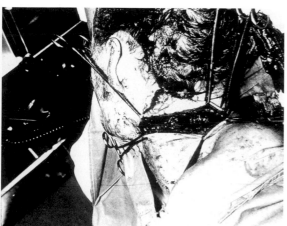

7, 8. Knife wounds inflicted on prison warders Ken Simmonds and Don Sprintall by Billy Hughes during the taxi journey from Leicester Prison to the court hearing in Chesterfield. It was a miracle either man survived.

9. The main living-room at Pottery Cottage, where Richard Moran was confronted by the sight of Billy Hughes holding a knife to his wife's throat.

10. Pottery Cottage on the night the murders came to light. Photograph taken by Scene of Crime Officer John Winston Slater, who used several reels of film documenting the property and the four bodies contained within it.

11. Tracks in the courtyard of Pottery Cottage. To the rear is the narrow gate through which Billy first entered the property from the moors. The body of Amy Minton lies in the snow behind the half-open garage door.

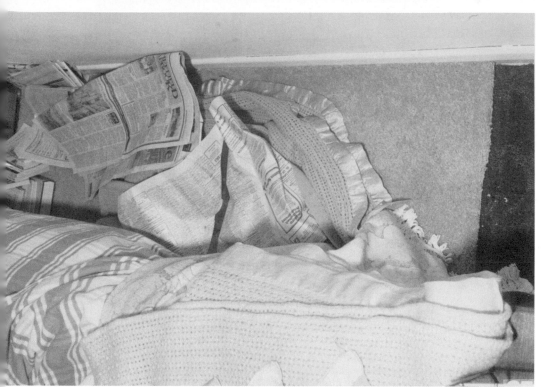

12. This corner of Sarah's bedroom shows the kitchen knife used as a murder weapon by Billy Hughes.

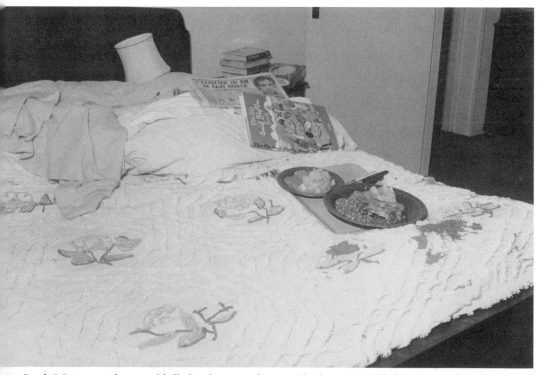

13. Sarah Moran was kept and killed in her grandparents' bedroom by Billy Hughes. He maintained the pretence that she was alive until the very end; the meal is one of several cooked by Gill for her young daughter, who had already been murdered. Also visible in the photograph is a local newspaper in which his escape was reported and the book he suggested Gill should buy for Sarah, knowing that she would never read it.

14. Rainow, Cheshire on Friday, 14 January 1977. Billy's reign of terror ended here when he was fatally shot by police marksmen, leading to the release of his hostage, Gill Moran.

15. Crime scene photographs of the Morris Marina reveal how dangerous the situation was for all concerned. An officer demonstrates the spot where the axe wielded by Billy Hughes caught in the vehicle's roof lining as he attempted to bring it down on his hostage, Gill Moran.

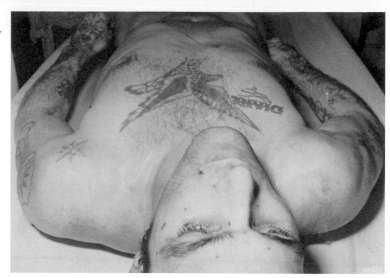

16. The body of a killer: Billy Hughes, 15 January 1977.

17. The Pottery Cottage murders were headline news for weeks afterwards in both national and local press.

18. The three men who brought the Pottery Cottage killer's reign of terror to an end: Detective Constable Alan Nicholls, Chief Inspector Peter Howse and Detective Sergeant Frank Pell, pictured after the inquest in April 1977.

19. A devastated Jean Hughes in 1977 with four-year-old Nichola, the daughter she bore Billy.

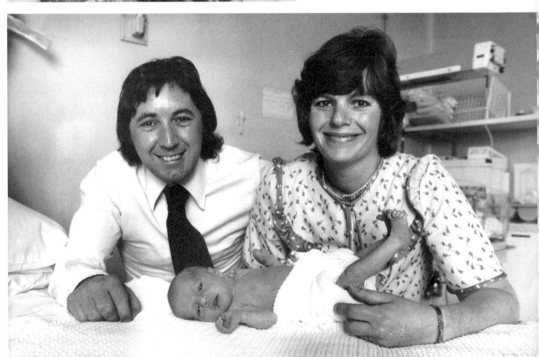

20. On 9 December 1978 Gill Moran married Jim Mulqueen after they met at a family reunion; his mother was one of Richard Moran's foster sisters. In June 1979 they became parents to Jayne, their only child. 'I'm picking up the pieces of my life again,' Gill told the press. 'I have found a new happiness.' Over forty years later, the couple remain together in a peaceful home far from Pottery Cottage and its memories.

Part Three:

Day 2, Thursday
13 January, 1977

Chapter Nine:

A Game of Patience

A T FIRST LIGHT, the search for Billy Hughes began again. Derbyshire's Assistant Chief Constable Arthur Mitchell visited the various static points and patrols that had been maintained all night, having discussed the case with senior officers. He thought the fugitive 'most likely' to be somewhere between the crashed Morris and the A6, and reiterated his instruction that within that region all houses were to be properly searched, all farmsteads explored and all isolated buildings examined.[1] Reflecting on the situation afterwards, he admitted that in light of his assessment, the site where Billy Hughes had taken refuge – Eastmoor – was 'completely in the wrong direction'.[2]

At Bakewell, Chief Inspector Peter Howse took a call that morning from his colleague Detective Constable John Burton, who informed him that the army had been forced to cancel an exercise in Farnborough and were offering two helicopters to aid the search. Burton was eager to join them. Howse granted permission immediately, but while the helicopters were air-bound he received an irate call from a more senior officer insisting that he should have provided proof that Burton was insured before allowing him to fly. Equally irate, Howse reminded him that all armed forces transport was classed as belonging to the Crown and therefore exempt from insurance. 'I don't know if that's true or not,' he reflects wryly, 'but it sounded good at the time! Unfortunately the helicopters had to be called off as a result of the weather anyway.'[3]

The search on the ground continued to be hampered by the poor weather, despite snowploughs having traversed the region during the night. 'Many schools in the area didn't open on Thursday because of the snow,' Howse recalls. 'So that cut down another line of inquiry because a child or teacher not turning up could have been an indication that something was wrong at home. The same thing applied to workplaces: normally someone has to account for their absence, but the weather kept scores of people at home. Everyone was affected, including those involved in the search. We knew we had to step up the search somehow, so members of the Special Operations Unit were deployed to carry out house-to-house checks in the nearest village, which was Beeley, and the traffic department did likewise at Rowsley. Because we hadn't received any sightings or information about his whereabouts we had to assume he was still with us. We set up a number of briefing rooms near each village and area within the search. Regardless of absentees, local schools, businesses, shops, pubs and post offices were visited and we appealed again to people to check on their friends and neighbours, etc., and to report any concerns, however insignificant, to us.'[4]

Howse then points out: 'I think it's important to say, too, that although we knew Hughes to be armed with a knife – at the very least – with which he had almost killed two prison officers – none of us were armed. Not a single officer. The best we could do was to ensure that those sent to explore farms and more remote locations were accompanied by a dog handler. I later heard from Inspector John Keen that the Chief Constable of Derbyshire, Sir Walter Stansfield, had visited the police control room at Ripley that night and was extremely displeased to discover some firearms had been issued to those involved in the search on Alfreton Division. He immediately ordered them to be withdrawn, declaring that firearms were only to be issued in exceptional circumstances and only on authority of an Assistant Chief Constable or rank above. But in view of what Hughes was already known to have done, you might well ask, "What are exceptional circumstances?" '[5]

'Get up, Gill.'

Already awake when Billy entered the room, she shuffled on to the edge of the bed, managing to sit up slowly. He untied the flex from her wrists and ankles, then told her she was going out: he wanted newspapers and to know if there were any roadblocks. He told her to do her hair and make-up as she usually would and to dress warmly. Then he left her.

In the bathroom mirror, Gill gazed at her reflection. Bruising crept up from below her dressing-gown, mottling her shoulders and neck. The bite mark was lost among the discoloration. She looked down at herself and saw bruises elsewhere, too.

After washing, she went back into the bedroom and opened her wardrobe. She put on a green polo neck and a skirt, then started applying her make-up. Billy appeared, sitting down on the bed to watch her. Her eyes met his in the mirror. 'Where's Sarah?' she asked.

'Sound asleep in Mum's spare room,' he replied, speaking as if he were family. 'I've covered her over.'[6] Gill tried to give him a smile of gratitude but could not. She finished her make-up quickly, anxious to get away from being alone with him. He seemed not to notice, telling her that he had fed the dogs and even checked on Sarah's rabbit, before following her down to the kitchen when she asked to make everyone a hot drink.

'I took a cup of tea upstairs to Richard and Mum,' Gill recalls. 'I saw that they were not gagged but they were still tied up. I held the cups for them while they drank the tea. I had some conversation with them and tried to comfort them.'

Suddenly she heard Billy shout to her from downstairs, telling her to look outside. She moved the curtain slightly in the spare room. In the gravel courtyard below, a huge council lorry was reversing, its sensors beeping. Billy shouted again and she went down to join him in the hall.

'Are you expecting anyone?' Billy asked, his face contorted with anger.

'Yes, but I'd forgotten. They've come to empty the septic tank.'

'Then deal with them,' he said fiercely. 'And act normal.'

Gill clenched and unclenched her fists to try to relieve the tension that threatened to overwhelm her. Then she took a deep breath and went outside.

Council worker Ernest Jones recalls arriving at Pottery Cottage around half past seven that morning with tanker driver Bobby Coles. He had never been to the property before, but saw the house sign on the wall and climbed out to open the gate. 'Bob Coles reversed the wagon in and parked it in front of a beige-coloured car, which was in the drive and facing the main road. It was just breaking daylight. After I had opened the white gate a young woman came out of the front door, walked towards me and said, "Will you be all right?" I said, "Yes thanks, I can see where it is." [7]

Bobby Coles edged his way along the seat inside the driver's cab: 'Just as I was getting out the woman came out of the front door and came round to the passenger side and said to me, "Do you want anything signing?" I replied, "No, not until we've emptied it."[8] She left them to their task.

Afterwards, Coles collected the invoice book and knocked on the front door. He glanced around; the snow had ceased, but the grey clouds bore a pink tinge that often heralded further flurries. He hunched his shoulders.

'The woman came to the door,' he recalled. 'I handed her the book and showed her where to sign. Whilst she was signing the book I said, "It's not very warm round here." She said, "No, it's always cold round here." She then handed me the book back and I gave her the top copy which she had signed. She thanked me very much and said, "Leave the gate open." '[9]

As the two men climbed into their vehicle, Gill stood on the doorstep, feeling drained. She had desperately wanted to say or do something – to whisper for help or to write that single word across the paperwork – but Billy was watching from a window, unseen. If the driver or his mate had reacted with shock, he would have known. And there would have been consequences, of a sort she could not bear to imagine. And so she closed the door, knowing that the mundane task of having to deal with the council workers represented something of far greater significance to Billy: her complicity. The perfect opportunity to betray him had presented itself and she had spurned it. Whether he understood why was of no consequence; all that mattered was her collusion.

As far as Coles and Jones were concerned, the endeavour was no different to any other, taking fifteen minutes from start to finish. 'The woman appeared to be quite normal,' Coles recalled. '[She] wasn't frightened at all.'[10]

Gill walked towards the lounge where the curtains were still closed across the wide picture windows. She caught sight of her father and stopped, heart pounding: 'He was still sitting in the same chair and he was covered up as far as his neck with something dark. He wasn't moving.' On the yellow armchair in front of the side window, Arthur lay beneath a blue anorak, his artificial leg at a peculiar angle.

Billy was suddenly there, seizing her arm, propelling her out of the room. 'I asked Billy to let me go to him but he wouldn't let me,' she recalls. 'I couldn't see whether Dad was injured or bleeding.' Billy told her that Arthur was merely sleeping and he had thrown the blue anorak over him for warmth. He refused to allow her anywhere near the lounge again, instead pushing her towards the telephone table, where he instructed her to ring the company she worked for and call in sick.

Gill's fingers trembled as she dialled the number, unable to think of anything but her father sitting awkwardly and unnaturally silent in the armchair.

Ann Burnage, secretary at John A. Roberts & Co., answered her call just before 9 a.m.: 'I recognised [Gill's] voice. She said, "I shan't be coming to work today, I'm not very well. Will you tell Mr Roberts?" I said, "Yes, I hope you feel better soon." She said, "Thank you" and put the phone down. She did not say what she was suffering from and I did not ask her. She appeared to sound normal except when I answered the phone by saying "John A. Roberts and Co.," when there was a long pause at the other end before Gillian spoke.'[11]

Billy stilled Gill's hand as she went to replace the receiver, prompting her, 'Now ring Sarah's school.' After a moment's hesitation, she called Wigley Primary, where headmistress Margaret Goodall spoke to her, remembering: 'She told me that Sarah would not be attending school because she was ill. Another pupil at the school was ill and I automatically replied, "Has Sarah got the bug as well?" Mrs Moran agreed that this was Sarah's illness. I then went on to explain to Mrs Moran that I had heard from the area office that Sarah would be unable to move to a senior school a year early as I had earlier proposed with her. She said, "Yes, I understand. You've told me that you've only known of one other child being able to do it." That concluded the conversation . . . Mrs Moran appeared to be her normal self. She is usually fairly reticent.'[12]

'Stay there,' Billy instructed Gill before running upstairs. He returned with Richard, who was no longer gagged and able to walk freely, although his hands remained tied behind his back. Billy told Gill to ring Brett Plastics while he held the phone for Richard.

Receptionist Gloria Holmes took the call. She was surprised when Richard failed to chat and joke as usual, instead telling her in an uncharacteristically curt voice that he had flu and would not be in to work. Gloria was concerned enough to speak to David Brown afterwards, telling him that Richard had rung to say he was ill but sounded 'odd'.[13] David rang him back to check there was nothing wrong.

Richard answered, repeating that he had flu and would remain at home. 'He said nothing during the conversation which gave me any grounds to believe everything was not correct,' David remembers. 'The conversation was confined to business matters. I thought his voice sounded upset but I thought that this was what was expected with flu. I had no more contact with Richard and spent Thursday night in London.'[14] Although he didn't mention it to Richard, David decided to call at Pottery Cottage the following evening, after collecting the French au pair who would help out while Glynis was pregnant; Richard spoke fluent French and David thought it would comfort the new girl to be able to converse in her first language.

As Billy replaced the receiver on its cradle, the phone rang again. He asked Richard if he was expecting another call. He shook his head. Billy warned him again to act normally, and lifted the receiver to Richard's ear.

'Hello, Richard, this is Sue.' Sue Silkstone worked with Gill and was worried about her. 'I'm just ringing to see how Gillian is. I hope I didn't get you out of bed?'

'No, I was coming downstairs to make a cup of tea,' Richard said. 'They're all in bed with flu. She should be back at work tomorrow.'

'I hope you'll soon be better.'

'Thanks, Sue, cheerio,' Richard replied before ending the call.

'He sounded normal,' she remembers, 'except that he sounded as if he had a cold and I remember he coughed once.'[15]

Billy gave Richard an impatient shove, following him upstairs before returning to Gill. She stood with her coat on in the hall, clutching her car keys and handbag as Billy had instructed. He nudged her towards the front door, unlocking it.

The world outside was cold and grey. Gill pulled her coat tighter.

'Get the papers,' he said as they walked across the snow. 'I want to see what they're saying about me. Get forty fags as well.'

She climbed into her car, pushing the key into the ignition lock.

Billy put a hand on the steering wheel and leaned in, his grey eyes on hers: 'I've got your family here, Gill. Don't do anything stupid.'

'I won't.' She kept his gaze. 'I promise.'

He stared at her for a moment, then drew back and closed the door.

Once she was travelling down the hill into Brampton, a dizzying sense of being disconnected from reality set in: how could everything be so normal beyond the confines of Pottery Cottage? As she drew up alongside the kerb on busy Chatsworth Road, she found herself watching people, utterly fascinated by the ordinariness of their lives. 'For them, it's just another day,' she told herself. 'They're all going to work as though nothing is happening. If only they knew what's happening at *my* house.'

She got out of the car, that same vertiginous sensation causing her to concentrate on each step towards the row of shops. She had called many times before at Parsons Newsagents for a paper or cigarettes, or a bar of her father's favourite Galaxy chocolate, but now it felt like stepping into another world, where everything was at once the same and yet completely unfamiliar. The bell jingled as the door opened and closed behind her, and the narrow aisles packed with provisions of one kind or another looked no different, but when she turned to the stand selling the local newspapers, all the headlines seemed to leap out from the page.

'Dangerous Hijacker Still Free Despite Moorland Hunt: Hostage Fear Among Police Theories' read the front page of the *Derbyshire Times*, juxtaposing a photograph of uniformed officers vaulting a five-bar gate on the snowy moors with a snapshot of the fugitive. Gill reached for the newspaper, her hands trembling so violently that she had difficulty reading the text: 'Theory one is that the 30-year-old man is holding a family hostage in an isolated house on the moors. Theory two is that the man could be suffering from exposure or even be dead after a night on the snow-covered moors, when temperatures plunged to seven degrees below. Theory three . . .'[16]

Gill snatched up the paper, and another, making her way to the counter where she heard herself talking to elderly Ellen Parsons. She pushed past other customers in her haste to reach the safety of her car, then threw the papers and cigarettes on to the passenger seat and switched on the ignition, screeching away into a gap in the traffic. She took a different route home as Billy had insisted she should, driving through Holymoorside where there was no sign of police. Relieved, she would not have been tempted to approach them anyway, 'because of the danger to my family'. Snow had begun to fall heavily again, but in some parts of the county the search went on, with four-wheel drives used to traverse the moors and higher ground. Life in mid and north Derbyshire, and some southern areas, drew to a standstill, however, and scores of officers were diverted from the search to help people in difficulties due to the weather.

'Where's Dad?' Gill asked as she entered the hallway of her home after parking the car in the drive. The big yellow armchair was empty. She noticed that two antimacassars had been placed on the arms in her absence.

Billy took the newspapers and cigarettes from her. He had drawn the curtains in the lounge and sat down on the sofa to read. 'In his bedroom,' he mumbled, absorbed in the relevant articles. Gill stood helplessly, knowing he would not allow her to go through to the annexe. With Billy's permission, she made drinks for everyone. He took the coffee for Arthur and a glass of Ribena for Sarah after directing her upstairs with coffee for Richard and Amy. In Sarah's room, Gill found her mother 'still gagged very tightly' and bound with her hands over her stomach. She gave her the cup to sip, then moved into the spare room to help her husband, who was bound but not gagged. As they talked together quietly, Billy appeared, indicating that she should go through to her own bedroom. He followed her, pushing her back on to the bed.

'He tied my hands in front of me and he tied my ankles together again,' Gill remembers. 'He did not gag me this time. He sat on the side of the bed, talking to me. Then he started to kiss me. It was a repeat of what he did before. He untied me and he told me to undress which I did. He committed exactly the same act as before. He was undressed also. When he had finished he put his clothes on and so did I. He didn't tie me up again and he went to Richard's room. They were talking but I couldn't hear what they were saying. He was still carrying the knife all the time.'

Gill sat slowly upright on the bed and put her feet on the floor, her body aching. Her mind was empty but for a single, repetitive thought: When will he go? Eventually, she went through to the spare room and asked if she could make something to eat. Billy agreed. She headed to the kitchen and emptied two cans of soup into a pan. While it was warming, Billy brought Richard downstairs, having untied the flex from his ankles. He made him sit on the kitchen floor while he fastened the bonds again. Richard slumped on the lino, back against the sink unit.

Gill looked down at her husband, appalled by his pained, exhausted face and the purple swelling of his hands from the flex wound tight around his wrists. She knelt down to help him eat, but he could barely sip the soup from the bowl she held to his lips. Billy had taken three bowls out: one for Amy in the spare bedroom, and two through to the annexe for Arthur and Sarah. He sat at the kitchen table to eat his soup, then pushed the bowl aside and looked down at Gill and Richard, sitting side by side on the floor.

He began to outline a plan. Money was the main objective apart from evasion, and he intended to visit a friend in lodgings at Sutton-in-Ashfield to recover his share of the money owed from a job they had done together. In order to ensure his own safety should the police catch up with him on his mission, Billy proposed taking Richard along as his hostage.

As he spoke, he traced an imaginary line with his fingernail on the kitchen table. Then he stopped, declaring, 'No, I won't do that. I'll take you instead, Gill. We can go in your car, Richard—'

'No, no, no! Billy, no!' Gill cried out, the tension finally snapping. She burst into loud, racking sobs. Billy frowned. While Richard tried to calm and comfort his wife, Billy fetched a bottle of whisky he had noticed and drank from earlier. He found tumblers in a cupboard and poured a large measure of whisky into one, then held it out to Gill: 'Drink.'

She took great gulps of it. Billy poured another glass for Richard, who drank more slowly. Billy untied the flex from Richard's ankles and when Gill's sobbing had subsided, he told the two of them to follow him upstairs, where they joined Amy. Billy handed her a glass of whisky, after removing her gag and bonds. He told them he fully intended to leave that evening, but until then, they needed to find some way of passing the time.

'Have you got any cards?' he asked.

Over the next couple of hours, a bizarre conviviality enveloped the four of them. 'Myself, Billy and Richard played rummy and then he tried to teach us a game called Chinese Patience,' Gill recalls. 'We played for money. We relaxed a bit as a result of drinking the whisky.' Amy picked up one of the newspapers Gill had bought and read it from cover to cover, while the other three

bickered amicably about who was winning. Billy shared the cigarettes with Gill, and all four of them drank large measures of
whisky, draining the bottle.

Billy made no attempt to contain his prisoners, confident in
the knowledge that each of them were tied to him by far stronger
bonds: those of automatic compliance, a psychological state
induced by extreme fear. There was nothing incidental in his
insistence that they should gather in Sarah's room with Amy
either; he knew that the little girl's implied presence would calm
Gill in a way that nothing else could under the circumstances he
had dictated. They sat close to the old-fashioned school desk that
Arthur had found on sale, Sarah's bright posters, the little trophy
she had won for sports, her Cycling Proficiency certificate and the
cot where her dolls slept.

'Ordinarily, when people move about in Mum and Dad's part
of the house you can hear them,' Gill told detectives three days
later. 'But we never heard another sound. We never heard the
toilet flush or anything.' Yet they believed Billy's remarks about
how the youngest and oldest members of the family were coping,
such was his control over them. In turn, Gill felt sure that Billy
'seemed to be starting to trust us a bit more'.

It began to grow dark outside. Gill said she was hungry and
needed something after drinking the whisky. Billy told her to
cook 'a proper meal', adding that they would join her in the
kitchen. 'The others sat down while I cooked beef burgers, chips
and tomatoes,' Gill recalls. 'I cooked some for Dad and Sarah and
Billy took it into the other part of the house. He wouldn't let
anybody else go. He let the dogs in. We ate our meal and then
Billy went and fetched the plates back from the other part of the
house. I saw that Dad's food was untouched and all the food on
Sarah's plate had gone. Mum said that perhaps Dad hadn't eaten

his food because he hadn't any teeth. I asked Billy if Dad could have his teeth and a bar of Galaxy, which he likes. He said he could. He took the teeth and the bar of chocolate into the other part of the house.'

When Billy returned, Gill finally found the courage to question why Sarah had failed to asked for her 'comfort towel'. As a baby, her daughter had never had a pacifier, but never slept without the same small towel rolled up into a sausage. That, and her little grey elephant, were Sarah's sleep essentials, yet both were lying in the lounge from the previous day. Gill wanted to know why she hadn't asked for them.

'She just hasn't,' Billy said with a shrug. 'She's never mentioned them. She's quite happy in there with your dad.'

Gill bit her lip. 'I can't understand it. She *must* want them. Would you take them through to her? Please?'

Billy pulled a face but took the toy elephant and rolled towel through to the annexe. Gill waited for him to return.

'She was really pleased to see them,' he said and Gill accepted that.

The telephone rang just before 4 p.m. Brett Plastics company secretary, Keith Bradshaw, wanted to know if there was anything he could do for Richard and remembers that Gill answered his call: 'We spoke for a few minutes. She appeared to be normal but I thought slightly on the miserable side. Gill told me that Richard was in bed suffering from flu and she had not been to work because she had caught a touch of it herself. I asked her what the weather conditions were like and she said it was snowing heavily.'[17]

Gill was about to say goodbye, when Keith asked, 'Have you heard about the loony on the loose?'

Gill froze. Billy was standing next to her; he had heard every word. She saw his jaw set in fury.

'I must go, Keith – I've got so much to do – I'm just going to say bye.' She dropped the receiver into place and turned to look at Billy.

He paced the hallway, up and down, up and down, then suddenly stopped. 'Loony?' he shouted. 'Loony? Why did he call me that? I'm not taking that – I'm not crazy.'

Gill tried to pacify him, grasping his arm to keep him still and telling him that Keith had never met him; he was only repeating what he had read in the newspapers, but everyone knew the press printed nothing but lies. Eventually, Billy's temper subsided.

'That's it,' he said. 'It is – it's all lies.'

Exhausted, Gill left his side to look out of the windows in the lounge. It was dark, but the darkness had a life of its own: the blizzard quickened and the wind tore in great gusts along the road, twisting the rope swing in the side garden and barrelling across the moors.

She flinched as Billy's breath warmed her neck where he stood behind her, looking out at the snow.

'This is right in my favour,' he said with a smile. 'They'll never track me now.'

Chapter Ten:

Roy's Café

NEITHER BILLY NOR Gill realised that a contingent of police officers had spent the afternoon working their way steadily down the eastern side of the A619. Eventually, they reached the Highwayman Inn, where manager Luis Lopez had a photograph of Billy, cut from a newspaper, propped up on his till. The search team checked the outbuildings to the rear and side of the pub, struggling with the frozen doors, but found nothing, returning to Chesterfield early in the evening. Just a few yards away, lights burned in the windows of Pottery Cottage.

Billy grew restless again, moving from one room to another. The television in the lounge remained silent, gathering dust, but the local news programme that evening featured the story of his escape. Alfred Horobin, head of Derbyshire CID, recounted the incident while standing before a map to point out places of interest, including the crash site on Beeley Moor. Horobin told the presenter: 'In essence, we're asking the public for any sightings of Hughes whatsoever. The one thing that we don't want the public to do is "have a go" at this man. So far as we're concerned, he's still armed with this knife, the knife he used to attack the warders with, and the last thing we want is for any member of the public to be injured whilst having a go.' Asked if Billy might put up a fight if confronted, Horobin replied: 'Well, I think in view of the present circumstances, undoubtedly this man could well have a go, yes, and stab some other person.' The final question put to him by the presenter was one which everyone familiar with the case wanted to know: how had the fugitive managed to get hold of a knife in the first place? Horobin hesitated before answering: 'That remains to be found out yet. One can speculate as to how the man came by the knife, but really, I'm not competent to speak about the prison side of it. That is down to them.'[1]

Blackpool Police remained on high alert, having been informed by Leicester Prison that an inmate had told a warder how Billy Hughes had confided in him a few days previously that he intended to escape on 12 January to kill his wife. While Jean and her children, together with Alice Swan and hers, had already vacated their home on Loftos Avenue for safe houses, Detective Chief Inspector Ken Mackay of Blackpool CID told a press conference: 'We have good reasons to believe Hughes may return here. We have made extensive inquiries in Blackpool and he has many connections in this town. We are treating the matter as serious and are acting accordingly.'[2]

At Pottery Cottage, Billy decided it was time to have a trial run at getting away. It was half past seven. 'He had sorted out things in the house that he was going to take with him,' Gill recalls. 'He had been listening to radios . . . all the time. He took Mum up to Sarah's bedroom and tied her up again but he did not gag her. He left the dogs with her.'[3]

At Billy's insistence, Gill and Richard followed him out to the Chrysler; all of them were surprised by the depth of the still falling snow. Gill climbed into the back of the car while Billy sat next to Richard, who drove towards Chesterfield. 'The roads were very bad,' she remembers. 'The car radio was on and we heard a report that the police had called off the search for Billy because of the bad weather. We told him that it was a good time to escape, if the police weren't looking for him, but he said it was a trick.' Billy had already instructed Richard to call for petrol and he pulled into the forecourt of a garage on Chatsworth Road where he had a business account. Afterwards, they continued towards the town centre, but the snow was falling so fast that Billy changed his mind, unwilling to risk getting stranded.

They arrived back at Pottery Cottage, where the snow seemed to fill the house with a cavernous silence. Gill made a pot of tea and carried it up to Sarah's room, where Amy was visibly relieved to see her daughter and son-in-law but shrank back as Billy entered. He sat down on the edge of the bed, talking at random. Then he mentioned his daughter, and drew out a handful of letters from her, filled with childish doodles. He passed them round and showed them Nichola's photograph, adding how much he loved her. His words gave Gill fresh hope for her own daughter's safety.

Billy tucked the letters and photograph back inside the pocket of a shirt he had taken from Richard's wardrobe, having had his pick of clothes throughout his time at Pottery Cottage. Then he noisily drained his tea, declaring that – despite the weather – he wanted to be on his way and needed to collect the money he was owed from his friend. He went through to the main bedroom while Gill padded after him. She watched from the landing as he heaved a grey suitcase belonging to Richard on to the bed and began filling it with his clothes, then found a plastic tote bag she used for work and pushed her belongings into it: a pair of shoes, jewellery, underwear and Tampax.

'Have you got a wig?'

Gill was startled by the question, although he had asked before. She had lied then, unwilling to hand over her expensive, fashionable wig, but now she found it for him. He tried it on. It looked surprisingly convincing; the length was no longer than many men wore their hair. She adjusted it slightly and he decided to keep it on. Then he returned to the bedroom, collecting the suitcase and one of Richard's suits, depositing them in the hallway before heading back to Sarah's room, where he tied up Richard and Amy once more.

'He left Mum tied up on the bed and Richard sitting on the floor with his back to the wall,' Gill remembers. 'He did not gag them. They were tied with plastic wire, fastened in a lot of small knots so that they couldn't be untied. He took a jug and two glasses from a dresser on the landing and he went to the bathroom and put some water in the jug. He left the water and the glasses on the floor with Richard and Mum so that they could have a drink.'

Billy closed the door and met Gill on the landing.

'Let's go,' he said.

The Newmans had arrived home later than usual that evening. Due to the heavy snowfall, it was around nine o'clock when they pulled into the driveway in their separate cars. Joyce noticed that Pottery Cottage was 'not as well-lit as usual' and that her milk order, which Amy Minton normally took indoors for her when she called to clean, had been left out.[4] Len spent an hour clearing the snow from his driveway before bed, ready for the following morning, but other than spotting Richard Moran's car parked near the road, he saw and heard nothing out of the ordinary.

At 10 p.m., when Len was shaking the snow from his spade before returning to the warmth of Seconds, Gill and Billy emerged into the courtyard of Pottery Cottage. Billy sprinted to the road in order to ensure that it was clear while Gill started the car. She stalled the engine as she reached the gate and the wheels became wedged against the tightly packed snow. Billy used all of his considerable strength to lift the car clear and she managed to get it going again. He jerked his head to indicate that she should move over, and as she climbed into the passenger seat, he opened the door and slid in behind the steering wheel.

They travelled in silence, Billy concentrating on the road ahead. On the back seat of the Chrysler lay the grey suitcase and plastic tote bag; Gill tried not to think about them. The weather helped in that sense: visibility was virtually nil as they drove at a snail's pace through Chesterfield to the M1 and finally, the slip road to Sutton-in-Ashfield. They had just reached the motorway junction when Billy said, 'I forgot some letters – we'll have to go back.'

'I was absolutely appalled, I almost cried,' Gill recalls. 'He said he needed the letters because the address was on one of them of the place where he intended to go.' She begged him to pull over to let her check the suitcase for the letters. He did as she asked. Searching fruitlessly for them, she finally conceded defeat and flopped down in her seat, swallowing her tears in order to give him directions to Alfreton for Pottery Cottage.

Gill had no idea why Billy was so determined to return, but as they drove through Brampton, she felt a nauseous rising wave of panic at the possibility that Richard and her mother might have got free and rushed into the annexe.

'Mum had said to Billy a number of times how worried she was about Dad,' Gill recalls. 'Billy had always replied that he was all right. He said that Sarah was looking after him. He said that Sarah was only tied with a pair of tights, that neither was gagged, and that Dad's hands had been tied at the front. I had asked him why Sarah didn't call out. He said it was because he had told her not to.'

Gill pleaded to be the one who fetched the letters when they arrived at the cottage, but Billy refused. He left her sitting in the car while he disappeared inside the house. He was soon back and said nothing as he turned the car on to the road again. She assumed he had the letters with him and that all was well, but was too wound up to ask.

Billy switched on the radio when they reached the M1. He became talkative, telling her about the crime he had committed with the friend he was going to see, 'but it all went in one ear and out of the other' as far as Gill was concerned. Billy did not seem to mind; he chainsmoked while parroting about his proficiency as a burglar, the stupidity of policemen, and repeated the tale about throttling two dogs sent into his cell, remarking, 'Alsatians never worry me. I can take care of them without any weapons. Dobermanns, though, they're different. I could handle one, but if they came at me with more than that, I guess I'd go under.' As for people, he went on, that was easy: he *could* kill but preferred to slit a person's throat in such a way that he disabled them but let them live. When it came to escaping, he'd known his chances were good because he was used to being on the run. 'If you're tough and ruthless,' he told her, 'you *always* succeed.'

When he finally took a breather, Gill ventured a suggestion.

'After you've collected that money,' she said, 'what about you let me drive home alone and you make your own way to wherever you intend to go?'

She took his silence as an indication that he was considering her proposal and went on: 'You can trust me. In fact, you can trust all of us – my family, I mean. We've supported you from the start – we've protected you – you know we have, Billy. And you're clever, you could easily get another car. I won't tell anyone, I'll just drive home, I promise. It would be better for you, actually – because, of course, no one will know which car you're travelling in, Billy. That's better, isn't it?'

He seemed to agree, telling her that she would have to stay with him until he got another car.

'Well, I can just drive you to a car park and you can take what you want,' she said.

For the first time, he laughed in genuine amusement. 'I don't want a car park. I'll just flag down a car and take the driver hostage. I'm afraid of no one. You know that. I'll just stop the car and open the door and get in.'

Gill's skin crawled at the thought of someone else falling into his hands.

'People are stupid,' he went on. 'They never think to lock the back doors of their cars. They stop at traffic lights and then you've got them.' He glanced at her. 'You want to remember that, Gill. Always lock all the doors of your car.'

She said nothing, knowing he would not let her go.

They reached the Nottinghamshire market town of Sutton-in-Ashfield at one o'clock in the morning. Despite the letters that Billy had insisted would lead him to his friend's lodgings, and switching seats so that he could look at the map while Gill drove, they were unable to find the café where his friend was supposed to be living. Eventually, they located the address but there was no café: Roy and Mary Johnson had closed down that side of their business some eighteen months earlier. Nonetheless, their boarding house on Huthwaite's Sutton Road remained known locally as Roy's Café.

Gill stopped the bronze Chrysler towards the corner of the street and peered out at the house, a tall, unattractive building that extended towards the back, in its own little plot with low walls. Inside, the Johnsons and their three children were asleep. There were seven other residents and a dog that never barked at intruders, having grown so used to lodgers arriving at all hours. As security, Roy kept a policeman's truncheon in the hall, hung on a hook with the dog's lead.

Billy blew on his hands and pulled on the yellow leather gloves Gill had bought on her honeymoon eighteen years earlier. He got out of the Chrysler and crossed the road, opening the small iron gate at the rear of the property.

Gill sat in the darkness, shivering and smoking a cigarette, dismissing any thoughts of escape when she realised he had taken the car keys.

She heard a noise. Billy wrenched open the car door and jumped in, panting.

'Where are the keys? Gill, the keys!'

'*You've* got them,' she said, bewildered. 'You took them with you. What's happened?'

He threw something heavy into her lap and fumbled in his pocket until he found the keys. He started the ignition, reversed, then accelerated away from the building. He looked in the rear-view mirror. 'I've knocked out a copper.'

'What! Why?' Gill panicked, realising that the object on her lap was a truncheon made of solid wood, about 12 inches long, with finger grips at one end and a leather strap.

Billy's breathing slowly returned to normal. 'I rang the bell at the café and knocked, but there was no answer.'[5] He lit a cigarette, then continued, 'A policeman came up and asked what I was doing. I thought he might recognise me, I headbutted him. I left him face down in the snow.'

He drew deeply on the cigarette. 'He'll come round in ten minutes or so.'

Gill sat in petrified silence, rolling the truncheon off her knee and on to the floor. Billy looked at her.

'Come on, Gill, don't worry. He'll be fine. That's his truncheon. I brought it for you as a souvenir.'

Gill said nothing. Billy repeated the entire story again, embellishing certain details, talking as if he were an actor in a film noir, clearly trying to impress her. The whole incident was fiction: there was no policeman at the café and none of the residents at the boarding house knew Billy or met him there. When the police later questioned everyone present that night, they discovered that a couple of lodgers had awoken early the following morning and found the kitchen light on, the private lounge door open and light on and the dining-room door wide open. The dog leads were lying on the floor at the foot of the stairs instead of on a hook.

As they travelled at speed along the M1, Gill asked, 'Billy, please could Sarah sleep with me? She must be so frightened. I want to be with her.' He seemed irritated at her lack of interest in his escapade and shook his head: 'No. Leave things as they are.' They both fell silent until reaching Pottery Cottage.

'As Billy drove into the gateway the car stuck in the snow and the engine stopped,' Gill recalls. 'He tried to start it but it wouldn't start. He said he would speak to Richard about it. We went into the house and I went straight upstairs to Sarah's bedroom. Mum and Richard were still tied up in the bedroom. I untied Mum and Billy untied Richard. Richard was tied up in such a way that Billy had to cut the bonds but I can't remember what he did it with. I suggested we all had a cup of coffee and Billy and I went downstairs to make it.'

Shattered from lack of sleep and burned out by unutterable stress, Gill nevertheless asked Billy again to let Sarah share her bed that night. 'When he refused I became upset and this seemed to make him angry,' Gill remembers. 'He became very tense. I didn't mention it again because he frightened me and I wanted to keep him happy. We took the drinks upstairs and drank them in Sarah's room. He showed Richard the policeman's truncheon and joked about it. We finished the coffee and I suggested we all sleep in that room that night. I said this because I was afraid that he would sexually assault me again. The very thought of it terrified me. Richard said he thought it was a good idea as well. We all agreed.' Gill had already told her mother and husband about Billy's attacks, recording in her witness statement: 'Richard wasn't in a position to speak but I could see that he was upset.'

She collected three sleeping bags before Billy could object, placing hers next to Richard on the floor. Her mother prepared to spend what was left of the night in her granddaughter's single bed while Billy hunkered down in a sleeping bag against the door.

Although it was three o'clock in the morning, Gill was too wired and emotional to sleep. After staring at the ceiling for an hour, she heard something that made her skin prickle with unease. She sat bolt upright and saw immediately that her mother was awake too, listening.

Richard slept fitfully while Billy was sound asleep.

Gill and her mother exchanged glances, both uncomprehending and fearful: from downstairs came the sound of slow, rhythmic thudding. Every possibility went through Gill's mind, each one centring on the safety of her father and Sarah. Thoroughly frightened, she decided to wake Billy, but had to thump his arm repeatedly to rouse him. She whispered to him and he listened. Then he tore open the sleeping bag and leapt to his feet. She heard him running downstairs.

He was gone only a few minutes, returning slightly out of breath.

Closing the door behind him, he sank down to the floor and slid back into his sleeping bag. 'It was the dogs,' he said softly. 'They wanted some water.'

His eyes closed. 'It was their tails we heard, beating on the door.'

Part Four:

Day 3, Friday 14 January, 1977

Chapter Eleven:

We're Going to the Police

L EN AND JOYCE Newman slept through their alarm on Friday morning, rising at 7.30 a.m. Observing that several inches of snow had fallen overnight, Len went out before breakfast to clear the drive. After they had eaten, Joyce tidied round the house, certain that the heavy snow would keep Amy Minton at home. Gathering her belongings, she noticed that the dairy door ('never left open except when Mrs Moran is gardening') was ajar.[1] Len left for work shortly before his wife, just after nine, and realised that Richard's car was not in its usual spot on the driveway. The Newmans attributed these small changes in their neighbours' routines to the abysmal weather but later they gained a new and terrible significance.

Sunlight reflecting from the snowbound moors filtered through the curtains in Sarah's room at Pottery Cottage. Billy got out of his sleeping bag, stretching like a cat. He saw that Gill was awake and told her to make everyone some toast. She washed and dressed quickly; despite her exhaustion she could not face being caught alone with Billy, and headed down to the kitchen before he emerged from the bedroom.

Waiting for the first round of bread in the electric toaster, Gill turned to look at the connecting door into her parents' quarters. It would take only seconds to cross the floor and push it open; half a dozen steps more and she would be with her father and daughter . . .

The toast popped up with a metallic jolt, startling her. Then Billy entered the kitchen, strolling across to the back door.

'Look at the bird table,' he said. 'Covered in snow. The poor birds won't be able to get any food.'[2]

He unlocked the door and walked across the terrace, using the flat of his hand to sweep the snow from the wooden tray, then scattering some crumbs where it was clear. Gill knew he was doing it for effect; he had no interest in whether the birds survived or not. She turned away, applying a thick smear of butter to each slice of bread.

Billy took two plates piled high with toast through to the annexe. Gill was already seated at the table with her mother and Richard when he returned. Billy scraped back a chair and sat down to join them, eating his breakfast hungrily.

He drank his tea in a single gulp, then looked at Gill and Richard. 'You two are going into Chesterfield to do some shopping. I need a lot of things, so make a list.'

Richard said nothing, but sitting next to him, Gill felt his entire body tense with anticipation. She stood up, rummaging in a kitchen drawer full of odds and ends for some paper and a biro, then sat down to write while Billy reeled off his list as if he were remembering items from the *Generation Game* conveyor belt: 'A gas camping stove, a saucepan, six tins of Irish stew, two tins of tomato soup, two tins of vegetable soup, four chops, two packets of glacier fruits, twenty-four cans of light ale, a half-bottle of Bell's whisky, a couple of packets of John Player Special, all the newspapers – locals and nationals – oh, and a tin opener.'

He leaned back in his chair, taking a small wad of crumpled notes from his trouser pocket. Gill knew he had taken the money from them earlier. As she counted out £25, Billy said, 'That's more than enough. Get a present for Sarah as well – she's been really good.'

'Thanks, Billy,' Gill forced herself to say. 'You are kind.'

He inclined his head and gave a smile of acknowledgement. Getting to his feet, he told Amy to go back upstairs, adding that he would be up to see her when Gill and Richard had gone. He waited for the couple to prepare – Gill pulled on her coat, pushing the list and cash into a zipped compartment inside her handbag while Richard threw on a blue raincoat and trilby hat, reaching for his car keys from the kitchen worksurface – then led them out to the Chrysler.

The snow had gathered in huge drifts about the courtyard; Gill noticed the swing her father had fashioned for Sarah from an old tyre and a rope which hung from a tree had been crowned overnight with a solid crust of white. She leaned against the car slightly as she made her way to the front passenger seat, sinking calves-deep into the snow. Richard put a hand to his hat as he bent down to slide in behind the steering wheel, telling Billy it might take longer than usual to reach town. Billy merely nodded, not even troubling to imply what might happen to their family if they betrayed him, which Gill recognised as a sign of his trust in them.

As Richard turned the ignition, all four wheels began spinning on the spot. He tried again: the car jerked slightly to the right but moved no further. Billy gestured for him to get out, then fetched two shovels from the garage. He handed one to Richard and they spent five minutes cutting the snow away from the tyres.

Billy told Richard to get back inside the car and wait. He dug deeper around the front wheels, then yelled, 'Try it now.' The tyres struggled to grip as the engine rumbled into life, but Billy gave an almighty push from behind, sending the bronze Chrysler forward in a spray of blackened snow. He turned away to clear the driveway further with the shovel, while Richard headed out on to the main road.

It was half past eleven as they drew level with the Highwayman Inn. 'This was the first time that Richard and I had been able to talk together freely,' Gill recalls. But they remained silent as the traffic edged down the hill towards Chesterfield. For despite every second taking them further away from the psychopath in their home, it was as if he were sitting directly behind them with the knife at their backs. When they did eventually begin to converse, it was in whispers.

Richard spoke first, his voice low and desperate: 'I can't take any more, Gill. We're going to the police.'

Gill twisted round in her seat, enraged by his suggestion. 'That's the very *last* thing you're going to do,' she snapped, glaring at him. All her life, she had been a passive character. Not weak, merely easy-going. She shrank from any form of aggression and was loath to cause unnecessary dissent, preferring to go along with the decisions of others. 'I'm not very good at giving orders,' she admits, 'but I'm very good at carrying them out.' Smart and extremely capable, until that morning she had never fought her corner aggressively. It simply was not in her nature.

But when she told Richard they were not going to the police, she meant it. There would be no breaking ranks: all the pain, fear and humiliation they had endured was borne solely to keep the police at bay. Any hint of their involvement would send Billy haywire, she was certain of it. She told Richard so, adding that a cavalcade of panda cars and firearms teams training their weapons on the house would see the whole family dead before the sirens had stopped wailing.

Richard grimaced in disbelief, telling her that reality was nothing like that – she was thinking in terms of the movies they had watched together. The police were skilled in dealing with any number of situations, including hostage negotiation—

'No!' she screamed.

Richard fell silent. He stared straight ahead, alienated by his wife's behaviour. Sapped of all his strength, having been bound and gagged repeatedly until every muscle in his body pulsated with pain, knowing that his wife had been subjected to sexual abuse by a criminal who left her mentally and physically scarred, above all else he was terrified for Sarah. He had thoughts that he could never articulate about what might have happened in the part of Pottery Cottage belonging to his parents-in-law.

Although Richard was a dynamic individual and enjoyed being someone to whom others looked for guidance, he had one trait that worked against him: he suffered from depression, and when the 'black dog' had him in its jaws, he resorted to a kind of passivity. His closest friends had noticed it at work, realising that where they would treat a setback as an obstacle to be overcome, Richard's reaction was different. 'What will be will be,' he would tell them. David Brown had once asked him about it when they were drinking together, and Richard had admitted to a belief that once a person was born, his life was already mapped out for him. David had laughed, pointing out that no one had changed his life as much as Richard himself. His friend agreed with a grin, but insisted that he still believed in fate, however crazy it seemed. 'It was really life and death he was fatalistic about,' David recalls. 'He used to say, "If God Almighty says, 'Come in, number ten, your life is up' – that's it. There's nothing you can do."' That was why, Richard told his friend, he believed in living for and in the moment, enjoying everything that life had to offer.

In the charged atmosphere within the Chrysler, Richard made one last attempt to persuade his wife. 'But I've had enough, Gill. How can we take any more?'

'Because we must,' she answered fiercely. 'We *must*. I'm telling you, Richard, if you insist on going to the police, I will never forgive you. Never!'

He watched the traffic lights change from amber to red, pressing his foot against the brake. His wife had not taken her eyes from him. He looked at her and then back to the glowing red light.

'All right, Gill,' he said quietly.

Richard parked near the shops they needed to visit on Chatsworth Road. He left Gill queuing at the till with groceries at the International store while he went next door to Henstock's Bakers to collect his mother-in-law's standing order for three loaves of bread every Friday. They then drove to Johnson's Ironmongers for the gas stove, a spare cylinder and other items before returning their shopping to the car. Finally, they walked together to the newsagents, where they were served by Ellen Parsons, who recalls: 'They came to the newspaper counter first and selected some newspapers and cigarettes. The woman then said, "I'm looking for a book for a little girl." At this time the man and woman were at the bottom counter where the books are on the shelves. The woman selected an Enid Blyton book off the top shelf. I got the book down and told her that it was an expensive one. I believe it was about £1.50. The woman said, "It's all right, it doesn't matter how much it costs." I put the cigarettes, newspapers and book in a bag. They paid me for them and then they left. The man didn't speak to me but he was talking to the lady. They both appeared to be normal ... Mr and Mrs Minton and their granddaughter Sarah Moran [visited] my shop every Thursday, Friday and Saturday for newspapers and television magazines.'[3]

Returning to their car, the couple headed further along Chatsworth Road to Kennings Garage. Forecourt supervisor Ivy Tinsley remembered them from the previous day and chatted to Richard about the weather as she filled the car with petrol and oil. Gill remained in the front passenger seat, unfolding the first of the newspapers they had bought.

'I looked at the *Derbyshire Times*,' she remembers. 'The story of Billy's escape was all over the front page with his photograph. It said that the police were checking houses. I had seen police cars on Chatsworth Road travelling quickly and I panicked because I thought they might be going to our house. Richard got back in the car and I told him what I felt. He asked me if we'd got everything on the list. We'd forgotten the glacier fruits. I said not to worry about them but Richard thought we ought to buy them. We stopped at Kirks on Chatsworth Road and bought them. We drove straight home.' Fearful that the police might arrive at the house in their absence, Gill kept up a steady but insistent mantra for the rest of the journey, telling her husband, 'Hurry, Richard, for God's sake, hurry!'

As soon as they turned into the drive, Gill thought her worst fears had been somehow realised: 'I could see there was a note pinned to the front door by what looked like a knife. I panicked and got out of the car. I ran to the front door.' A screwdriver had been inserted through the paper into the wood; in Billy's neat slanting hand, the note read: 'Gone next door. Billy and Mum.' Gill stood tense with anxiety, wondering what could have happened. Then she heard Richard shout, 'They're here!'

She ran to the top of the drive and saw the two figures returning from Seconds.

'What were you doing?' she exclaimed, more sharply than intended. Billy frowned, then explained that he had gone next door to look for money. 'He didn't find any money,' Gill recalls. 'Mum realised that she hadn't got the Newmans' key when she came back. Billy let her go on her own to look for it. She came back with the key, it had fallen out of her pocket.' Gill and Richard exchanged a look of disbelief, amazed at the recklessness of Billy's own actions.

Billy carried the shopping bags into the kitchen, checking that they had bought everything on the list. He asked Gill to boil as many eggs as possible. Thirteen went into pans on the stove; while they simmered, Amy managed to speak briefly alone to her daughter.

Whispering, Amy told Gill that she was 'so worried' about Arthur after hearing from Billy that morning that her husband had wet himself. 'I don't know what to do about it,' Amy said tearfully. 'I asked Billy if he'd let me go through and help him, but he wouldn't.'

Gill was equally upset and sought out Billy, pleading with him to allow Amy into the annexe. He refused again, insisting, 'There's no need. I've cleaned the old man up. I took him to the bathroom and did it.' Seeing Gill's doubtful expression, he added, 'It almost made me sick, but I did it and he's all right now.'

Gill accepted his explanation, then asked about something else troubling her: 'Billy, I can't understand why Sarah hasn't asked for any fresh underwear – she's so particular about cleanliness.' When he didn't respond, she asked if he would take Sarah a pair of clean knickers which she had already fetched from the airing cupboard upstairs. He agreed to that and found Gill waiting for him afterwards. Seeing the question in her eyes, he said, 'Sarah was glad to have them, but she made me turn my back while she changed.'

A hot wave of relief rushed over Gill; she knew that was exactly the sort of thing her daughter would say. 'She's all right then,' she said gratefully.

'All right?' Billy replied. 'She's even got the radio on.'

And Gill believed him.

There was no snowfall that day, but some areas were already experiencing drifts of ten foot and higher, while roads across the north remained dangerously icy. Abandoned vehicles caused further problems with access as the police search intensified. While static checks were maintained, the intelligence that Hughes might be heading for Blackpool resulted in repeat searching in certain regions, with a general push towards the north-west.

Derbyshire's Assistant Chief Constable, Alfred Mitchell, guaranteed every available manpower for Buxton South Sub-Division and by midday Chief Inspector Peter Howse was in charge of seventy officers combing the area. He decided on some solitary searching, heading home to Wye Bank, five minutes from the police station, to change out of his uniform into a tracksuit. He drove to Beeley village, parking his car near the pub, and jogged up the steep, winding hill to the spot where the abandoned taxi had been found.

'By now there were no visible traces of the incident,' he recalls, 'but I stood where Billy Hughes must have stood and tried to think where he would have gone. I took the most likely route: up to the line of trees, around the hillside, and then along the crest of the hill where the A619 road came into sight. I paused there, knowing that if he had taken a right, that would have led him back towards Chesterfield, past the Highwayman pub. Because that was on Chesterfield Division, I headed in the opposite direction to the Robin Hood pub on my sub-division. It was closed, but I spoke to the landlord, a former comptroller at Chatsworth. He had already been visited by police officers and hadn't seen anything unusual. Because of the weather he had decided to remain closed until the weekend.

'I then ran down to Baslow where I met Sergeant Bob Hodgson at the Devonshire Arms. He had arranged a refreshment room in the pub for all those involved in the search. I looked at my watch: even in these conditions it had taken me less than an hour. Bob gave me a lift back to my car and after changing into uniform again, I went back to the station. I asked if anyone had reported seeing a lone figure running on the moors at the back of Chatsworth; I had been open in my movements, yet there hadn't been a single call. So much for all the publicity – people were more concerned about the consequences of the weather than an escaped prisoner. But I spoke to Alf Mitchell again and he informed me that extra officers would be available for door-to-door inquiries over the weekend. But if there was still no sign of Hughes, then he couldn't guarantee further resources. The extra officers comprised of three coachloads of men from other divisions who were freed up by the cancellation of the Derby County football match due to the weather.

'It was to be the final push,' Howse concludes. 'And we would have to make the most of it.'[4]

At Pottery Cottage, Gill decided to cook a proper meal.

Amy stood at the sink preparing the vegetables, remembering the last time she had done so – just prior to Billy's intrusion. Unable to stomach any food when it was served, she climbed the stairs to Sarah's room, needing to be alone.

Gill and Richard ate with Billy in the kitchen, after he had taken two plates through to the annexe for Sarah and Arthur. 'Richard and Billy drank some beer,' Gill recalls, 'and I washed up. The three of us then went upstairs to Sarah's room. It would be about 2 p.m. Billy asked me if I could do something with his hair because he had seen his photograph in the paper and his hair was short. I got the wig he had worn before. He asked me to cut off some of his own hair, which I did, then he put the wig on. It was too long and I trimmed it for him.'

While Gill busied herself with the wig, the telephone rang downstairs. It was their friend John Grosvenor, director of a catering company and fellow member of the Chesterfield Round Table, calling to invite Richard and Gill to a lunch party at his home that coming Sunday. He had already rung Brett Plastics and found out that Richard was at home on sick leave.

'I didn't get a reply for some time,' he remembers. 'I was about to put my phone down when there was an answer. The phone bell had rung about ten times before it was answered by a woman who I immediately recognised as Gillian. She gave the number and I said, "Hello, Gill, it's John Grosvenor here. How are you?" I invited her and Richard to the party and she said, "Yes, we'd love to come." We did not chat for long and she sounded quite normal except that perhaps she was a little subdued . . . I asked her about Richard's health and told her that I hoped he would soon be well.'[5]

Gill returned upstairs with Billy to Sarah's room, where he tried the wig in front of a mirror. He seemed pleased with his appearance, grinning. 'I look quite sexy, don't I?' He then went downstairs again but was gone no more than five minutes, informing them, 'I've just been through to see Sarah and Dad. Sarah said, "Oh, Billy, you do look nice."'

Gill stared at him, her stomach churning.

He then decided to have a bath, propping a toy drumstick belonging to Sarah against the bedroom door as a precaution. But Gill and her mother and husband sat talking in hushed voices, feeling quietly confident that he was now preparing to leave. Hearing him splashing in the bath, Gill called out, 'Don't wash your neck too much – you'll get your wig wet.'

She glanced at Richard, her eyes bright with something akin to excitement. The sense of an ending was almost too much to bear. 'We didn't think of escaping, we just wanted him out of the way,' she recalls. 'We couldn't take the chance of anyone getting hurt.'

Wearing a clean shirt and tie with his suit, Billy joined them in the bedroom, pondering where he might acquire some cash. 'He asked Richard if there was any money at his firm,' Gill remembers. 'Richard said there was only petty cash. He said Richard and myself would have to take him to Richard's firm . . . Billy tied Mum up and left her in Sarah's room. He tied her hands and feet but he didn't gag her. He left the dogs with her for company, he left the radio on, and he left her some water.'

The three of them headed out into the snow once more. It was dark but a clear night as they climbed into the Chrysler. 'Richard drove and I sat in the front, Billy sat in the back,' Gill confirms. 'Billy had the knife with him. I felt very guilty about all this and I prayed that there would be a lot of petty cash so that he would go and leave us alone. All I could do was hope.'

The telephone rang at Pottery Cottage in their absence. It was David Brown on his way home from London, hoping to speak to Richard. He had met the sixteen-year-old French au pair at Heathrow earlier that day; to his consternation, the young girl sobbed throughout the journey northwards, convincing him even more that it would be useful to introduce her to fluent French-speaker Richard. Tired and disconcerted by the girl's evident unhappiness, David missed the junction that would take him to Eastmoor and had to continue to the next, past the factory in Staveley, into deep snow. He looked at his watch: 6.45 p.m. The young girl at his side wept quietly and he decided it might be wiser to get her settled under the maternal care of his wife. He drove home without calling at Pottery Cottage, but has wondered ever since what might have happened if he had.

In Staveley, the Morans' bronze Chrysler pulled on to the well-lit forecourt of Brett Plastics. Richard glanced at his watch: 7.30 p.m. 'The night shift is already on,' he told Billy. 'I'll have to go into the factory and tell them that I'm here. If they see my lights on in the office and don't know it's me, they'll come and investigate.'

He got out of the car, spotting quality control officer Phillip Bagshaw at the far end of the warehouse. He had a quick word with him about the lights being already left on in one office. Bagshaw replied that it must have been done by accident.

'Richard then said that he was going down to the office to get some papers and do some work,' he remembered. 'I asked him if he was feeling better, because I had been told he had been off ill. Richard said he was feeling a lot better . . . [He] was dressed smartly as usual. He was wearing a suit and a collar and tie. He appeared to be cleanly shaved and I noticed nothing unusual about him except that he had red rings around his eyes . . . He spoke in his normal voice. He did not appear in any way upset or distressed.'[6]

Richard returned to the car, driving only a few yards to the office block. He took out his keys – one of six sets – which included a key for the accounts office, plus keys for the safe and cashbox. 'We all three went in,' Gill recalls. 'We went to the accountant's office. [Billy] made me and Richard sit in a corner. Billy had the keys from Richard and he asked him which was the safe key. Richard told him and he unlocked the safe. There were three wage packets and two £1 notes in it. He then went round the room pulling out files and things. Then he opened desk drawers and in one of them he found a wad of notes and some bags of silver.' One of the bags burst, sending coins rolling across the bristly carpet tiles. Gill began scrabbling for them until he told her tersely to stop, having realised to his chagrin that he had misplaced the knife. 'He found it under some papers,' she confirms. 'We left the building and Richard locked up after us. Billy then took the keys from Richard and we all got into the car.'

As the car bumped on the uneven snow through the gates, Billy wound down his window, drew back his arm and threw the keys away. He closed it again to count the pilfered money. 'There's two hundred and ten pounds here,' he said approvingly.

Gill's eyes met his in the rear-view mirror. 'Don't worry,' he said. 'I'll soon be on my way.'

They headed back upstairs to Sarah's room at Pottery Cottage, where Amy lay listlessly on the candlewick bedspread. Billy told Gill to feed the dogs and let them out, then make a drink. He moved from room to room. Eventually, he asked her to get all his shopping together. When he entered the kitchen a few minutes later, she was waiting and pointed to the bulging bags: 'Everything's ready, Billy.'

'You're coming with me,' he said.

Gill stared at him. 'No.'

'It's all right,' he said, plainly irritated by her lack of enthusiasm. 'I'll stop another car on the way, rob the driver and transfer everything into that car, then take him or her with me. I'll leave you the Chrysler and the keys.' He paused. 'It's up to you what you do then.'

He lifted the bags of shopping and headed out to the car, returning for the grey suitcase and plastic tote. Gill ran up to Sarah's bedroom while he was outside, telling her mother and husband what Billy had planned. To her own surprise she was not as frightened as before, convinced that he would do as he said – let her go after he had hijacked another vehicle.

They heard his footsteps on the stairs; he appeared carrying new lengths of flex and a couple of Richard's ties. As he bound Amy and Richard as before, he told them in an almost placatory tone, 'This is the last time.' He left the gags off and put a jug of water nearby, then signalled to Gill.

She looked at her husband and mother. Words had left her and she turned to follow Billy, each tread of her feet on the stairs feeling oddly heavy. Outside, she stood shivering next to the car, gazing up at the star-filled sky, her breath a white cloud.

Billy threw one of Richard's suits on to the back seat and told Gill to get into the car. She opened the door and was met by a gust of hot air; he must have left the heater on with the engine running while he packed everything else into the boot. There was an unpleasant smell from the paper bag containing thirteen hard-boiled eggs on the back seat.

She glanced at Billy as he climbed into the driver's seat. He looked at her, then grasped the steering wheel with both hands. 'Right,' he said. 'We're going.'

Gill believed the nightmare was almost over; she could sense it.

Chapter Twelve:

On the Run

'BILLY DROVE TO Chesterfield,' Gill recalls. 'We got as far as the island at Queen's Park and he said he'd forgotten Richard's map.'[1] She was aghast at his insistence that they would have to return to Pottery Cottage when they were already several miles into his attempt to flee the area.

'But it's ridiculous!' she shouted, momentarily forgetting the danger. 'All the roads are signposted and we can stop at any garage to buy a map book! For God's sake, Billy, keep going!'

He shook his head, turning towards Chatsworth Road again. 'No. I'm going back to get Richard's book.'

She felt like screaming at the top of her lungs, refusing to accept that there was no possibility of changing his mind. 'I tried to persuade him to go on without it, but he wouldn't . . . When we got to the house, he said he wanted to change his clothes and put on one of Richard's suits, which was in the car.' Billy's sinister reasons for turning back and taking the outfit with him remained unspoken as Gill watched him disappear into the house. She then did as he had instructed, climbing into the driver's seat and reversing the car to drive straight out when he returned.

She smoked a cigarette while waiting for him, trying to settle her nerves. He was gone longer than she had anticipated. To save petrol she switched off the ignition, listening to the wind soughing through the black, winter trees. Suddenly she heard him call from the lounge window, 'I won't be long, Gill, I'm going to see Dad and Sarah.' She made no reply, lighting a second cigarette and smoking it more slowly than the first.

He appeared at a run, wearing the suit from the back seat of the car. Gill moved across into the passenger seat as he approached from the driver's side. She caught a glimpse of a wild look in his eyes before he leaned forward to start the ignition.

Nothing happened.

He turned the key again; the car wheezed but failed to start. He tried several times, replicating the same lack of success, then turned on her, yelling: 'I told you not to turn the fucking thing off!'

'I'm sorry!' she shouted back, despite knowing that he had said no such thing. She thought to herself: The alternator's gone; Richard kept meaning to get it fixed. She began to cry, desperate to get away and set Billy on his own path, not to be stuck there with him.

'Stop crying,' Billy said with an effort, regaining some semblance of calm. 'We'll take your car.'

She gaped at him through her tears. 'What? No! It's hopeless – we'll never get it out of the garage! The snow is piled up against the doors!' She swallowed several times, then said, 'Look, the alternator's gone on this. If we leave it to dry out, we might be able to get it going. Just give it a few minutes – I'll go inside and make us some tea.'

He flatly refused, telling her that they didn't have time, he was worried about the burglary he had committed a couple of hours ago at the factory in Staveley; for all he knew the police might be on their way to question Richard. He nodded towards Seconds, where an outside light issued a bright white beam. 'Go next door,' he said, 'and ask them to give us a tow – there's a rope in the boot.'

Gill was panic-stricken: 'I can't! I can't involve them, Billy.'

'Well, go and flag a fucking car down!' he shouted.

She got out of the Chrysler. 'I went into the road and tried to stop about three passing cars,' she remembers, 'but none of them would stop.' She moved as fast as she could in her wellingtons through the thick snow until she was leaning in at Billy's open window, telling him that no one wanted to help.

He was incensed at the time she had wasted, barking, 'Go next door and make up a good story.'[2] She began to shake her head but he insisted: 'Tell them your friend is in hospital and you need to get her husband there. Go on – quick!'

Gill's nearest neighbours had arrived home early that afternoon due to the schools closing because of the weather. At 7 p.m., the Newmans ate their evening meal upstairs in front of *Nationwide*. When the programme finished, Len went out to potter about the garage while Joyce picked up the *Derbyshire Times*. 'I read about the incident concerning the escaped prisoner,' she recalled, 'but the places mentioned did not really cover the Eastmoor area.'[3]

After about ten minutes, Joyce heard the terrace doorbell ring. 'I thought my husband would either see the person or, in fact, that it was he who was testing the bell, so I ignored the first ring. The bell then rang again so I came from our bedroom/lounge into what we call the east bedroom which overlooks the drive [and] saw Mrs Moran talking to my husband.'[4]

Gill had stumbled across to the Newmans' side of the property where light peeped from the garage-door frame. She rang the bell, shouting for Len, and heard him call from the garden, 'Who is it?'

'It's me, Gillian.'

Len opened the gate at once, then stared at Gill in surprise. In the stark beam of the security light she looked terrible, he thought: her face was ashen, her hair unkempt, and although her clothes were neat – a white sweater and skirt worn with wellington boots – her hands worked frantically at the fabric of her green coat.

'What can I do for you, Gillian?'

Her words came out in a tumble: 'Len, can you do me a big favour and give us a lift, I mean a tow, can you get your car out and tow our car for me?' She shifted her weight rapidly from one foot to the other, adding, 'I've got to run my friend's husband home.'[5]

Len frowned. 'Where's Rich?'[6]

Gill's eyes narrowed. Her voice dropped to a whisper as she leaned forward: 'He's tied up in a chair, you know.'[7]

Len drew back. Then he put his hands gently on her shoulders, asking, 'Gillian, what is it? Are you drunk?'[8]

She gave a small, high laugh, patting him on the cheek with her hand. She whispered again, 'It's the man from the moors, he's listening.'[9] She rocked backwards and forwards on her heels, saying softly, 'He'll kill us all.'[10]

Finally, Len understood. 'I'll get my car,' he said, thinking quickly about how to reach a telephone; there wasn't one at Seconds. 'Just give me a moment—'[11]

'We've got a tow rope,' Gill said more normally.[12]

Len retreated swiftly behind the gate, telling her, 'I've just got to get the dog in and I'll be with you.'[13] Panic-stricken himself, he hurried across the terrace and grasped the dog's collar. He glanced up and saw that Sarah's bedroom window was wide open. He ushered the dog into the house, where Joyce had just reached the bottom of the stairs, curious to know what had brought Gill to their door.

'It's the moors man,' Len blurted. 'He's got Richard tied up in a chair and wants me to tow Richard's car with him and Gillian in it. That's why she came round . . .'[14]

They talked frantically about what to do next, deciding that he should go along with the charade and give Gill and the fugitive a tow while Joyce followed in her Mini Cooper. Once the Chrysler was on its way, Len would find a telephone at the first opportunity and call the police.

Joyce pulled on her boots. Len left the house by the French windows, intending to reach his car in the garage by crossing the terrace. 'I was desperately trying to think,' he recalled, but what he saw next shook him profoundly.[15]

In the shadowy garden of Pottery Cottage, Amy Minton leaned against the low wall, excruciating pain distorting her face. 'Len . . .' Amy's voice was faint. 'Len . . .'[16] She tried to call out again, but whatever strength she had left disintegrated and she fell, disappearing from sight.

Len dashed into his garage, searching for something with which to arm himself. Realising he had no time, he grabbed a spade, unlocking the car with his free hand. Joyce came into the garage. He told her that things were even worse than he had imagined, warning her that they were both now 'in mortal danger'.[17]

Terrified, Joyce got into the car quickly, ready to reverse it at speed on to the drive once her husband had opened the garage doors. For all they knew, the fugitive might be waiting on the other side, but it was a risk worth taking. At a nod from Joyce, Len threw down the spade and flung open the double doors.

The driveway was empty.

Len ran to the car, shouting at Joyce to move over. As she climbed over into the front passenger seat, he dived in behind the steering wheel, reversing 'at full speed' out of the garage.[18]

Gill had returned to the stationary Chrysler at Pottery Cottage, waiting with Billy in the dark. Disorientated with adrenalin, she wondered what Len would do. Billy smoked a cigarette, twitching his legs and demanding to know 'what the hell' Len was doing. He nipped the tab end, flicking it out into the snow.

'Go and hurry him up!' he told Gill, just before tyres screeched on the nearby drive as Len's car hurtled on to the main road in a blaze of headlights, turning towards Chesterfield.

'You've fucking told him!' Billy yelled.

'I haven't! Billy, I haven't!' she screamed back, burying her face in her shaking hands, mumbling nonsensically about having 'only said Richard was in the bath'. Afterwards, she reflected, 'That's the only lie I ever told him.'

Billy gave a sharp intake of breath.

Gill lifted her head. She too gasped at the sight of her mother emerging from the front door of Pottery Cottage. 'I couldn't believe it,' Gill states. 'She was supposed to be tied up. She staggered very slowly towards the car. She was making a dreadful noise. It was like a moaning noise. I started to get out of the car to help her. He pulled me back.'

'Stay in the car!' Billy shouted fiercely to Gill as he leapt from the vehicle.

Amy lurched towards them, a glutinous black stain seeping from her throat on to the blue checked housecoat she habitually wore. Billy caught up with her just as she collapsed; he seized her by the arms, hauling the dying woman backwards towards the garage, leaving shallow trenches in the snow where her stockinged heels had dragged.

'Mum – Mum – Mum!' Gill's hysterical scream spiralled up into the night sky. 'Mum!'

Gill's fragile grip on reality was now at breaking point. She was dimly aware of Billy straddling her mother, who lay in the snow. 'It all happened so quickly,' she reflects. 'I can't remember getting out of the car but I must have done, because I was then outside the car and I could see Mum lying on her back in the snow. Whereas, when I first saw her leave the house she was on Billy's side of the car. It was dark and whilst I realised she was injured I couldn't see what had happened to her. I was petrified and I broke down. I was at my wits' end.'

Billy was suddenly in front of Gill, shoving her into the garden. He looked terrified himself but raging at the same time. 'Stay where you are and don't move!' he shouted, then vanished.

Gill stood in the bitter air on the snow-covered stone flags, looking up at her daughter's bedroom window. '[It] was open and the light was on,' she recalls. 'I broke down and I thought about all sorts of things. I thought he'd thrown Richard out of the window. I looked up at Dad's side of the house and there was no light on. I thought there couldn't have been any lights on for three days.'

She shook uncontrollably, murmuring, 'Is it true? Am I going mad?' She answered herself, 'Yes, this is madness. It can't be true. It's me. I've gone mad, I am insane.' Then she turned and ran towards the gate, meeting Billy coming from the opposite direction.

'He reached the gate as I did,' she remembers. 'He said, "Come on." He took hold of me by the hand and we ran up the drive. I was screaming, "What have you done with Mum?" She had gone from where I'd seen her and I couldn't see her anywhere. He said he had taken her into the kitchen and she was lying on the floor. I realised that he had harmed Mum and I didn't believe him when he said he had taken her inside. I thought he had probably dragged her further into the snow.'

Billy's fingers tightened around Gill's wrist. As they reached the top of the drive he pulled her onwards, running towards the Highwayman Inn whose lights glimmered through the skeletal trees. 'Every time a car came along he pulled me into the ditch,' Gill states. 'He made me lie down on my face in the ditch by pushing me down. When I held my head up hoping that someone would see me he pushed my head down again. We ran off again when there was nothing coming. He climbed over the wall of the Highwayman pub and then he helped me over. I said, "I can't climb walls." He said, "I'll help you over." He still held me, he never let go of me.'

They dropped back down into the ditch when another vehicle flew by in a spatter of slush and mud. 'I just couldn't think how it was going to end,' Gill admits. 'I thought I might die of exposure.' They crawled on through the ditch in the darkness, keeping to a low wall until they reached what seemed to be an endless garden filled with trees. They ran blindly through the grounds, past a sprawling property in the centre and down a long, tree-lined avenue to the main gate.

Billy stopped, gasping, on the roadside. He nodded at two cottages opposite, asking, 'Who lives there?'

Gill pointed to the semi-detached cottage on the right, Summit House. 'The Frosts,' she said, equally breathless. 'Mr and Mrs Frost live in that one. Ron – he's a motor mechanic.'

Billy made a low noise of exclamation, running a hand through his hair. 'Then that's where we'll go. And be normal.'[19] He pushed open the gate, reaching for Gill's hand, squeezing it tightly.

'We went round the back,' she recalls, 'and I knocked on the door.'

The Frosts were sitting comfortably on their sofa, having just watched *The Bionic Woman*. It was half past eight and *The Sale of the Century* was about to start. The Anglia Television logo depicting a silver knight revolving on his horse appeared, followed by the jaunty voiceover: 'And now, from Norwich, it's the quiz of the week . . .'

There was a knock at the back door. Reluctantly, Madge Frost got up to answer it. Hearing a woman's voice calling to her, she expected their immediate neighbour, Mrs Clarke. She was surprised, therefore, when she opened the door to Gillian Moran, whom she knew lived just down the road, and a strange man. 'He had dark hair, longish, straggly, wet, clean shaven,' Madge recalled. 'He was wearing a blue suit, patterned, shirt and tie [and] a light brown glove on one hand.'[20] The other hand was full of tattoos.

Gill stood there, 'frozen and soaked', not knowing what Billy intended to say or do. Eventually she explained: 'We've broken down. Is Ron in?'[21]

'Yes, come in, he's watching television,' Madge replied, thinking privately that it was 'funny for Gillian to bring a strange man to the house' when she was married. She led the two of them towards the sitting-room, calling to her husband, 'Gillian's here.'[22]

Ron came out into the passage to meet them. 'They want a tow,' Madge explained. She looked more closely at Gill and Billy. Both of them were soaked to the skin, filthy and looked fit to drop. Then she saw Gill's lips move in a silent entreaty: *Help me.*

'I'll get my boots on,' Ron said, heading through to the back porch with a reminder to his wife to switch on the outside light.[23]

As they were leaving, Madge asked, 'Will one of you two be able to tow?'[24]

'We'll be all right,' Billy replied.[25]

Madge shut the door, locking it behind them. She climbed the stairs and peered through the bedroom window, just in time to see the tail lights of a vehicle passing the Highwayman towards Baslow. She thought it must be her husband's pick-up. Her mind raced, remembering Gill's silent plea and the younger man's bedraggled, baleful appearance, blue suit and tattoos. She made a decision, then rushed downstairs and outside, locking the door behind her before banging her fist on her neighbours' door.

Ron's pick-up truck had passed the Highwayman by then. Billy sat furthest away in the driver's cab near the passenger door, with Gill in the middle. 'I clung to Ron, he was safety to me,' Gill recalls. For his part, Ron was alarmed by her odd behaviour: '[Gill] was very close to me and all the way down the road she was digging me in the ribs with her hand, this action was done out of sight of the man. I thought this was very strange but before I could recollect my thoughts we had arrived at Pottery Cottage.'[26]

Ron saw the tow rope hanging from the Chrysler, but warned, 'I'm not backing my truck across the road.'[27]

'There's no need to,' Billy replied, 'the rope's long enough.'[28]

The two men climbed down from the truck, leaving Gill alone inside the cab. Billy tied the tow rope on to the truck, nodding as Ron told him to 'try it in second or third gear, but wait till we get out of the drive'.[29] Ron had hoped for the chance to speak to Gill without Billy overhearing, but she had already sat down in the Chrysler, so he got back into his pick-up and started the engine.

The Chrysler began to move, but instead of steering it straight, Billy tried to take a short cut through a snowdrift, causing the rope to snap. Ron reversed the truck and got out again, feeling '80 per cent sure' that Gill's companion was the escaped prisoner: 'I didn't know whether to drive off or what but Gillian was alone with him and I wondered where her family was with her house being in darkness.'[30]

Ron managed to get a closer look at Billy as they pushed the car out of the snowdrift, but 'he seemed perfectly calm and normal'.[31] A second attempt at towing failed, but when Ron attached the rope a third time, wrapping it round and round before securing it, he succeeded in pulling the Chrysler clear of the drive.

'Ron towed us for some distance,' Gill recalls. 'I don't know how far. Then Billy realised he hadn't turned the ignition on. When he turned the ignition on, the car started. He gave a couple of hoots to Ron and we stopped.'

Ron jumped down from the truck, unfastening the tow rope from his vehicle. He used his own axe to hack off the rope attached to the Chrysler, passing the long length to Billy, who threw it on to the back seat.

Reaching inside his jacket, Billy offered, 'Here, let me treat you—'

'No, no, it's all right.' Ron shook his head, raising a hand in farewell.[32]

Billy accelerated towards Baslow as Gill watched the pick-up truck growing smaller in the rear-view mirror. 'I was thinking, My help's gone, now I'm on my own,' she recalls.

Ron tried to make out the Chrysler's number plate before it vanished over the horizon but it was impossible in the darkness. His previous conviction that Gill's companion was the fugitive sought by police faltered slightly; the man was 'so calm and collected' and Gill hadn't said a word since arriving at Pottery Cottage to indicate that something was seriously wrong.[33]

With a deep sigh, Ron turned the truck around and headed back along the A619. But as he approached Gill's home before his own, he saw figures in the road, flagging him down.

The police had arrived at Pottery Cottage.

Chapter Thirteen:

Pursuit

A T 8 P.M., butcher Charles Smart heard 'a terrible hammering' on the back door of his home, Crossgates Farm, some 250 yards from Pottery Row on the opposite side of the A619.[1] While his wife Winifred waited in the sitting-room, he opened the door to Len and Joyce Newman, 'waving their arms about wildly' and looking 'very agitated'.[2] Len told Smart to 'ring the police, quick, that madman's holding Gillian and Richard hostage in the bottom house!'[3] After calming the couple down, Smart suggested that Len should use the telephone himself.

Chesterfield Police logged the call at 8.09 p.m. 'I'm at Smarts' farm, Eastmoor,' Len said. 'I've been told that the escaped prisoner has a family at ransom up here. I'll wait for your officers.'[4] When the call ended, Smart loaded his shotgun and telephoned other farmers nearby, urging them to arm themselves.

A short distance away, Madge Frost spoke to her neighbours, retired couple Jean and Thomas Clarke, who listened in horror to her story; they knew the Morans and Mintons only by sight. 'Have you rung the police?' Jean asked.[5]

'No, I daren't,' replied Madge, close to tears. 'I'm frightened that chap might hurt Ron.'[6]

Jean Clarke returned with Madge to her home, telephoning another neighbour, Jeffrey Edwards, to ask him to call round while they waited for Ron. Edwards lived at Wardlow Wells Farm, 500 yards from the Highwayman Inn; it was through his gardens that Gill and Billy had run when seeking help with the car. Edwards remembers the call and Jean 'crying for help. She said, "Come quickly, come quickly, it's terrible . . ."'[7] Locking his wife indoors, he ran across the road armed with a carving knife and found Madge Frost 'in a state of hysteria'.[8] After listening to her tale, he decided to head for Pottery Cottage, but 'Mrs Frost blocked my exit from the house until I undertook not to call the police, because she feared for her husband's life'.[9]

Edwards departed, running along the road with the knife held out before him. As he neared the Highwayman Inn, three men peered at him from the forecourt. He tucked the knife inside his jacket and slowed his pace, relief flooding through him when he realised the men were police.

'Thank God!' he exclaimed. 'You're just the people I need – the madman is ahead of us at Pottery Cottage, he has a girl hostage and is with Mr Frost, who's trying to start a car—'[10]

The three officers had been dispatched from Chesterfield Police Station in response to Len Newman's call. They reassured Edwards, requesting that he return home; their superior, Detective Inspector Frank Hulme, had Pottery Cottage surrounded. Among the arriving officers was Constable Chris McCarthy, who remembered Billy Hughes from the Queen's Park rape and GBH case. McCarthy had recently been accepted into Chesterfield CID on a temporary detective constable basis. He was accompanied that night at the Highwayman Inn by Detective Sergeants Graham Rason and Bill Miller, Detective Constables Fran Muldoon and Bob Hassell, and their Divisional Commander, Superintendent Tommy Hoggart, who coincidentally had led the investigation into the Queen's Park attacks. Briefing his officers on the forecourt while waiting for more back-up, Hoggart directed them to reconnoitre Pottery Cottage and report back.

Ron Frost appeared in his pick-up truck as the five men walked along the road. They flagged him down and he confirmed what they had been told about his encounter with the fugitive. Frost returned home to his wife while the officers continued towards Pottery Cottage. They reached the white gate at precisely 8.53 p.m. A further police contingent soon joined them in the driveway.

The house was ablaze with light. Behind curtained windows, music blared from somewhere within. DS Miller approached the front door in the glare of a security light and found it locked. Banging his fist against the glass, he shouted: 'Police! Is there anyone in here?'[11]

No reply. The music continued to throb.

Miller walked to the back of the cottage with DC Hassell, leaving their colleague Fran Muldoon knocking repeatedly on the door and windows facing the road.

The two officers approached the garden gate. At their feet, meandering through the snow like a moorland stream, was a rust-red trail. It led towards the garage, but Miller forced the gate where it had been held fast by banked-up snow. Entering the garden, he and Hassell saw all the lights were lit. The kitchen window blind was drawn and a curtain had been pulled across the door. From a downstairs room came the sound of two dogs barking frantically.

Miller pointed up at Sarah Moran's open bedroom window. The music appeared to be coming from a radio inside the room. The curtains blew wildly in the wind.

'Police!' Hassell shouted. 'Is anyone in there?'[12]

Hearing movement nearby, they turned to see a group of shadowy figures behind the garden wall: more police, approaching from the fields.

Ascertaining that all ground-floor windows and doors were secure, DS Miller stood in front of the casement kitchen window and brought his elbow down sharply on the glass. It shattered, leaving several shards, which he knocked out before reaching in to release the catch and lift the roller blind. He and Hassell climbed inside, looking around the kitchen and hearing 'a slight bumping noise, which appeared to be coming from upstairs'.[13] Hassell unlocked the back door, allowing other officers access to the property.

Miller and Hassell led the way upstairs. Patches of blood spread across the stair carpet, some of it freshly congealed. They trod carefully until they reached the landing, stopping suddenly at the sight before them.

Richard Moran lay face down on the carpet, head against a chest of drawers. Blood saturated his pale blue patterned shirt, much of it still wet. His legs in their neatly pressed navy blue slacks were slightly drawn up with one black loafer resting against his blue stockinged feet. White flex was pulled tight in a crude knot about his ankles. A length of orange flex had been used to secure his arms behind his back but he had almost managed to work them free before being stabbed to death. Blood pooled on the carpet from a knife wound to his throat, and two knives lay beside him: an ivory-handled kitchen knife and a wooden-handled cutlery knife.

The officers edged past his body to check the rest of the Morans' quarters, which proved to be empty.

Downstairs, DC Muldoon and DS Rason had found another body. The lights in the Mintons' lounge were off, but when Rason flicked a switch he immediately saw, in the adjoining room, a figure partially disguised with heaped clothing on the parquet floor. Closely followed by Muldoon, he pushed past a table and chairs to investigate.

Arthur Minton lay on his back next to the long, drawn orange curtains. His feet in their polished brogues rested on the stone wall, his artificial leg slightly detached at an awkward angle. Among the items thrown over his body were a suede coat and an anorak, and a large teddy bear dressed in blue and white pyjamas had been thrust on his face in a cruelly stupid gesture. Blood bloomed on Arthur's white overcoat, a favourite from his many years as a popular neighbourhood grocer. More flex had been used to tie his arms rigidly behind his back. On the floor beneath his raised body were the scattered remains of a meal: ketchup-smeared crinkle-cut chips and a slice of tomato. Near the wall lay a wooden-handled fork.

Miller and Hassell entered the room as Rason bent down to confirm that life was extinct, although it was obvious from the appearance and temperature of Arthur's body that he had been murdered at least two days before. None of the men spoke to each other, instead turning away to head for the kitchen, where a decision was taken to leave the remainder of the house unexplored until the two dogs had been removed.

Miller returned to the garden, leaving by the gate to follow the trail of blood in the snow. He saw clear signs of disturbance against the white wooden doors of the garage and stepped closer, moving the snow lightly with his foot. Beneath it lay the body of

Amy Minton, face down beside the wall, right arm outstretched. She had been stabbed multiple times and her throat cut. It was obvious that she had died earlier that evening.

Side-stepping the body, Miller checked the double garage but found nothing, returning with Hassell to their Ford Escort, parked at the Highwayman Inn. Hassell informed the Operations Room of their discoveries, maintaining wireless communication and keeping a log of the incident.

At ten past nine, DC Muldoon showed a dog handler into Pottery Cottage where the sliding doors into the Morans' dining room had been tied shut. Unfastening the knot, the dog handler checked the Labrador and basset hound, who rushed out eagerly, and led them to his van for safety. Muldoon then searched the remainder of the house with DC Brian Bunting.

Moving through the annexe, Bunting entered the Mintons' bedroom and stopped at the door. Ten-year-old Sarah Moran lay in a foetal position on her grandparents' thick green carpet. Curled between the double bed and an armchair, her wrists and ankles had been tied with softer material than the flex, but secured with force. She was gagged equally tightly, the fabric knotted beneath her blonde ponytail. Wearing pink socks over her dark tights and a jumper under a short-sleeved dress, the injuries to her chest and the deep wound at her throat had bled profusely. Nearby, tucked up in an old pillow case for a bed, a favourite doll slept soundly; Sarah's last act before being murdered.

The two officers withdrew.

While searching the rest of the house, Muldoon heard Bunting shout that he had discovered another body. He went through to the bedroom where his colleague stood sheepishly in front of a wardrobe door. Bunting explained that he had opened it and found a human leg, but on closer examination realised the limb was a spare prosthetic belonging to Arthur Minton. Retreating, Muldoon reported back that there were definitely four bodies, not five.

At the Highwayman Inn, having been informed of the discoveries, Superintendent Hoggart dispatched three Regional Crime Squad officers to pursue the fugitive: Detective Inspector Geoff Cooper, Detective Sergeant Brian Slack and Detective Constable Bob Meek. Eager to accompany them, McCarthy jumped 'without asking' into the back seat of their green Morris Marina.[14] No one objected as he hunkered down next to DC Meek. DI Cooper occupied the front passenger seat with DS Slack at the wheel. 'Off we went,' McCarthy confirms. 'I distinctly remember commenting to Brian, who was driving at excessive speeds on the icy roads, "Just go steady, Brian, there are enough dead already." Brian sped on through the dark, wintry hills of north Derbyshire. There were no street lights and the roads were bordered by dark drystone walls into open fields. It was pitch black. Geoff Cooper continuously gave a radio commentary as to our progress but we received nothing back at all.'[15]

The bronze Chrysler had gained substantial ground with its head start but the Marina was fast. 'We drove off towards Baslow,' recalls Gill Moran. 'I was frozen so I had a drink of whisky which was in the car. [Billy] had some as well. He put the heater on full blast. He still hadn't said where he was going, but he asked me how we could get to the M6. I said, "You can go Macclesfield way, but that's over the tops, or you can go to Chapel-en-le-Frith, which will be a better route." He said, "Oh, we'll go that way then." We weren't driving too fast. My feet were cold and wet and I told him that I was going to take my wellingtons off. I suggested he did the same. I held the steering wheel while he took his shoes off.'[16]

Completely oblivious to the fact that her home was now a charnel house containing the bodies of her mother, father, husband and child, all murdered by the man at her side, Gill desperately tried to settle her nerves by swallowing mouthfuls of whisky.

'There's a car coming up behind us fast,' Billy said, frowning at the rear-view mirror.

Gill twisted round in her seat. She could see the car: a Morris Marina with its headlights on full beam.

'It's a fucking cop car,' snarled Billy.

Gill's heart leapt. She sought some indication that he was right, but saw nothing. 'It's not,' she told him.

'It fucking *is*,' Billy slammed his foot against the accelerator and they leapt forward.

The Crime Squad officers conferred inside the Marina, having spotted the Chrysler just past the turning for Litton on the A623, ten miles from Pottery Cottage. Slack sped along the flatter road at Tideswell Four Lane Ends, where the Anchor pub stood back from the crossroads, lights pooling on the grass verge. He overtook the Chrysler, then braked sharply, jumping out with his colleagues into the middle of the road, braced to tackle the other driver.

But the Chrysler maintained its speed; Billy's contorted, determined face edged closer to the windscreen. 'He's not going to stop,' McCarthy shouted.[17] The car ploughed towards them, sending the four officers scattering, then overtook the Marina. Scrambling back into their seats, the men cursed the madness of Billy's actions. Slack shoved the accelerator towards the floor, racing after him. Cooper shouted into the radio but reception was sporadic; they all agreed that someone would have to get out at the Wanted pub in Sparrowpit to request assistance from headquarters.

'I didn't intend it to be me,' McCarthy admits, 'so I just kept quiet. We continued the chase towards Peak Forest. Bob Meek jumped out of the squad car at Sparrowpit and made contact with our colleagues, but we had to leave him so were not aware of that at the time. We stayed close to the Chrysler. Several times the driver swung an axe out of the window and he kept slowing right down, then speeding off. It was a miracle we didn't crash into the back of them.'[18]

The two cars raced along the icy, hill-bordered A623, reaching speeds well in excess of 80mph. They were heading towards Barmoor Clough, where a roundabout split the A6 in two: left to Buxton and right to Manchester. 'I can't remember where we drove,' Gill concedes. 'Billy was saying, "fucking this" and "fucking that". He was going faster and faster. I told him to slow down or he would kill us both.'

The roundabout came into view. Positioned right across the junction, its beacon flashing, was an unmanned police car. The Chrysler swerved past it, hitting a row of bollards, then careering around the island. With the Marina on his tail, Billy headed down the A6 towards Chapel-en-le-Frith, gaining distance until he lost control on a right-hand bend. The car shot across one side of the road, then the other, before spinning round and skidding into a drystone wall.

The impact shot driver and passenger forward. 'It was the back end that went into [the wall],' Gill remembers. 'We stopped, he was trying to smash the windscreen from the inside with an axe . . . It wouldn't smash. A man came up to my side of the car.'

The occupants of the Marina leapt out, running towards the Chrysler. Cooper yanked the handle of the passenger door as Billy reared over Gill, pulling her head backwards with his left hand and holding a knife to her throat with the other.

Cooper remained at the door. 'Come on, Hughes. You've had a good run. Give yourself up—'[19]

'Back off, copper! Everybody fucking back or she gets this!' Billy yelled.

'He means it – please!' Gill screamed, shaking uncontrollably.[20]

Cooper withdrew a couple of paces, shouting at his colleagues to do the same. He turned back to Billy, asking calmly, 'Look, what's the point in this? Don't make things worse for yourself.'[21]

'I'm not fucking arguing!' Billy snapped. 'Back off and get me a car full of petrol or she' – he pressed the knife against Gill's throat – 'gets this.'[22]

'You can have what you like,' Cooper said, 'but there's no point in killing her.'[23]

'Get me that car now or else!'[24]

Cooper held up his hands. 'All right. Take the Marina. It's an unmarked police car, the ignition keys are in, and it's full of petrol.'[25] He made the offer in the knowledge that a force Range Rover was at their disposal nearby; he had spotted the vehicle seconds before the crash and the fully briefed officers inside it were standing off round the corner.

'I'll have it, now back off,' Billy told Cooper, who retreated a few more steps.

'Further!' yelled Billy, and Cooper joined his colleagues.

Gill had heard the exchange without grasping what was being said. She kept her head low, whimpering in fear, arms wrapped about her body. Then she felt Billy's hands seize her shoulders.

'He pushed me out,' she recalls. 'He got out of the same door. He pushed me to another car. I didn't know it was a police car, there were no signs on it. I could hear crackling from that car and I thought it was going to catch fire. I said to him, "We can't get in this car, it's going to blow up, it's been in a bump." He said, "No, it hasn't, it's a police car, get in." I could see policemen around and I felt relieved by their presence and that I had not been killed. I felt like running to them, I didn't want to get in the other car, but I had to because he forced me. He had got me. He pushed me into the passenger seat. I knew he'd got the axe. I don't know how he got in the car.'

The Marina roared away with Billy at the wheel and Gill sitting next to him. As soon as the Range Rover turned the corner, driven by a constable with a sergeant at his side, McCarthy, Cooper and Slack scrambled into the back seat. They then sped in pursuit of their previous vehicle.

Inside the Marina, Gill gazed at the whisky bottle in her hand. She had no memory of carrying it from her husband's car.

Billy glanced at her. 'Put that down,' he ordered. 'Get the radio working. Go on!'

Gill set the whisky bottle between her feet. She pressed and rotated the dials but Cooper had disabled the radio deliberately. Raging and mistrustful, Billy shouted into the microphone none-theless: 'Listen, you bastards! Listen to me. I've got a hostage. I want another car and I want it full of fuel and no police around. Do you understand? Listen to me . . .'

The car squealed around a corner. Gill sank back against the leather seat. 'I kept seeing signs for Stockport and Manchester,' she recalls. 'I didn't know where we were going and he didn't. He was really panicking and was driving at a very fast speed. At one point he slowed right down, he wound his window down and he was trying to shout to the policemen. I can't remember what he said. He was giving them instructions but they didn't hear. He tried to work the radio in the car and he had me fiddling with the knobs. He held the mike and he spoke into it. He said, "Come in, you fucking something or other." Then he told me to speak into it. He told me to turn a few knobs and try a few switches, but it didn't work. He was driving dangerously and fast. I had put the seat belt on and I got down in the seat.'

Convinced they were about to die, Gill slipped further down in her seat and shut her eyes.

Chief Inspector Peter Howse had just reached home, shedding his uniform for casual clothes, when the telephone rang. It was Sergeant Eric Cross, whom Howse had instructed to call if there were any developments in the search for the missing prisoner. Cross had plenty of sobering information to pass on: four bodies, including that of a ten-year-old girl, had been found at a house named Pottery Cottage in Eastmoor, and Hughes had taken a woman hostage in a vehicle now being pursued by a Crime Squad car in the north.

Howse asked Cross to collect him at once. Banging down the receiver, he pulled on a coat and shoes, then dashed out of the house, sprinting to the main road. Sergeant Cross was only minutes away. When the car drew up, Howse greeted Detective Constable John Burton sitting in the back seat as he jumped in front next to Cross, reaching for the radio handset to inform the control room that they were on their way. After a short delay, he received a message from the Deputy Chief Constable telling him to take charge of the operation on the ground. Howse acknowledged his direction, but first they had to make up lost ground and catch up with those already engaged in the pursuit.

Several miles away, the five policemen in the Range Rover watched incredulously as the Marina tore around bends, roaring past the Victorian terraced houses of Furness Vale and Newtown. Cooper maintained contact with radio control as they approached a set of traffic lights; behind the Range Rover was a fleet of police vehicles that had responded to messages about the fugitive. These now included the car containing Chief Inspector Peter Howse, who had joined the chase at Chinley.

Billy veered towards the traffic lights. A panda car attempted to prevent him jumping the red light, but he swerved it and raced on to the small town of New Mills, high above a rocky gorge. From there, he took a convoluted route back to Chapel-en-le-Frith through the villages of Birch Vale and Hayfield in the precipitous Dark Peak, where roads and rivers twisted amid wooded valleys.

In the canal basin town of Whaley Bridge, Constable Paul Gardner of Macclesfield Police had been told to 'stop the car without fail'.[26] He and a colleague used their patrol car and another vehicle to block the Buxton side of the A6 where it joined the A5002 at a set of automatic traffic signals. Gardner recalls how 'without warning, the offending car appeared from the direction of Chapel-en-le-Frith, travelling at a fast speed. The car passed by us, headlights full on and with the horn being sounded continually. The car was being pursued closely by a police Range Rover and five or six Ford Escorts of the Derbyshire Police.'[27] Gardner and his colleague jumped back into their patrol car to join the police convoy following the Marina.

Six miles south, in the tiny village of Rainow, another Macclesfield officer was busy setting up a roadblock. Police Constable Eric Harris had taken a quick look around the village, where stone cottages clustered on the steep slopes above the valley of the River Dean, and decided the best spot would be near the top, on the Whaley Bridge approach. Nearby, a huge snowdrift of around six-foot high narrowed the road before a sharp right turn on to Chapel Lane.

Harris parked his patrol car broadside across the road with its headlights lit, blue light flashing and 'Police' sign illuminated on the roof. Just before 10 p.m., a fully occupied green Crosville single-decker bus arrived from the direction of Whaley Bridge. Harris flagged it down, requesting that the driver and his passengers disembark. All those present, including a group of teenage girls bound for a Macclesfield disco, headed to the local post office, which had been opened to give them shelter. Harris angled the bus across the road before the patrol car. Any vehicle attempting to pass would have to mount the offside pavement to avoid the massive snowdrift, thereby risking collision with the bus or the stone wall to the right.

A little over two miles north of Rainow, Billy misjudged a sharp bend shortly after passing another pub bearing a Highwayman Inn sign. Several pedestrians leaving the pub had to leap to safety, causing Gill to stifle a scream. She told herself it was almost over; they could not go on much longer. 'I don't know where we were,' she muses, 'but I know we were climbing. I said to him, "We're climbing, we're going over the tops." He said, "Where can we get to this way?" I said, "I don't know."'

In the village below, Constable Harris heard via radio control that the Marina was approaching. He ran back to his car for a 'Police Accident' sign and had just set it down some fifty yards from the bus when the Marina hurtled round the bend at 70mph. Spotting the headlamps burning at the top of the hill, Harris ran for cover.

The Marina flashed past, hitting the Police Accident sign with a loud crack and trapping it beneath the wheels, emitting a shower of sparks. Billy raced on towards the roadblock, unable to do anything other than mount the snowy pavement and scrape past the bus in an ear-splitting shriek of metal on metal, before swerving to avoid the patrol car. His attempt to make the sharp turn into Chapel Lane ended with the Marina hitting the stone wall with such force that the low structure disintegrated, embedding the car in the gap.

The fleet of pursuing police vehicles had to slam on their brakes, skidding at all angles across the road. There were shouts, screams and the sound of breaking glass as Billy smashed the two rear passenger windows with the axe.

Inside the Marina, Gill Moran lifted her head. She kept her eyes tightly closed. She didn't know where she was or what had happened; all she could hear was a deafening silence that rang at an impossible pitch.

Slowly, she opened her eyes and realised that 'suddenly, there were policemen all around'.

Chapter Fourteen:

Rainow

A SLEW OF UNIFORMED and CID officers gathered behind the crashed car, with several breaking away to warn locals to stay indoors. The bus passengers who had sought refuge at the post office were stunned by events; the postmaster switched on the television to keep the younger teens distracted from what was happening nearby. At the village institute less than fifty yards from the roadblock, forty women who had been enjoying a Mothers' Meeting party were told to continue their revelries but to remain inside until further notice. Two constables also visited the Robin Hood pub within sight of the accident to advise the proprietor to turn down the lights, keep the punters quiet and the doors locked. Meanwhile, the resident with a ringside view – fifty-eight-year-old farmer Robert Dunning – had been too preoccupied with his business accounts to notice that part of the wall surrounding Elmwood House had been destroyed. 'I didn't realise for some time that anything was happening. Then I looked out and saw about eight police cars.'[1]

Miraculously, neither Hughes nor Gill were injured by the crash. Hughes moved quickly, kneeling on the driver's seat over Gill, back to the dashboard. 'He put his left arm around my neck from behind very tightly,' she recalls. 'I could hardly breathe. His body weight was almost covering me from the front and he held the axe in his right hand, inches away from my face. I was petrified.'[2] Her entire body shook from the shock of it all, making him roar, 'Can't you keep your bloody legs still?'

Chief Inspector Howse ran to the Marina, hoping to reach the car before Hughes had a chance to recover. But when he bent down at the shattered nearside window to peer into the dark interior he saw that Hughes had turned towards him from the driver's seat and was swinging a sharp-bladed axe dangerously close to Gill's head. 'I never saw Gill's face because she was sitting with her back to me,' Howse recalls. 'She was hysterical, terrified, as you can imagine. He was in a great rage, forcing her head backwards over the seat.'

'If you come any closer I'll fucking kill her!' Hughes shouted. 'I've got a knife.'

Gill whispered, 'Billy, you haven't.'

He leaned forward until his mouth touched her ear, hissing beneath her hair: 'I know that and you know that. But they don't.'

'He's got a knife to my heart,' Gill screamed, obedient in her terror.

Howse had no way of knowing whether that was true or not, but the axe was all too visible. A single blow from either weapon would be enough to kill her; even if he leapt through the open window it was doubtful that he would be fast enough to stop an attack. As things stood, Hughes was in total control of Gill's life and so Howse held up his hands. In order to pacify Hughes, he shouted for everyone to get back. He then made a show of approaching those closest to repeat the order, rapidly briefing his colleague John Burton on the situation in the car and instructing him to put an unseen containment in place to prevent any chance of Hughes's escape.

Walking back to the Marina, Howse assessed the situation around the car. The stone wall was low but could potentially provide cover for someone inching forward on their stomach to the driver's side. The car itself was tightly wedged on the snow-laden verge with the engine cut out. It seemed unlikely that it could be driven without mechanical help and if that was so, then Hughes was trapped – but so, too, was his hostage.

And Gill was the main concern. Howse had no doubt that attempting to arrest Hughes would result in him attacking her. The only option was negotiation, to persuade Hughes to release her and give himself up. But Howse had no plan, relying instead on the training he had been given in hostage situations and his own ability to respond appropriately to Billy's wildly fluctuating moods. The only strategy he had was to seek levels at which he could get through to him.

Over forty years later, he reflects: 'From what I knew about hostage situations there was no panacea. But the longer I could delay things, the better. I was prepared to take as long as it took. Gill Moran was Hughes's only means of escape and if he didn't get what he wanted, he might just kill her anyway. In order to try to persuade him to give himself up without harming her, I had to reduce his state of frenzy and bring him down to a level of relative calm so that negotiations could take place. I picked up his Christian name from the hostage, who was pleading, "Billy, don't kill me, Billy." And throughout subsequent events, I referred to him as Billy whenever I spoke to him.'

Howse knew a lot about the fugitive's past from having read his criminal record, but nothing about his hostage, except that her family had been murdered. 'I did have concerns about Gill's state of mind,' he recalls. 'For instance, if she had been kept in captivity for the last three days then there might be elements of so-called "Stockholm Syndrome", in which the hostage fears the actions of the police as much as those of the captor. I had to convince both Hughes and her that they were in no danger from me. She had every right to fear that if we, the police, tried to obtain her release, Hughes might kill her. That's why at no stage did I ever threaten him or give the impression that I would attack him. I purposely adopted a relaxed attitude and pose and tried to converse with him in a friendly and confidential manner, in an attempt to reduce his obviously dangerous mental state.'

Howse continues: 'I didn't know, however, that although Gill was absolutely under his physical control he had lost his hold on her mind. She had partially witnessed his attack and subsequent murder of her mother, which changed everything. After three days of terror and indecision, Gill now knew that she could not trust Hughes or believe anything he said. On that final journey from Eastmoor to Rainow, he had maintained the fiction that her husband and daughter at least were still alive. If they were, then he was no longer in a position to harm them. Thus, only Gill was in immediate danger. She must have realised that he wouldn't kill her while she remained useful to him, but if that was no longer the case, then she was in grave danger. In that respect, she still had to seem to be on his side, supporting him. But it must have felt like a time-bomb ticking away in that car.'

So Howse began to talk, crouched down again by the broken rear window, raising his hands to show he was not armed. He addressed Hughes, but Gill listened, feeling some of the terror that had gripped her over the past three days begin to ebb, just a little. 'I have never heard such a wonderful voice in the whole of my life,' she reflected afterwards. 'And I will never forget it as long as I live. It had such kindness in it. Such gentleness. And it gave me so much comfort.'

Having positioned himself in such a way that he could look directly into Hughes's face, with some six feet between them, Howse's opening gambit was to convince him that there was no immediate danger.

'There's only me here now, Billy,' he confirmed. 'All right? So let's talk. There's no need to harm Gill, just calm down.'

'You're too close,' Hughes rejoindered. 'I warn you: try anything and she's dead.' He paused. 'I want another car.'

'All right, I won't try anything. Just let's talk. There's nothing to bother about. I couldn't get at you anyway if you did try to kill her, and everyone else is too far away. But I don't think you really want to harm her, do you? Come on, she's been all right with you.' Howse attempted to appeal to him in another way, reminding him, 'You're a family man yourself. You've got a wife—'

'I'm not fucking bothered about *her*!' Hughes shouted in fury. His reaction was the reverse of what Howse had set out to achieve. 'No fucker cares about me – and I intend to take every fucker with me if I have to.'

'All right,' said Howse. 'But think about this lady here – she's looked after you for three days, hasn't she? She's done everything for you. And you must think a lot of her after all she's done. Be fair now, give her a chance. You don't want to hurt her.'

Gill said softly, 'Please, Billy. Please . . .'

'I'm not fucking bothered about anybody, but she's been all right,' he said grudgingly. 'But you try anything and she's dead.' He jerked his head towards Constable Eric Harris's vehicle, parked in front of the bus. 'I want that car with a blue light and a radio.

Try and stop me and she's for it.' He raised the axe closer to Gill's skull, causing her to scream.

'Steady, Billy, steady.' Howse lifted his palm. 'Look, this isn't your scene. Holding a woman hostage? Come on, you've fallen a long way if that's what you've got to do. You can see she's terrified. Now, I know all about your background – you're a hard man—'

Gill interrupted hysterically, 'He's not a hard man, he's not! He won't hurt anyone if they're all right with him! He always keeps his word, don't you, Billy?'

'All right,' said Howse. 'He'll keep his word. But he's still a hard man who shouldn't need a woman hostage with his reputation.' He paused, then tried another tactic, offering: 'Right, here's a thought – just give yourself time to consider it. How about I take her place, Billy? If you let her go unharmed, I'll have a car brought forward and you can take me as your hostage.'

'I'm not that fucking green!' Hughes snorted. 'You'll bloody jump me, you will.' Then he said fiercely, 'Listen to me: I want a car with a blue light and a working radio. I'll take her with me but I'll let her out on the motorway.'

Gill asked in a small voice, 'Is that right, Billy? You'll let me go?'

Hughes nodded. 'You're coming with me but I'll drop you off, you'll be all right.'[3]

Gill said nothing. 'I'd got past believing him then,' she recalls. 'All this time, he still had the axe near my face, he hadn't changed his position and I was still shaking. I just couldn't possibly think how I was going to get out of that car. I just couldn't imagine it.'

Howse shook his head. 'You can have the car, Billy, but I want the woman. Give me your word on that and you can have the car.'

'Billy, please,' Gill begged. 'Give him your word.'

'Look at me, Billy, I want your word.'

Hughes glared at him. 'Just get that car brought up here.'

Howse switched tack, rebuking Billy as a friend might in familiar language: 'Fucking hell, Billy, what are we talking about? It's
all over. You know I can't let you go. Give me the axe and the
knife and we'll go and talk about it. There's a pub up the road,
we'll even go and have a fucking pint if you want. You have my
word there'll be no rough stuff.'

Hughes relaxed slightly, but said, 'I'd sooner have a car.'

'I dare say, but how far do you think you'll get?' queried Howse.
'You know where you stand with me. You might as well give yourself up now. What can they do to you except send you to prison
for a while? You'll be out again some day.'

His expression altered. 'I'm not going to fucking prison ever
again! I'll take all the bastards with me when I go before that
happens!'

He was right, of course, Howse knew. After what he'd done,
he would be incarcerated for the rest of his life. Having
stabbed two prison officers and killed four members of the
same family, including a ten-year-old girl, his time inside
would not be an easy one either. Like Brady and Hindley, who
had murdered children and buried their bodies on the moors
not far away, he would be unlikely to receive much sympathy
from his fellow inmates. Howse decided to concentrate on
persuading him not to harm his hostage in order to convince
him that people would be more forgiving if he let her go. The
ruse of introducing his wife into the conversation had proved
spectacularly misplaced, but Howse was certain there must be
someone who cared about him, whatever he had done. Prison
was inevitable, but he had to try to think of reasons to make
Hughes want to live.

Intuitively, Gill grasped what Howse was trying to do. From
the front seat, she pleaded, 'He doesn't mean any of it; he thinks

a lot of his daughter. He loves her – he'd never harm her. He's been so good to Sarah, my daughter.'

Howse was certain then that the ten-year-old girl whose body had been found bound and gagged in her grandparents' bedroom was Gill's daughter. His eyes lit upon Hughes, who returned his clear, direct gaze with a penetrating look of his own, followed by an almost imperceptible shake of his head. The two men understood each other, but Hughes had no reason to fear Howse might speak of the murders; he had no intention of doing so for Gill's sake.

'Let her go,' Howse repeated. 'Come on—'

'What about guns?' Hughes demanded. 'Who's got them?'

Howse held up his hands. 'You know better than that, Billy. We don't carry guns. If we did, then I'd have one, wouldn't I?' While Hughes considered that, Howse changed the subject. It was another bitterly cold night and Hughes had only a lightweight suit to fend off the chill. Hoping to conjure up images of somewhere warm and inviting, Howse blew on his own hands and rubbed them together, exclaiming, 'Fucking hell, it's freezing, isn't it? Wish I'd worn gloves.' Then he added, aware that most of Hughes's crimes were associated with drinking: 'I wouldn't mind that pint either.'

Hughes cocked his head on one side, suddenly interested in the police officer. He asked more calmly, 'What's your name, anyway?'

'Peter Howse.'

'Where are you from?'

Aware that people from the same background often have a greater affinity than with those who are not, Howse said, 'Well, I'm based at Bakewell but from Glossop originally. It's a mill town,' he added, emphasising an immediate similarity with Hughes's home town of Preston.

'What's your rank, then?'

'Chief inspector.'

Hughes snorted, 'Fucking hell.' He obviously felt a twisted pride in being deemed dangerous enough to warrant a high-ranking officer's time, especially one who was off duty. Then he asked curiously, 'Was your dad a cop?'

Howse shook his head. 'No. Both my parents worked all their lives in the local paper mill. My dad worked twelve hours a day but he was made redundant when the mills closed. He didn't have much of a life after that, to be honest.' Having shared personal information, he felt encouraged when Hughes continued the exchange.

'My dad died a couple of years ago. A bloody soldier and a hard bastard – he used to give all us lads a good beating from time to time. I hated him . . . still do.'

Howse recognised the lack of conviction, thinking that Hughes was not only at war with the world but probably at war with himself. In addition to that, he would be loath to let his hard-man image slip in front of Gill. After all he had told her about his brutal past, he could never back down. And yet, Howse pondered, as much as he wanted her to think him tough, he would not be able to face her finding out that he had killed her family. With this in mind, Howse began, 'So you hated your dad?'

Hughes nodded.

'As much as you hate your wife?'

Hughes frowned, then nodded again.

'What about Gill?'

He looked puzzled. 'What do you mean?'

'Well, whatever you've done and whatever you're doing now, she shouldn't be part of it, should she? We agreed, didn't we, that she's done nothing to harm you? So let her go. Everyone will think better of you if you do.'

Hughes reverted to his previous mood, snapping, 'I might. But I'll kill her for sure if you don't get me another car.'

'I'll do that,' Howse said. 'But I can also do a lot more for you than she can. If you let her go, I'll get you the car and you can take me as your hostage. I'll drive and you can sit behind me with your knife and the axe. I'll drive you wherever you want to go.'

Hughes pursed his lips, considering. 'And you're a chief inspector, right?'

'Yes.'

'You're not squad?'

'No. I was, but I'm not now.'

'So what the fuck are you doing out after dark?'

Howse gave a short laugh. 'I've got a lot more right to be out than you do.'

Hughes gave a quick nod in consent.

'Come on, Billy, I'm giving you the chance to take the easy way out,' Howse urged. 'Give me the axe.'

'I want a car.'

'Okay, we've established that. You can have a car if you let her go unharmed.'

'Get the car first.'

'No, I want your word, Billy. About her. Look at me.'

'All right then,' he said.[4]

An outside security light clicked on in a nearby property as he spoke, illuminating the entire area around the car, causing Hughes to 'go berserk', Howse recalls. 'He threatened the hostage with the axe and accused me of trying to trap him. Then he noticed two officers crouched down about twenty-five yards away from the car and demanded that they retreat and that all lights should be switched out.'

'Get those two bastards with sticks to fucking *back off*.' Hughes shouted.

Howse got up, slipping slightly on the ice. He turned, calling for the men 'with sticks' to withdraw and the light to be switched off. The two men were, in fact, holding shotguns and he was relieved that they had been too close to the shadows for Hughes to realise it.

Howse turned back to the car, where Hughes demanded immediate action. 'I had to adopt a calming and coaxing approach,' Howse recalls. 'I felt that I was rapidly losing the advantage I had been working for, and which I had the impression I was achieving before the light was suddenly switched on.'[5]

'Just simmer down,' he told the agitated fugitive. 'None of that was my doing; you know that, don't you, Billy?'

'All right,' said Hughes, still glowering. 'But time is running out.' He began making specific demands about the car, which he wanted to be parked facing Macclesfield, in the road a few feet to the left of the Marina. He also wanted some cigarettes. Having already secured his 'unconvincing' promise to release Gill unharmed, Howse left to do his bidding, hearing him shout that no one else was to come near.

Heading further away than before, Howse was surprised by how thickly the area behind the bus was strewn with vehicles, personnel and a large crowd of onlookers, who had no intention of leaving until the drama was over. He sought out Constable Eric Harris, who had set up the successful roadblock less than an hour before, and told him to bring his car slowly down to the side of the Marina. Harris recalls: 'I was then requested by the Chief Inspector to turn my patrol car round to face Macclesfield and to leave it with the engine running, the door open, the headlights on and the blue flashing light on. This I did, and had just got out of the vehicle when Hughes suddenly started screaming for the lights to be extinguished. I reached in the vehicle and put the lights out as requested . . . then moved back to the bus.'[6] Harris handed Howse the keys, adding that his Chief Superintendent had established another roadblock further down the hill. Howse was about to turn away, when Harris called, 'Sir? The Chief Superintendent wants to know if you'd like a psychiatrist?'

Howse gave him a quizzical look, inclining his head towards the Marina. 'For me or him?'

Harris hesitated, nonplussed. 'For him, I think, sir.'

Howse shook his head. 'It's too late for that, Officer. Make sure you move back to a safe position behind the bus.' He had already spied four men whom he knew from Buxton and was keen to speak to them. Two were firearms officers: fifty-year-old Detective Constable Alan Nicholls, a highly respected 'old school' officer, and an experienced, even-tempered detective sergeant, thirty-two-year-old Frank Pell.

Despite Howse's recent assurances to the wanted man, both Nicholls and Pell were armed. An hour earlier, Derbyshire's Deputy Chief Constable had given orders for them to be dispatched to the scene with police-issue Smith & Wesson .38-calibre revolvers, each gun loaded with five bullets. Accompanied by Detective Inspector Peter Burgess – a tough, uncompromising man whom Howse had found to be efficient and trustworthy – Pell and Nicholls were driven to the scene by Detective Sergeant Derek Beale, arriving at 10.30 p.m.

Howse took the opportunity to brief Nicholls and Pell, who were confident they could get close enough to the driver's side of the car to ascertain exactly what was happening and to be in a position to shoot if necessary. Burgess confided that an armed response team was on its way but he had no idea when they would reach Rainow. Howse was fine with that; he knew there were no better men than Alan and Frank, who were steady of hand and head.

Howse outlined his plan: when Hughes moved to Harris's car, now parked alongside the Marina, no doubt using Gill as his shield, he would attempt to free her. They all agreed their best chance of saving her life was by getting her out of the car. Burgess would provide the necessary back-up and Pell and Nicholls were prepared to shoot Hughes if it came to that; the same conditions would apply if he tried to kill her inside the car.

Howse remembered the cigarettes. DI Burgess produced a packet from his pocket and shook out its content, then replaced two, saying, 'Give him these. He's bound to want more, so you've got an excuse to come back if you need one.'

As Howse approached the Marina, Hughes shouted for him to chuck the cigarettes on the back seat and stand well back. But he seemed less keen than before on switching vehicles. Howse recalls: 'He clearly wasn't ready, for some reason. Then after a good deal of muttering to himself – almost as if he were trying to find something he had misplaced – he said he wanted a police cap, a pair of size-eight shoes and some more bloody fags.'

Howse returned to his gathered colleagues, asking loudly if anyone was a size-eight foot. The mumbled denials led him to suspect that there might well be a size eight among them but no one wanted to hand over their shoes in the snow.

Howse walked a short distance uphill, where Constable Chris McCarthy stood with the other Crime Squad officers. 'Nobody owned up to being a size eight,' McCarthy remembers ruefully, 'until Mr Howse said to me, "What size are your shoes, Officer?" "Eight, sir," I said. He replied with a wry smile, "Give them here." I was then duly obliged to stand in the road in my socks. However, a kindly traffic officer supplied me with a pair of wellingtons from the back of his vehicle and from somewhere else I was handed a navy blue gabardine raincoat. I stood in the road like Paddington Bear.'[7]

Holding McCarthy's shoes, together with a cap and more cigarettes collected from Beale, Howse walked back down to the Marina, talking to Hughes on his approach and then through the front nearside window. He did so in order to distract him from the back of the car, where the two firearms officers were gradually moving forward with their guns. Howse then retreated a couple of paces, dropping the shoes, hat and cigarettes on the back seat of the car.

Hughes insisted on Howse retreating while he put on the shoes. He obeyed, then crouched again at the open rear passenger window.

'Get some lights on,' Hughes demanded, 'I want to see what you're all up to.'

Howse called out and Constable Harris switched on the headlamps of the single-decker bus, illuminating a wide area of the road with its myriad vehicles and onlookers and the deep black shadows beyond of house and hill. Howse kept speaking to Hughes, but realised 'he had reached a stage where he was going to try something. I told him that the waiting car was his for the taking, including me as a hostage if he would let the woman go. It became obvious from his attitude that there was little chance of this happening. If he was going to make a run for it, the hostage was his only chance of escaping again. I think the hostage realised this as well as she became hysterical and began pleading with him again.'[8]

Hughes again told Howse to back off, but the officer held his ground, determined to stay close enough to react to whatever happened next. He had already made up his mind to tackle Hughes when he left the Marina, intending to 'go for his legs, hoping he would slip on the ice as I had done and that I might be able to pin him down until others arrived. But everything had gone very quiet and the light was extreme: bright white around us and then impenetrable black elsewhere, like a stage, almost. I could feel the icy wind getting up and heard from somewhere nearby the creaking of shoes on snow. The car rocked gently in the stiffening breeze. Behind me I could hear the low throbbing of the getaway car, whose doors lay invitingly open.'

But it was not to be. Howse speculates now that perhaps the lights from the bus were brighter than Hughes had expected. It would certainly have been better for him to make his move under cover of darkness, but the light was there at his request. Howse took a step to one side to avoid acting as a barrier to Hughes reaching the other car, but the headlamps cast a long shadow, causing the officer to appear more foreboding than before. Suddenly Hughes leaned towards Gill, telling her to get ready to move, but she was a long way past following his instructions.

'She was more petrified than ever,' Howse recalls, 'and understandably terrified at the prospect of leaving the car to be alone with him in another vehicle. She shouted that she didn't want to go. Her shoulders shook as she began to wail, repeating that she didn't want to go and wasn't going to go with him. Hughes became angry, then incensed. He said something to her that I missed and she shook her head violently. Their relationship as hostage and captor had reached breaking point: if she refused to act as his shield, he would have to drag her, leaving him vulnerable to attack.'

And then Hughes lost control. After a stream of threats and expletives directed towards Gill, he did what he had done so many times in his life before: he blamed someone else for problems of his own making. Howse heard him scream at Gill, 'It's your fucking fault!'

Frank Pell crept closer, holding the pistol ready. He had a clear view of the three of them: Howse, Gill and Hughes.

'You're too close!' Hughes yelled at the chief inspector.

'Just release her, Billy—'

But Hughes had finally snapped, shouting. 'Your time is up!' as he swung the axe at Gill. She shrieked, diving forwards towards the car door.

Howse sprang up. Plunging through the rear window, he grappled with the raging Hughes, who struck Gill a glancing blow on the side of her head with the axe. She screamed and shrank further into the corner.

Hughes brought the axe down again, this time on Howse's forearm. It was a dead weight but had landed on its side rather than on the blade.

'I don't know what happened then,' Howse admits. 'It was utter confusion. I tried to protect her head with my left arm and to work the axe out of his hand with my right, but in such a dark, strange and confined space it was the blind fighting the blind.'

A shot rang out.

Frank Pell had fired at Hughes through the shattered rear passenger window. The bullet skimmed off the door and penetrated Hughes's scalp, where it remained embedded. 'Bloody hell,' Hughes groaned, yet fought on, struggling with Howse for possession of the axe. Gill cowered, screaming, against the door as the weapon's blade snagged on the roof lining above her head.[9]

Pell raced to the driver's door, firing a second shot. The glass splintered and blew in, showering those inside.

Pell's second bullet entered Hughes's left shoulder blade, travelling up into his thorax. Despite being severely wounded, Hughes battled against Howse's attempts to wrest the axe from him.

In disbelief, Pell pulled the trigger a third time. It missed and he was about to fire again when Nicholls reached his side, taking slow and perfect aim.

He fired a single shot straight through the windscreen. There was a loud crack as the bullet left a starburst in the glass on its fatal trajectory.

Inside the vehicle, Howse felt Hughes's entire body shudder. A moment later, the injured man fell backwards, leaving the axe safe in the chief inspector's hands.

'No more shooting!' yelled DI Burgess, running forward.[10]

There was chaos everywhere: doors slamming, lights going on, shouting, and feet pounding on snow. In the middle of it all, Howse prised himself from the car, his arm numb from the blows of the axe. Blood beaded from tiny cuts on his hands and forehead where shards of glass had flown in with the second bullet. He straightened up as Burgess appeared at his side and saw Gill still cowering in her seat.

She had no idea what had happened. 'There were a lot of bangs,' she recalls. 'Something came from the direction of the passenger window in my door and hit me in the face. I don't know what it was. I heard somebody say, "Get her out."'

Together, Howse and Burgess helped Gill from the car. There was blood on her forehead. She blinked in the white light, confused, thinking that her face was wet because she had been shot but then realising it was only a trickle of blood. 'I never thought they had guns in England,' she remembers saying to herself. 'It's just like America – just like the TV.'

Howse looked down at himself. There were bloody axe marks

on the sleeve of his coat. He kept checking himself to make sure he hadn't been shot: 'After it was all over I looked in the car and saw a bullet hole in the door just inches from where I had entered.'

Then he turned to Gill, who stood in a trance between him and DI Burgess.

'Are you all right?' he asked.

She moved her head slightly, staring straight ahead.

'Get her out of here,' Howse said quietly, and DI Burgess took Gill away, handing her to Constable Harris, who helped her into his patrol car. 'She was bleeding from a cut which was from the left side of her forehead,' he recalls. 'I then started for Macclesfield Infirmary. Approximately one mile later I halted at a further road-block and [Mrs Moran] was then transferred to a waiting ambulance to be taken to hospital. I then made my way back to the scene to assist.'[11] She had not cried at all; her face was a pale, blank disc and her eyes remained fixed on a point that no one else could see, even as she was lifted into the ambulance by kind hands.

The fugitive lay slumped against the dashboard of the green Marina. Officers reached in, dragging him from the car, where a red vortex of blood smeared across the door, dripping down on to the pristine snow. At 11.10 p.m., he was driven from the scene in an ambulance, accompanied by Glossop-based Police Sergeant Tony Gregory on a journey lasting less than ten minutes.

At West Park Hospital in Macclesfield, twenty-eight-year-old William Thomas Hughes was pronounced dead on arrival.

Part Five:

Aftermath

Chapter Fifteen:

My God, She's a Brave Woman

T HE TWO FIREARMS officers unloaded their guns at the scene. Pell handed his pistol, two live rounds and three spent cartridge cases to DS Beale, who also took possession of Nicholls's pistol, plus four live rounds and one spent cartridge case from him. A spent bullet was recovered at a later stage from underneath the mat in the driver's footwell of the Marina, while another had to be carefully prised out of the nearside quarter-light pillar.

Figures soon began to emerge from the streets, houses, pub and village institute, milling about in the shadows. The media had already been alerted and were on their way; the three men involved in the shooting were taken into a nearby building by Derbyshire's Head of CID, Alfred Horobin, and Detective Chief Inspector Sydney Thompson, to ensure that they were not approached by either public or press. 'We were now part of the investigation process,' Howse explains, 'and as such we were given a swift debrief then removed from the scene to make our statements separately. There were many witnesses to the incident, but the only one to have observed events at close quarters was DI Burgess. As I left, he gave me a handwritten note which described everything he had seen, from the moment I leapt into the car through to us helping Gill out to safety. It seems incredible, but the whole episode in Rainow had happened in the space of under an hour.'

There would be no further communication between Howse and Burgess, Beale, Pell and Nicholls until the inquest three months later. Driven to Buxton Police Station, Howse spent a couple of hours typing up his report in an empty office. 'It was not the ending I had been working towards,' he admits. 'Hughes was dead, after all. But the main objective – saving the hostage – had been achieved. I was still typing at 2 a.m. when the Divisional Commander, Jack Barker, came in to ask if I was all right. He apologised for interrupting but said he just wanted to see how I was holding up. After watching me in silence for a few minutes he left, quietly shutting the door. I spoke to no one else that night except Sergeant Cross, who had been waiting to drive me home. He made no mention of what had happened until I got out of the car. Then he said, "You know, people will say that what you did tonight was either very brave or very stupid." I replied, "Well, it was neither, really – we did what was necessary to save Gill Moran's life."

'And that's still how I see it today.'[1]

A nurse helped Gill Moran into a crisp white hospital bed, arranging the blankets neatly.

'Where am I?' Gill asked, completely numb in body and spirit.

'Macclesfield Hospital, love.'

Gill nodded, 'Oh.'[2]

She remembered arriving at the hospital with the bottle of Bell's whisky and the shopping list she had written out that morning, and wondered how those two things had remained in her possession. A policewoman had taken them from her and then she had been shown into this room with its starched sheets, soft overhead light by the bed, pale blue curtains and clean floor. She was never alone; the small space was perpetually crowded with what seemed to be an army of police officers who were working shifts just to keep her company. 'At last,' she thought, 'I'm with people I can trust', and yet she did not ask them the only question that mattered because she instinctively knew that they were not allowed to tell her.

Someone touched her forehead and when she put her own hand to it, she realised the small wound had been sutured. Somebody else – or perhaps it was the same person – injected her with a warm liquid. It made her feel very strange. She lay still on the narrow bed. It all kept flowing through her mind, the events of that night. She had not expected Billy to die. But she had trusted him and he had lied to her. To what extent, she did not know, but she could hear voices from the past telling her that she was gullible. Her schoolfriends had always said so. 'You'll believe anything,' they used to tell her. And she did.

A nurse was watching her. Not in an unpleasant way, but with an expression Gill had never seen before. She could not put a name to it, but it made a tiny nerve leap in her throat to see it. She pulled the covers up with exaggerated slowness, over her chin, her mouth – all the way to her forehead, like a child – and shut her eyes. But she did not sleep.

*

The Senior Investigation Officer, Frank Hulme, arrived at Pottery Cottage that night with his team to view the bodies and set in motion the process of preserving, gathering and recording all the evidence. Simultaneously, Scene of Crime photographer John Slater pulled up in a van with his colleague Peter Sowery, who had taken Hughes's fingerprints after his arrest for rape and GBH the previous summer.

Slater got to work photographing the outside of the house first, from the deep trenches in the snow where the Chrysler had been towed on its final journey to the bloody drag marks in the grey slush towards the garage, where Amy Minton's body lay prone against the wall. 'It was one of the worst scenes I've ever worked on,' he reflects. 'When I reached Richard Moran's body on the landing, I realised we had met. I'd been called out to Brett Plastics some time earlier – I can't remember how long ago – but there had been a burglary at the offices and I spoke to him then. Obviously, there's no such thing as a commonplace crime scene but Pottery Cottage was very disturbing. Apart from the bodies, there were small details that stayed with me. Hughes had pretended that everyone was still alive when, of course, the grandfather and the little girl had been dead for a couple of days. But he'd had the mother, Gill Moran, still making meals for them and on another landing I photographed a plate of uneaten toast and a cup of tea with the skin across its surface, both left on a chair. I was there all night, documenting every room.'[3]

At midnight, two hours after the local police surgeon had provided official confirmation of four deaths, eminent Home Office pathologist Dr Alan Usher arrived to view the bodies in situ. A veteran of almost 800 murder investigations, he verified that all the victims had been killed as a result of severe knife wounds to the throat and multiple stabbing injuries to their chests. Once Usher had completed his duties, Detective Constable Fran Muldoon began methodically collecting items as part of his responsibilities after being appointed exhibits officer. He was also tasked with drawing up a plan of the building and its grounds to show where each of the bodies had been found. Scene of Crime Officer Sowery subsequently identified seventeen fingerprints belonging to Hughes within the property.

Harold Lilleker & Sons, funeral directors, arrived at 1.25 a.m. in a large, windowless van. The four bodies were then transported to Chesterfield Royal Hospital mortuary. Buxton Scene of Crime photographer Anthony Pearce travelled in the opposite direction to Macclesfield Hospital mortuary, having taken a number of black-and-white images of the Marina at Rainow. 'The car was empty and there was blood on the snow,' he recalls. 'In addition to photographing the car, I took samples of the blood inside it and pieces of the rear-view mirror, which had ended up in the passenger footwell at the front. A senior officer told me to head for Macclesfield Hospital, where Hughes's body lay in the mortuary, in order to search him.'[4]

Pearce began examining Hughes's clothing at 2.25 a.m. He removed £187 in notes from the inside breast pocket of his jacket, two packets of cigarettes, part of a pen, a key, a red handkerchief and pieces of glass from his other pockets. 'Usually, I hated having to deal with dead bodies,' Pearce admits, 'but I checked over Billy Hughes with a certain grim satisfaction. The bullets were still embedded in his flesh and I remember the pathologist looking down at the corpse and musing, "It's rare to find a body of such muscular quality." It's weird, the things that stick in your mind!'[5]

Post-mortems took place on the four murder victims a few hours later. John Slater had taken a total of 168 photographs – fourteen rolls of film, each containing twelve shots – at Pottery

Cottage, before documenting the autopsies. Usher was unable to judge the order in which each victim had died, but from Gill's testimony it was clear that Amy Minton had been the last, murdered shortly after Richard Moran, while Arthur Minton and Sarah Moran were almost certainly dead within hours of Hughes infiltrating their home.[6] DC Muldoon was also present at the post-mortems, taking possession of clothing and objects, all of which had some significance, however slight: a pocket in Amy's housecoat yielded her biro, handkerchief, a polo mint, and the whistle she had used to summon the Newmans' dog whenever she exercised him.

Formal identification was mandatory, but there was no question of asking Gill, the victims' next of kin, to fulfil that obligation. Seeking to obtain details of other relatives, a police officer telephoned Richard's colleagues Paul Goldthorpe and David Brown. The calls were made around 5 a.m. on Saturday morning. 'I was baffled at first,' Paul remembers, 'to be awakened at that hour by someone asking about Richard's next of kin. I replied that would be Gill and her parents. Who else? the officer wanted to know. I said that Gill had a sister in Paris but I didn't know her address. I wondered what on earth was going on and ended up calling Charles Dauncey, a friend of mine who lived not far from Pottery Cottage. He picked up straight away when I called and told me about the murders. It turned out that he had given my details to the police as someone who might be able to help. I can't even begin to describe the shock I felt. Then David turned up at my house and we drove together to Pottery Cottage. We couldn't get past the police cordon, but spoke briefly to Len Newman, then headed for Staveley.'[7]

The two men arrived at the Brett Plastics factory around 8.20 a.m. 'As I walked past the accounts office, I noticed that the door was open,' David recalls. 'I looked inside and saw the room in chaos. The safe had been ransacked and the door left open with the key in the lock. Coins were scattered all over the floor.'[8] Fingerprints lifted from the safe by Peter Sowery were later identified as those of Billy Hughes.

Thirty miles away in Buxton, Chief Inspector Howse walked into the police station where he was based 'and everything went quiet. The word from on high was that no one was to speak to me about the previous night's events, no doubt to avoid compromising the forthcoming inquest. But when the inspector left the station on his rounds, our longest-serving officer in Buxton, Eric Glover, came up to my office and shook my hand in silence. Then one by one, all my other colleagues came up to do the same.'[9]

The woman whose life Howse had saved was likewise met with a wall of silence. Gill Moran was now desperate for someone to answer the question that felt as if it were burning a hole in her heart. But everyone she asked reacted as if they had not heard, immediately speaking of other, much less consequential matters. A young nurse took her off for a bath, sitting close by all the while. 'How strange,' Gill thought, 'I've never had a bath with a woman watching me before.' Afterwards, the nurse helped her dress, holding her hand very tightly as she led her back to bed, where another young woman, a WPC, sat nearby. After the same warm liquid had been injected into Gill's veins, she and the two women talked about the weather over cups of tea, just as if they had met up in a café in town.

Then, during a lull in the conversation, the policewoman said gently, 'Superintendent Morris is coming to see you in a minute, Gill. He's ever so nice. We all think he looks like Father Christmas.' And when he entered the room, Gill agreed, remembering how, only three weeks ago, she had celebrated Christmas in her dream home with her family.

Morris approached Gill's bedside. The nurse brought him a chair and Gill listened as he told her everything, measuring out his sentences as if each one bore its own weight and had to be carefully balanced. When he had finished speaking, she said steadily, 'There's no one left then?' Morris reached for her hand and said in a voice thick with emotion, 'No, love. No one.'

Gill turned her face to the wall.

That same day, Arthur Minton's nephew identified the four bodies in the mortuary at Macclesfield Hospital as those of his family. Len Newman provided further confirmation.

Just after five o'clock, a small, slim woman with her hair newly permed and dyed chestnut brown followed a detective sergeant through the corridors of Chesterfield Royal Hospital. He led her down to the mortuary, where she stood apprehensively as an attendant drew back the canvas sheet from the body on a steel gurney.

Jean Hughes nodded, 'Yes, that's Billy.'

Afterwards, she made a statement, concluding that she had 'never heard of the Minton or Moran families and to the best of my knowledge, neither did my late husband'.[10] She then travelled back to her home on Blackpool's Loftos Road, where she and her children had been allowed to return for the first time since Wednesday afternoon. The following day, she lifted her four-year-old daughter on to the brown sofa in the white sitting-room and tried to explain.

'My mum told me [Dad] had gone to Baby Jesus,' Nichola recalls.

'I asked if he'd come down and see me. I was crying because he'd gone away. My mum used to say, "He's watching you, looking after you." All I can recall from that time is that she never got dressed but just sat on the couch, crying. She cried that much she had sores where she kept wiping the tears.'[11] Nichola herself 'sobbed for days' and insisted on sleeping with her father's last letter under her pillow.[12] In his neat, slanting hand he had written that he loved her and would soon be taking her to the Pleasure Beach again, where he'd buy her a shandy in the pub and pretend it was beer. The margins of his letter were filled with colourful, adept drawings of her favourite Disney characters: Mickey Mouse, Goofy and Donald Duck.

At a press conference called by Derbyshire Police, Assistant Chief Constable Alfred Mitchell confirmed that the same man who had sent such enchanting letters to his toddler daughter had murdered three generations of one family over a period of three days. The story exploded in the press like another gunshot, particularly since it was the first time in British history that a prison escapee had been shot dead by police. 'It was obvious,' Mitchell told the gathered journalists, 'that had the officers not acted, the woman would have been killed. He was armed with an axe. The woman did suffer injuries, despite what the officers did. There is no question about it – there was a frenzied attack taking place on the woman inside the car.'[13]

Forensic investigations continued apace, as Scene of Crime Officer Anthony Pearce examined Richard Moran's Chrysler in the garage at Buxton Police Station. Once again, the items removed from it provided texture to the details of the case: 'Axe from the offside of driver's seat, knife from under mat in driver's footwell, dark brown wig from front passenger seat, two sheets of paper with reference to Roy's Café, reddish sweater from back seat, light-coloured raincoat from back seat, grey case containing clothes, red torch from front passenger seat, wallet containing £36, credit cards and driving licence in name of Richard Moran' and various other effects.[14] Examination of the toilet facilities Hughes had used at Trowell Services eliminated any possibility of the purloined prison knife having been planted there.

Anthony Pearce was dispatched to Macclesfield Infirmary after searching the Chrysler. 'I was sent to photograph Gill Moran's injuries,' he recalls. 'She was sedated and almost supernaturally calm. Awake but with no emotion whatsoever. She was able to talk quite normally but was obviously suffering from severe shock, in the clinical sense. I documented her wounds, which were fairly superficial under the circumstances.'[15] Gill had begun talking to police and over the course of that weekend, she gave a full account of the three days during which she and her family had been held hostage. Her twenty-nine-page statement was taken by Chief Inspector Sydney Thompson with Detective Policewoman Butler assisting.

Years later, when he and Thompson were on a course together, Peter Howse discussed the matter with him: 'Those interviews with Gill had affected him very deeply. Sydney Thompson was a quiet, intelligent man with a wealth of experience. He was particularly sensitive to Gill's needs and allowed her to progress at her own pace, rather than asking questions. When we talked, he was particularly vitriolic about Billy Hughes, for both the atrocities he had committed and the sexual acts he had forced Gill to perform.'

Howse recalls that he and Thompson were especially disgusted by unfounded, pernicious gossip among locals who claimed that Gill had known Hughes prior to his escape and that there had been some sort of relationship between them: 'It was categorically untrue and utterly shameful. It beggars belief that people would wish to inflict further pain on someone who had already suffered so deeply. Gill's evidence told the full story. Sydney Thompson listened, letting everything come to the surface. Further questioning would have been necessary only if there were any doubts about the veracity of the evidence. There were no such doubts in this case.'[16]

On Sunday afternoon, Police Chief Superintendent Arthur Morris visited Gill a second time, declaring afterwards: 'My God, she's a brave woman. There's a remarkable difference to when I last saw her. She appears much better, much brighter.'[17] Gill's main concern was for the family's pets, who were a precious connection to her lost family. 'She was worried about whether they were all right,' Morris recalled. 'We were able to tell her that neighbours are looking after them.'[18] Gill was especially touched to hear that Bobo the rabbit had been collected from his hutch by the mother of Sarah's schoolfriend Jenny Sydall.

Family and friends visited throughout the day, helping with Gill's sedated surface equilibrium. Her sister Barbara had been traced in Paris, where she was informed about the murders as she arrived home from a wedding reception. Barbara had been widowed, and her four children left fatherless, only three years earlier, when her husband was killed in a car crash. She flew to her sister's side on a private plane provided by Richard Moran's friend, Billy Martin. In the meantime, Richard's grieving foster sisters – Margaret, Ann and Eileen – arrived at the hospital. All three were astounded by Gill's 'amazing bravery'.[19] Ann recalled: 'When we saw her in hospital, just for five minutes, she said, "Don't feel sorry for me, feel sorry for the ones I've lost." '[20]

The Goldthorpes and Browns were next to visit. They found Gill sitting up in bed, surrounded by flowers. Ann Goldthorpe entered the room first: 'As soon as Gill saw me, she held out her arms and cried, "Oh Ann, thank goodness you didn't come to us that Wednesday – he would never have let you get away." '[21] David Brown remembers that Gill broke down while they were there, 'but she was heavily sedated, nonetheless. Bits of reality kept breaking through, however, coupled with confusion. At one stage she said very matter-of-factly, "I've got to go to the cottage and scrub the blood from the floors." It was very disturbing and painful.'[22]

Doctors decided the following morning that Gill was 'medically fit in the clinical sense, sufficient not to be detained in hospital'.[23] Her close friends, Grenville and Linda Browett, smuggled her from a rear exit into their car to avoid the waiting press. She accompanied them to their Matlock home, Tigh-Na-Rosen, a pretty stone cottage not unlike her own with similar spellbinding views of the moors. Gill and her two dogs stayed there for several weeks. Grenville recalled that for the first few days he and his wife kept trying to impress on Gill that she was not a guest in their home: 'Instead ... we'd expanded to a family of three.' The Browetts worked out a rota to ensure that Gill was never alone, with Linda taking leave from her job as a teacher. The police were ever-present, along with concerned neighbours and friends bringing food, drinks and helping with chores such as the washing. Chesterfield Round Table, the organisation where Richard had been a member alongside Grenville, gave unstinting support and practical assistance. But Gill retains only scant memories of that time, stating: 'In the beginning people would be in the room, talking and I'd look at them and I could hear the sounds but I didn't know what they were saying.'

In the months preceding the inquest, the media laboured to produce stories about the case, which captivated the public imagination. Interviews with those closest to Hughes and the Mintons and Morans were highly sought, but the former, especially, were extremely cautious about their links to the man now regularly referred to as 'Mad Billy'. Teresa O'Doherty spoke to the press only a handful of times from the Chesterfield house she shared with her daughter Rosie. She was angered by the 'malicious gossip' of neighbours who believed she had secretly received thousands to discuss her relationship with Hughes, insisting, 'I haven't had a penny . . . I can manage on my dole money.'[24] She expressed fathomless revulsion towards her former partner, but was keen to extend her sympathies to Gill Moran, 'and I really do mean that'.[25]

Hughes's widow gave several interviews without realising she could have commanded large fees for her story. Declaring to the *Lancashire Evening Post* that she no longer loved her husband but was 'sorry it happened for him this way', she discussed her belief that a violent death had been inevitable for him: 'He asked for it . . . He would probably have hanged himself or something like that. He had got to the end.'[26] Her sorrow was reserved for 'the people who died, especially the child' and her own daughter 'because she still talks about him'.[27]

Jean continued to share her home with Alice Swan, who had survived an axe attack by Hughes and admitted gratefully, 'I feel really safe now. Thank God he's dead.'[28] Alice's partner, Hughes's brother Alan, remained living with them on Loftos Avenue, but Jean's attempts to reach out to other members of the Hughes family had largely failed; May Hughes avoided people as far as it was possible to do so in the wake of the news about her first-born. A practising Roman Catholic, Jean was troubled by what would happen to her husband's remains, but found his mother 'non-committal over the situation'.[29] Despite her tangled emotions, Jean wanted him to be buried in Blackpool in accordance with the rites of his faith. She consulted her priest, Father Robert Dewhurst of St Cuthbert's Church, who later told enquiring reporters that there was 'no question' of Hughes being excommunicated, explaining: 'He was obviously a psychopathic killer and by virtue of this is exonerated from guilt.'[30]

Hughes's younger brother David was his only blood relation to speak to the press, who tracked him down to his workplace, a discount warehouse in Ipswich. Having made it clear that there would be no further interviews, David confirmed that he intended to 'pay my respects' at his brother's funeral and was of the view that 'William must have had a mental breakdown. I think he knew he would go to prison for a long time. The police have always tried to put him away for a long stretch. The break-up with his girlfriend and the rape case would have been on his mind and in one way he took an easy way out. His marriage had broken up but if his wife did not want it to work, she should not have married him when he was in prison. She knew what he was like – that he had been in and out of jail.'

David admitted to having pleaded with his mother and sister to move away from Preston, after they had 'gone into hiding to get away from the stares. People are staring at me and they give me dirty looks . . . I don't like the way history will remember my brother but it's just something I'll have to live with.'[31]

On the cold, grey morning of Friday 21 January, 1977, a cavalcade of press, together with a few members of the public, gathered at the entrance to Brimington Cemetery, north of Chesterfield town centre on the road to Staveley. The gates had been manned since dawn, access barred to all those except one hundred invited mourners, who each had to produce the small card that verified permission to attend the funerals of Richard and Sarah Moran,

Amy and Arthur Minton. In the Victorian chapel on the hill, which had a regular capacity of eighty, four coffins stood in a row at the end of the aisle bearing sprays of beautiful flowers: red roses and white carnations for the adults; pink roses and spring daffodils for Sarah, with five posies from her friends at Wigley Primary School.

Among those attending were Derbyshire Chief Constable Walter Stansfield and Assistant Chief Constable Alfred Mitchell. Gill and her sister Barbara were last to arrive, having to switch cars after leaving Matlock in order to avoid the press. At half past nine, the black Daimler carrying the two women drove through the gates with a police escort. Grenville Browett was waiting outside the chapel and tucked Gill's arm firmly in his as they made their way to the front pew. 'The only thing we could see were those four red coffins,' he recalls. 'I felt her body sag.'[32] Gill had deliberately specified that the dimensions of the four caskets should be the same. 'I don't think I could have borne it if there had been a little one for Sarah,' she admits.

Canon Stanley Branson, rector of Old Brampton, conducted the short service. He looked round at the congregation, proclaiming, 'People ask the question, "How does God allow these terrible things to happen? How can a God of love allow these things?" The answer is that God is love and because He is love, He gave man freedom of will and freedom of choice. These things happen because of man's freedom of choice. Nevertheless, His love is sufficiently strong to support us in times like this.' Canon Branson then turned to Gill: 'Don't feel you have been deserted. Although you have lost all your nearest and dearest, there are many friends who will help and support you.' Nonetheless, he later disclosed feeling 'amazed at [Gill's] courage. She stood up very well until nearly the end. I tried to comfort her.'[33] Gill recalls hearing him say, 'They're never dead as long as they're in your heart' and found that she 'couldn't bear to leave. It was my family, all I had, I wanted to stay with them.'

A few hours after the cremation took place, a farmer inspecting a dyke that ran through the fields of his home, Rod Knowle Farm in Eastmoor, found a set of papers in a plastic folder: the route order and magistrates' court warrant dated 12 January 1977. He handed them in to police, who arrived in vast number – 130 officers – the following day to search the snowy landscape between the farm and the A619. They found a cache of scattered documents: letters, Christmas cards and a solicitor's brief. The search went on until an officer made a discovery in a field near the drystone wall on to the main road: a black-handled knife, rusted from exposure but still bearing its deadly blade. It lay some 300 yards from Pottery Cottage. Subsequent forensic examination established beyond doubt that the knife was that reported missing on 3 December 1976 from the kitchens of Leicester Prison.

Chapter Sixteen:

Justifiable Homicide

J EAN HUGHES WAS unable to afford the cost of transporting her
husband's body from Chesterfield to Blackpool. Since it was
normal policy for the Home Office to pay for prisoners' funerals,
the authorities decided that Billy Hughes should be buried in
Boythorpe Cemetery, close to his last address.

The news caused a storm of protest when it was aired in the
press. A group of local women whose relatives were laid to rest in
Boythorpe Cemetery flooded Chesterfield council with
complaints. One of those spearheading the campaign was Mrs Pat
Millan, Teresa O'Doherty's sister-in-law, who declared: 'We don't
want him buried here. He comes from Preston. I've been in touch
with local councillor Ron Jepson and the Town Hall. He doesn't
deserve to be buried here. He's not a Chesterfield man. It's a
shame for the town. He should not go through the gates of
Boythorpe Cemetery. He ought to be buried at Leicester Jail, with
the other murderers.'[1] The protestors threatened to dig up
Hughes's body if the burial went ahead.

As a result, the funeral at Boythorpe was cancelled and covert arrangements were made to cremate Hughes's remains. Protestors unaware of the change descended on the cemetery the night before the funeral, attaching a set of chains and a padlock to the gates on Hunloke Avenue. They then hung a board, signed by scores of nearby residents, from the railings, which read: 'Hughes – we don't want him here. Take him where he belongs.'[2]

By dawn on 25 January everything had been removed from the gates and the first vehicle to pass was a panda car. Gathered journalists reported that a 'female chorus of hate' preceded the rain-lashed funeral of 'Mad Billy', with twenty women of all ages running into the cemetery to 'claw at the grave where he was to have been buried. In torrential rain, their hair hanging in rats' tails, they dug at the clay with their bare hands, hurling lumps back into the sodden grave. They seized spades and planks of wood to fill it in.'[3] Meanwhile, the Chesterfield Taximen's Association announced their refusal to carry Jean Hughes in their cabs: 'We have studied her picture from the newspapers and last night we decided not to carry her as a protest.'[4] But Jean had already made arrangements for travel from her home in Blackpool. She left early that morning in a car with Father Dewhurst and two other passengers. Minutes before the ceremony had been due to begin, their car was diverted four miles to Brimington where, purely as a result of the protests, Hughes's funeral took place in the same chapel and crematorium as those of his four victims.

Ten people, including two of Hughes's brothers, attended the service. A single posy from Jean and her daughter Nichola lay upon the coffin. 'It is not for us to judge,' began the priest. 'Judgement should be in God's hands . . .'[5] Outside, twenty rain-soaked women with grave dirt beneath their fingernails demanded entry to the cemetery grounds but were held at bay by police officers. Waving a banner proclaiming 'Holy Ground Not For Killers', the protestors jeered the mourners as they left the service.

'Sick and disgusting' was how Jean viewed the campaigners. 'They say he shouldn't be buried on Holy Ground – then they shouldn't either,' she declared. 'They aren't Christians, just hysterical, publicity-seeking women.'[6] Attending the funeral had been 'the hardest thing' she had ever had to do, 'but wild horses wouldn't have kept me away. I used to love Billy. I don't now. I shall never forgive him for what he did, but I believe he was ill and needed treatment.'[7] She lay the blame squarely at the feet of all 'the judges and magistrates who heard his case, and all the prison doctors and psychiatrists and probation officials who just let things drift. The system failed in Billy's case – and that poor family have been wiped out as a result.'[8] Jean told reporters that she hoped to hold a memorial mass at St Cuthbert's and that Blackpool Police had agreed to hold on to his ashes until the service, but a chief superintendent was swift to discredit her assertion: 'There is no question of the police being involved with these ashes. They will not be kept at the police station.'[9] Jean later disposed of the ashes privately.

Gill Moran refused to comment when contacted by the press for a reaction to the protests at Hughes's funeral. Reporters followed her every move nonetheless, and eventually she sought advice on how best to deal with the constant intrusion. A solicitor recommended granting one newspaper exclusive rights to her story, which would negate much of the interest from other media outlets. David Brown assisted as a bidding war ensued; approaches were made via Gill's solicitor but he agreed to meet journalists in order to sound out the most sympathetic and trustworthy. As a result of the *Daily Mail* making the successful bid, the redoubtable Lynda Lee-Potter was dispatched to meet Gill. Three years her senior, Lancashire-born and married with children, Lee-Potter had been the *Daily Mail*'s star columnist since 1972. Over the course of several interviews which provided the basis for the serialisation, the two women became genuine friends.

Lee-Potter's first encounter with Gill was at the Browetts' Matlock cottage, where the younger woman sat apprehensively on a sofa. 'Her hands were icily cold, she was wearing black trousers, a white polo-necked sweater; slight and frail with the wide, soft mouth, the sweet, diffident smile,' she recalled. 'Horror and grief annihilated her and she wept convulsively with her arms tightly wrapped round her body, swaying backwards and forwards. Grenville came in and knelt down in front of her, putting his arms around her as though she were a child, leaning his forehead against hers, rocking her to and fro very gently, stroking her hair.'[10]

The reporter spoke at length to those closest to Gill and visited the sites associated with her story, including Pottery Cottage. The police had completed their forensic investigations and she was able to walk through the house with Gill's permission, noticing that 'the mug inscribed Granddad is still in the kitchen . . . Sarah's National Cycling Proficiency certificate, the rocking horse, the tinkling musical box are still in the crowded, charming, little girl's room. The room in which three terrorised hostages spent two days and a night with a killer surrounded by dolls, a teddy bear, the Christmas decorations still on the windows which stare out over the rolling misty, menacing moors.'[11]

Gill's story ran in the *Daily Mail* for eight instalments, beginning on 14 February 1977 and ending with Lynda Lee-Potter's own reflections ten days later, in which she declared that Gill 'has no self-pity, remarkably little bitterness, no irritation when the thirty-eighth person today will say, how are you? [But] it's reminders of normality that threaten to destroy her. Laying the table in Linda's house and remembering the countless times she's thoughtlessly, happily done it in her own. The mention of the new series of *Just William* on television because her mother had said, "You must let Sarah see it, she'll love it." But she doesn't want people to be careful. She doesn't want them continuously monitoring every word in case it upsets her because life isn't like that.'[12]

Although the serialisation had opened with the words: 'Pottery Cottage: when you read this you will have understood everything', one of the overwhelmingly persistent questions remained: why had Gill and her husband 'thrown away so many chances' to raise the alarm?[13] Derbyshire's Assistant Chief Constable, Alfred Mitchell, touched upon the subject in an internal report, stating that in the last few hours of her young life, Sarah Moran had shown 'more pluck than her parents. Hughes made life appear quite normal at the Moran household and Mr and Mrs Moran, by their willing cooperation, enabled him to do this. Both Mr and Mrs Moran had several opportunities to escape and give warning without there being any further danger to their family, but for some reason they chose not to avail themselves of their chances. Whatever happened at the house did not cause the slightest suspicion to anybody in the neighbourhood.'[14]

It fell to Richard Moran's foster sister, Ann Wintle, to explain: 'Gillian did not know that her family had been killed. She thought they were still alive. She thought she would be the hostage for that lunatic and that he would let her family go if she went with him. All the others were still tied up. He didn't kill them until just before she left the house and she didn't know . . . She thought she had saved her family.'[15]

But the majority of criticism in those first three months after Hughes's death was directed at all those agencies involved in his incarceration, escape and last days of liberty. Reflecting on the matter, Peter Howse responds: 'The problem with sensationalised stories is that people remember the headlines far more than the content. A lot of it was based on speculation anyway because of the constraints impinged upon the information that could be released publicly prior to the inquest. The real concerns about why such a dangerous man was being ferried to and from court in a taxi, how the knife came to be missing from the prison kitchen and why Pottery Cottage was not visited by the police were all perfectly justifiable questions that required explanations, but it took time to examine each issue thoroughly in order to establish the facts beyond doubt. There were two inquiries – one government led, the other an internal study by Derbyshire Constabulary – but the findings of both remained largely *sub judice* until the inquest.'[16]

In the meantime, news outlets continued to speculate and questions were also raised in parliament. Jeremy Thorpe, Liberal MP for Devon North, wanted to know how it was that 'those responsible for transferring this man did not inform themselves or those responsible for his custody about his violent propensities'; Shadow Home Secretary William Whitelaw called for a review into the policy of transporting prisoners by taxi, and north-east MP Tom Swain, in whose constituency Pottery Cottage lay, questioned how Hughes had purloined the knife while incarcerated at Leicester Prison.[17]

Derbyshire's Assistant Chief Constable, Alfred Mitchell, made inquiries into the logistics of the police search. His report ran to thirty-two pages, deeming that 'there was intelligence and information which indicated that Hughes was making towards Preston in Lancashire and, therefore, a very reasonable assumption that he would do just this. The other main possibility was that he would seek shelter in Chesterfield and the appropriate action was taken for both of these circumstances. There was nothing to suggest that he had gone up hill in the direction of Eastmoor and when looking at the terrain between the abandoned car and Pottery Cottages, it appeared a most unlikely and difficult route for any person to take. Shelter and cover were more readily available in the westerly direction . . . It will be appreciated that much of what is contained in this report, the statements and documents is *sub judice* until after the Coroner's Inquest.'[18]

A further exploration was conducted at the instigation of Home Secretary Merlyn Rees, who requested an 'inquiry into the security arrangements at Leicester Prison, and for the escort of prisoners to courts, with particular reference to the escape of William Thomas Hughes on 12 January 1977'.[19] Gordon Fowler, Chief Inspector of the Prison Service, whose career began as a housemaster at Rochdale Borstal, thus compiled a fifty-seven-page report that was published on 10 March 1977. Based on copious documents and interviews with Leicester Prison staff, Fowler concluded that 'the primary failure in respect of the escape of Hughes concerned the searching procedures within the prison', where management and staff failed 'to coordinate or pursue with sufficient vigour the search for a boning knife which had been reported missing . . . standard searching procedures were not followed . . . and no records kept of any searches made by staff'.[20] Furthermore, 'information conveyed to the prison authorities from the police and other agencies when Hughes was first received was insufficient to identify him as a person prone to extreme violence or as a potentially dangerous psychopath'.[21] Regarding this last point, Fowler urged immediate discussions between chief police officers and senior members of the prison service, although he found that Hughes's 'demeanour and behaviour were not dissimilar to that of a large number of prisoners, and his subsequent actions were wholly untypical of his behaviour while serving his prison sentence'.[22] Fowler judged the frequency of remand prisoners' appearances in court, especially during the currency of a sentence, to be 'both expensive and hazardous to security'.[23] Suggestions for improvement followed, together with a grid showing the number of escapes by prisoners from escort vehicles in the six years preceding the Hughes case; in 1976 alone, fifty-six prisoners had bolted.

The appendices included a report by Leicester Prison's Senior Medical Officer, Dr Alex Sutherland. Although he had never met Hughes, he was asked to review his prison records in order to comment on 'any clinical features which might bear relation to the final dreadful series of offences which culminated in the death of Hughes'.[24] Access was denied to the autopsy reports, photographs and all other forensic evidence relating to the murders. Nevertheless, Sutherland was confident enough to state categorically that, 'even in hindsight, there is little if any psychiatric evidence which would indicate, even to experts in this field, that Hughes was to terminate his criminal career in such a horrific way – a way which appears outwardly to bear the hallmarks of a study in terror. In this respect, I am mindful of the case of another prisoner, a notorious rapist [Peter Samuel Cook, the so-called 'Cambridge Rapist'], who was a patient in my care in this establishment during the remand period. In his case, even though he had been in Broadmoor Hospital for a spell, this was not because of any deviant sexual proclivities on his part but because he was regarded as a psychopathic personality requiring and being susceptible to treatment. However, he could not be contained in an ordinary psychiatric hospital because he was prone to abscond. Consequently, his transfer to a Special Hospital became necessary. The fact remains that there was nothing in his past history which could be construed as likely to herald the enormity of the offences of which he was later found guilty.'[25]

Sutherland's memorandum ended: 'The case of Hughes bears similarities to the foregoing. He was a recidivist, his criminal career beginning as a juvenile. Offences of an acquisitive nature followed one upon the other with remorseless regularity. These occasionally involved the use of violence, notably against police officers, but in fifteen years' experience as a full-time Prison Medical Officer, I would have seen scores of lists of previous convictions not dissimilar to that of Hughes, formidable though it is . . . He was never regarded as suffering from any form of mental illness and his intelligence has been regarded by most as being in the low average range. There was never any question that he was subnormal within the meaning of the Mental Health Act . . . This man appears from the records to have been an inadequate, antisocial, unstable, irresponsible and unscrupulous individual.'[26]

The Home Secretary's public response to the Fowler Report was to guarantee that the seventeen recommendations aimed at reducing the risk of prisoners being able to leave prison with unauthorised articles in their possession would be implemented immediately; another eight related areas were to be put under further review. Rees himself was adamant that there had been 'errors of judgement' in the Hughes case but none of were 'grounds for considering disciplinary action; these were failures of the system rather than of particular individuals'.[27]

The inquiry received a huge amount of coverage in the press, who approached Gill for her response. Photographed while shopping in

Chesterfield, she replied: 'I am pleased that the inquiry has been held and I hope that as a result, similar tragedies may be prevented. People have been wonderfully kind, unbelievably so. I have had hundreds of nice letters from people all over the country.'[28]

But Derbyshire's Chief Constable, Walter Stansfield, was irked by one particular point made in Fowler's report. In a letter dated 26 April 1977 to the Derbyshire Police Committee, Stansfield insisted that his officers had categorically and without question provided HMP Leicester with ample warning about Hughes's psychopathic tendencies: 'In accordance with the guidance issued by the Home Office we notified the prison authorities in writing and by telephone on August 26, 1976, that in our opinion Hughes presented a special risk because he was likely to try to escape, he was of a violent nature and he had suicidal tendencies. Nothing further was required of the police at that stage and – I repeat that in this particular case – we had no additional information. Some of the reports in the media conveyed the impression that the written notification of special risk was sent by us to the wrong place. That is not so.'[29]

The inquest into the shooting at Rainow finally took place the following day, 27 April, in Chesterfield. Frank Pell (promoted to inspector), Alan Nicholls and Peter Howse (then a superintendent on attachment to the Home Office research branch) all gave evidence. Pell told the court that 'the shots were fired solely to save Mrs Moran', after which Coroner Michael Swanwick asked Nicholls if it had been necessary to shoot Hughes to save Gill Moran from a 'murderous attack'.[30] Nicholls replied firmly: 'That is correct, sir.'[31] Howse then described how he had negotiated with Hughes for almost an hour in the hope of making him realise 'the futility of the situation, make him give himself up and surrender Mrs Moran to me'.[32] He added: 'She would not have been alive today if we had not taken the course we did.'[33]

Pathologist Dr Alan Usher confirmed that Richard and Sarah Moran and Amy and Arthur Minton had each died from shock and hemorrhage caused by multiple stab wounds inflicted by William Hughes, who had died from gunshot wounds, one of which had cut through his aorta, the main artery from the heart.

Swanwick then addressed the all-male jury in what he felt to be 'the most horrible and tragic' inquest he had ever conducted, explaining that Gill Moran had not been called because 'she has already suffered enough'.[34] He singled out Howse as having displayed 'great presence of mind and gallantry', adding that 'it is well established that a person is justified in killing another one – not only a police officer but any citizen – in order to prevent a murderous crime'.[35] Finally, he directed the jury to find that in the case of the deaths of the four family members the 'proper verdict is murder'.[36]

Less than twenty minutes later, the jury returned unanimous verdicts of murder regarding the Mintons and Morans, and justifiable homicide in the case of their killer. Foreman of the jury Clifford Gladwin stated that he hoped their sympathy would help to sustain Mrs Moran, and that Howse might be considered for a commendation.

Afterwards, Detective Constable Nicholls declared that he had no regrets: 'If I were called out on the same type of incident I would feel just the same. I would try to go about it as calmly as possible. You have to, when lives are at stake and it is what we are trained to do.'[37]

As a result of the inquest, a death certificate was issued for William Thomas Hughes, 'occupation unknown, no fixed abode', showing his date and place of demise as 14 January 1977 in Rainow. Cause of death: 'Gunshot wound of Thoracic Aorta sustained when he was shot by police officers.

'JUSTIFIABLE HOMICIDE.'

Epilogue: Pottery Cottage for Sale

L ONG AND OFTEN endless shadows were cast over many lives by those three days in January 1977.

Leicester Prison warders Don Sprintall and Ken Simmonds expected the Criminal Injuries Compensation Board to help them cope with injuries that they attributed to 'faults in official procedures'.[1] Sprintall's neck would remain numb for the rest of his life and Simmonds suffered a permanent loss of feeling in his right hand; unable to face further escort duties in the region, he was transferred to work in HMP Brixton. In 1978, Simmonds was offered £943 to add to the £913 he had received under the industrial injuries scheme, while Sprintall was offered £1,226 to supplement his £677 payment. The former colleagues did not begrudge Gill Moran's £75,000 fee for the serialisation rights to her story, but felt 'resentful' that Jean Hughes was said to have received a 'substantial sum' for her memories and photographs, which later proved not to have been the case.[2] The Prison Officers' Association (POA) considered the proffered amounts derisory, pointing out that members of the IRA had received greater compensation.

In June 1979, the POA provided legal representation for the two men at the Criminal Injuries Compensation Board in London. Forensic photographs showing the horrific wounds each man had sustained were presented and as a result, Simmonds and Sprintall had their individual awards raised to £3,000. When Sprintall died in June 2012, his daughter Sharon (who had been twenty-one years old at the time of the attack) said that in his later years her father had 'liked telling the story because it was such a defining part of his life, and because it was part and parcel of the job, which he did for nearly thirty years . . . It was his fifteen minutes of fame – he was on television and in all the papers – and I'm really proud of how he came through it.'[3]

A different sort of financial compensation was made to Chief Superintendent Alfred Horobin, who successfully sued the *Daily Telegraph* over an article that claimed that while head of Derbyshire CID he had been 'in charge of the hunt for killer William Hughes, the conduct of which led to questions in Parliament and the press'.[4] The article implied that his transfer to uniform branch was connected to the problematic search, but Horobin demonstrated in court that his request to leave the CID was made long before 'the Hughes incident'.[5] He was awarded £4,000 in libel damages.

Chris McCarthy, the constable with size-eight shoes, was eventually reunited with his footwear, which had a single spot of blood on an inside heel. 'They were my best shoes,' he remembers with a hint of a smile, 'I had paid £25 for them from Ravel and was reimbursed for the full amount. I received a commendation for my part in the apprehension of Hughes and went on to serve forty years as a regular officer with the Derbyshire Police. I'll always remember that incident with Hughes as one of the most momentous of my service. Many accounts have been given since the event and most have been inaccurate, including claims that Cheshire Police officers were responsible for the shooting of Hughes. It wasn't true. Frank Pell and Alan Nicholls from the Derbyshire Constabulary shot him and I witnessed it.'[6]

Pell is currently enjoying his retirement, describing himself with characteristic modesty as 'a cricket buff and granddad who likes messing with computers'.[7] His fellow marksman retired in 1978, following thirty years in the force, and died in 2009; a plaque honouring Alan Nicholls is now on display at Derbyshire Police Headquarters in Ripley. His son Simon recalls that when his father arrived home that night after the shooting 'he said to my mum, "I've shot the bugger dead." But he just saw it as part of his job. He was an old-fashioned officer, he worked hard and got on with it.'[8]

After the inquest into the Rainow incident, Peter Howse received a call from Derbyshire's Assistant Chief Constable Alfred Mitchell, informing him that he had received a request from local magistrate, Brett Plastics director Francis Hall, asking if could arrange for Howse to meet Gill Moran as part of her recovery process. Howse agreed immediately. He worked at the Home Office in London during the week, but returned to Derbyshire every weekend. Mindful of the intense press scrutiny, Francis Hall drove Gill to the quiet surroundings of the Grouse & Claret pub in Rowsley, having ensured that no one else would be present, then chatted to the licensee at the bar while Gill and Howse talked for an hour.

'It was the first time we had met face to face,' Howse recalls. 'During my negotiations at the car in Rainow she had been sitting with her back to me and we were both whisked away from the scene after Hughes was shot. Nor had she been called to give evidence at the inquest. We made no mention of what had taken place that night, or at Pottery Cottage. We simply discussed how she was bearing up. The physical effects were obvious: she had lost a great deal of weight and chainsmoked throughout our meeting. Medicated and receiving some counselling, she was taking her own steps to get on with life, helped by relatives and friends. She said that she hoped to get back to work the following week and I encouraged her. Then we parted. I felt humbled by the experience. She had endured the most terrible losses and yet she was slowly but surely trying to put the pieces of her life back together.'[9]

Howse was awarded the Queen's Commendation for Brave Conduct in December 1977 for his actions at Rainow. In 1991, one year before his retirement from the police force as Deputy Chief Constable of Norfolk Constabulary, he received the Queen's Police Medal, whose recipients have performed acts of 'exceptional courage and skill at the cost of their lives, or exhibited conspicuous devotion to duty'.[10] He remembers the Chief Constable seeking him out at an awards ceremony one year after the murders: 'I asked him, "What would have happened if Gill Moran had been killed and Hughes had survived?" The Chief Constable said, "Ah! That would have been a different story." We both knew the line between failure and success was very thin indeed. I've been conscious of it ever since that night in Rainow.'[11]

Retired Scene of Crime photographer John Slater spent more time than anyone else in the presence of the victims at Pottery Cottage, an experience that left him profoundly affected. 'I still have nightmares about it,' he admits. 'They're always the same: it's the early hours of the morning and I'm going through the house alone with my camera and rolls of film, photographing everything. Then I reach the grandparents' bedroom in the annexe of Pottery Cottage and kneel down next to the body of ten-year-old

Sarah, who suddenly sits bolt upright and says, "But I'm *not* dead." Then I wake up in a cold sweat, my heart pounding. A psychologist would have a field day, but I think it all comes down to one thing: no one who worked on the case could understand why Billy Hughes had murdered Sarah Moran. Especially when he was himself the father of a little girl.'[12]

'Nicky loved her daddy and often visited him [in prison] with me,' Jean Hughes reminisced after her husband's shooting. 'Now she can't believe he's dead. She writes him letters on children's paper once or twice a day and posts them, telling him to come home quickly and she'll make him better with a bottle of medicine.'[13]

If Jean's life as Billy Hughes's wife had never been easy, it was no better when she became his widow. She remained in the house at Loftos Avenue, but was the only adult there: both her house-mates were in prison. Alan Hughes was serving an eighteen-month sentence in Haverigg Open Prison, Cumbria, for burglary, while his girlfriend, Alice Swan, was likewise incarcerated on an unrelated charge a short while after the murders at Pottery Cottage. Jean did her best to care for her closest friend's three children as well as her own daughters. As a result of trying to make ends meet, Jean appeared at Blackpool Magistrates' Court on 29 September 1977, charged with failing to notify the Department of Health and Social Security (DHSS) that she was working as a machinist while claiming supplementary benefit. She had obtained £52.69 more than she was entitled and the DHSS wanted compensation.

Prosecutor Bert Stillings declared that Jean was subject to suspended prison sentences totalling eighteen months, imposed the previous year for offences of theft and handling stolen goods. Yet he was not unsympathetic to her predicament, referring to the years she had spent as 'a battered wife' to Billy Hughes, and how since his death, she had been left to care for five children on a pittance.[14] This last sentiment was picked up by Jean's solicitor, Hugh Pond, who spoke of his disgust at the attitude of the DHSS, whom he said allowed 'other, important people in more privileged positions' to escape prosecution, adding, 'I don't wish to dwell too heavily on this but my client was given no opportunity to repay the money. Other people, particularly in Blackpool, appear to be given this chance.'[15]

The clerk to the magistrates interrupted, 'Do you mean that people who have committed offences in this town have been able to buy themselves out of being prosecuted?'[16]

Pond replied, 'I am not going so far as to say that but the DHSS appear to be choosy who they prosecute, particularly in Blackpool.'[17]

Jean's family physician, Dr Joseph Cox, gave evidence that Jean 'is in such a poor state of health that she should never have been prosecuted', expressing admiration for the quality of her care for five children on such a low income.[18] He told the court that the benefits to which she was entitled were miserable: 'I just don't see how anyone could do it in this day and age,' and concluded that the prosecution brought by the DHSS was 'a farce'.[19]

Solicitor Pond then revealed the truth behind the widespread misconception that Jean had received a fortune for the story of her marriage to a multiple murderer. He provided proof that she had only been paid three small sums: £15 from the *Daily Mirror* and £50 each from the *Daily Mail* and the *News of the World*. Finally, Detective Superintendent Arnold Sanders, head of Blackpool CID, spoke in Jean's favour, describing her as showing 'great consideration' to the children in her care, adding that he held her in the highest esteem for her efforts to 'improve the home conditions' without proper assistance from any individual or organisation.[20] The court hearing ended with the magistrate ordering Jean's immediate release and refusing the compensation claim by the DHSS.

As the years went on, Jean's efforts to protect Nichola from the reality of her father's death and what preceded it were severely undermined by others in the vicinity. Nichola remembers that 'the neighbours and the kids at school were nasty. They'd bang into me and say, "Your dad was a murderer." I stuck up for him and fought back. I'd throw the bricks back through their windows, so then they'd say, "Oh you're just like your dad – you're a psychopath." '[21] Jean confessed the truth when Nichola reached the age of fourteen, having discovered newspaper accounts of the case. 'Why didn't you tell me?' Nichola screamed, devastated to read about the murders, especially that of ten-year-old Sarah. 'I couldn't see my dad doing that because he never hurt me,' she recalls. 'Even though what he had done was wrong, at the end of the day he was my dad and I loved him to bits.'[22] She found it hard to forgive her mother for keeping it from her 'because he was my father and I felt I had the right to know'.[23]

At fifteen, Nichola left school to work in a café, her world seemingly falling apart. 'I was fighting with my mum,' she admits. 'I wasn't the normal Nicky, I was nasty. If Mum asked me to do something for her, I'd refuse. There were lots of arguments and she'd tell me, "You've got a temper just like your dad's." Everyone seemed to be sending me sort of crazy, and I'd think that maybe I was a psychopath. I wanted to get a gun and shoot the policeman who killed my dad. Maybe I'd snap like my dad had done. I used to go up to my bedroom and kick the door and bang my head against a wall to get the temper out of me. Eventually my mum said she was taking me to the doctors. "You'll end up like him," she said. "You need to see a doctor to sort your head out." '²⁴ The doctor suggested counselling, but Nichola became addicted to antidepressants.

Tormented by her daughter's pain, Jean began drinking heavily. She too grew dependent on prescription drugs, specifically carbamazepine, a mood stabiliser used to help manage bipolar disorder, alcohol withdrawal and to control seizures.

The constant desecration of the present by the past proved unendurable. On 13 May 1998, Jean took an overdose of paracetamol and carbamazepine in the bathroom of the house on Loftos Avenue, then tied a plastic bag over her head. By the time she was found, it was too late. Jean was fifty-two years old when she died. An inquest later returned a verdict of suicide.

Seven months later, on the evening of 11 December 1998, Nichola kissed her sleeping children goodbye and lay down on the same bathroom floor with a handful of pills, intending to die. 'I couldn't handle it any more,' she admits. 'I was depressed and my life was a mess. I wanted things to be like they used to be before my dad died. I wanted to be with them both, like a proper family.'²⁵ But Nichola was found in time. She was rushed to hospital, where she remained unconscious for two days. The shock of what she had so nearly achieved was enough to provide her with the necessary impetus to change her life for the sake of her children. On 7 March 1999, she moved out of 45 Loftos Avenue, weeping as she locked the door for the last time. 'I needed to make a fresh life because there were too many bad memories in the house,' she confirms. 'The place was sending me crazy. It was still upsetting, though, having to leave.'²⁶

Five months after her departure from Blackpool, Nichola reflected: 'I've got new friends. I don't feel as if I'm being blamed any more for what happened at Pottery Cottage. I'm no longer known as "mad Billy Hughes's daughter". The only thing the children know is that Nana's with Granddad Billy now. My five-year-old has started asking questions but I don't think it's fair to tell her at that age. Which was the same choice my mum faced. When is it ever the right age to tell a child something like that?'[27] The nightmares continued for a long time – 'about when he was shot, about the killings, the bodies on the floor' – but eventually Nichola learned to separate the man who committed the murders from the father she loved. She had no choice but to make that distinction, for the sake of her own sanity.

'Some days, I get up with so much anger inside me,' Gill Moran admitted a few weeks after the funeral of her parents, husband and daughter. '[But] I think, I won't be beaten. I won't. I know Mum, Dad, Richard and Sarah are watching me, willing me somehow to be able to go on. I believed in God. I *believe* in God, but why me, why leave me, why take Sarah? I always used to say, "I don't know how I can stand it when anything happens to Mum and Dad", but they had a life. Sarah was growing into such a lovely girl, and Richard – it was all happening for him. It was right at the beginning of the good times for Richard. He tried so hard for us and, oh, I did want Richard to be proud of me.'[28]

Gill got through the coming months day by day, sometimes hour by hour, or minute by minute: 'Some days I just want to go upstairs and scream and scream and pull my hair. I've so much hate in my heart for Hughes. I'd never hated anybody before in all my life. Thank God, *thank God*, he's dead. If he'd been alive he'd haunt me forever.'[29] She felt guilty at having to force the memories at bay occasionally: 'Some days I want to think about Richard and Sarah, but I can't. I daren't. If I let them come into my mind, I'd go mad. I have to black them out sometimes just so I can get through the day.'[30]

Gill returned to her secretarial job under the paternal eye of her boss, John Roberts, who told her there was no rush, but understood that work was another cog in the slowly turning wheel of her recovery. She thought about finding a home of her own, even though the Browetts pleaded with her to stay until she was certain the time was right. The income from the newspaper serialisation, coupled with her own money and the proceeds of Richard's will, amounted to more than enough to buy her a lovely home, but there was always one consideration: she already owned a house.

Pottery Cottage.

The *Morning Telegraph* reported in August 1977 that her home was about to go on the market. 'I don't know what I'm going to do about the cottage yet,' she insisted. 'I don't want to comment.'[31] In October that year, the *Derbyshire Times* published the story from a more disturbing angle: 'Reports that a movie company is to use Pottery Cottage to film the horrific saga of the Billy Hughes killings have been denied by Mrs Gill Moran's solicitor. Mounting speculation over the fate of Pottery Cottage – which has lain empty since the killings ten months ago – has begun to spill over in to reports in the press that a film company is to buy the cottage and begin shooting the final chapters of the Hughes story. But the Chesterfield solicitor has written off the rumour as "gossip".'[32] With exaggerated patience, Gill's solicitor declared: 'The situation is just the same as it has always been. The house has not been sold and Mrs Moran has no intention of selling it to a film company. I have had several calls from the press inquiring about this, but it is totally untrue. I've even had it put to me that she's playing the starring role in the film.'[33] That last fabrication aside, it was a matter of record that a YTV film about the murders was in development with a script written by Colin Shindler. Production stuttered over a number of years, until it was finally shelved in January 1983, partly due to cutbacks compensating YTV's advertising losses on the new television network, Channel 4.

In November 1977, local and national newspapers were able to announce truthfully that Pottery Cottage was for sale with Sheffield-based estate agents Henry Spencer & Sons, renamed and priced at £33,000 freehold. It seemed unnecessary to state the obvious, but nonetheless, newspapers informed their readers that anyone wishing to view the property 'will not be shown around by Mrs Gill Moran, the sole survivor of the murders'.[34] While speculation mounted as to whether the cottage would find a buyer or not, the press refused to let Gill settle back into obscurity. Consequently, her habitually placid and soft-natured black Labrador, eight-year-old William, became headline news in June 1978 when he attacked a poodle, which later died. Friends had been walking William on Gill's behalf and were so keen to keep his owner's identity secret that it caused the injured animal's owner greater distress, leading to a court case. Gill's solicitor accused the press of blowing the incident out of all proportion, describing her as 'very much upset by the publicity the incident received'.[35] He told the court that Gill felt 'deep affection' for William, who was 'very dear' to her because of his links with the past.[36] Now living in a house in Chesterfield, Gill pledged to keep William within the grounds of her home, which had high fencing around the garden.

Unbeknown to the media, Pottery Cottage had sold; its new owners were a young married couple, Richard and Carol Coggins, and their two daughters. Seeking a house in a rural location within easy commuting distance of Sheffield, where Richard had recently begun working for a steel company, they short-listed five properties, one of which was Pottery Cottage. The estate agents were candid about its history before showing them around. 'We were a bit apprehensive when we set off,' Carol admitted shortly after moving into the house. 'But we're not superstitious and we didn't have any strange feelings when we walked around it. But we wouldn't have bought it if Billy Hughes had been in prison. I don't think we could have lived here knowing that he might come back.'[37]

The interval between their offer being accepted and the legal formalities reaching completion gave the couple a chance to change their minds, but they were convinced that it would be 'a super place to bring up our children' and in September 1978, they took possession of the keys to the property.[38] Ironically, given the many reports about Pottery Cottage's 'isolation' during the period when Hughes was at large, the only drawback as far as the new owners were concerned was 'the level of traffic that pounds past the front door on the main route to Manchester from Chesterfield'.[39] Carol Coggins accepted that many people would shudder at the thought of living in a house with such a horrifying past but as far as she and her husband were concerned it was 'just walls and a roof' and 'what had happened involved another family . . . There's nothing spooky about the place.'[40] The estate agents confirmed that they had 'always believed there would be a buyer' and ventured confidently that, 'if the house is offered for sale again, it will be much less of a problem to sell'.[41]

The surrender of Pottery Cottage marked a turning point for Gill. Ann Goldthorpe recalls: 'We saw her only a few times after that. She invited us to a party at her place in Chesterfield and we were surprised, but very pleased, to discover that she was in a new relationship.'[42] Gill's new partner was thirty-four-year-old James Mulqueen; his mother was Richard Moran's foster sister Ann. He and Gill met again at a family reunion when she was considering her future in Derbyshire. 'I had thought of leaving the area after the tragedy,' she recalls. 'I was sick of all the gossip and people pointing at me in the street. They were saying wicked things about me, and I nearly left to start again where no one knew me. I have some good friends here. They know the truth – and that's all that really matters.'[43] Jim helped make it possible for her to stay; he sold his shopfitting business in Tottenham, where he had been living after his divorce from the mother of his two sons, and moved to Derbyshire to be with Gill. With the proceeds of her previous home six miles away, they bought Alden Cottage, a country idyll on Sydnope Hill, in the lovely village of Two Dales.

The media's discovery of their relationship resulted in several disparaging and scurrilous front-page articles that shunted the Jeremy Thorpe affair into a side column. While Jim responded to requests for interview with the plea: 'All we want is to be left in peace, but we are being hounded', Gill was unwilling to be drawn on her private life, telling journalists: 'It's a bit early yet to talk about marriage. But I'm picking up the pieces of my life again. You could say I have found a new happiness.'[44] The couple did marry, on 9 December 1978. The following June, Gill gave birth at Chesterfield Hospital to their daughter, whom they named Jayne Sarah, in memory of the half-sister she would never meet.

With the new life she had battled for continuing apace, Gill gradually lost touch with most of those whom she had socialised with during her first marriage. 'We didn't see Gill again after the party in Chesterfield,' Ann Goldthorpe reflects. 'There were Christmas cards for a short while and then that stopped too. We didn't know she had moved away. It was as if she had to cut almost all ties with the past in order to move forward. But we understood that, all of us. She stayed in touch with the Browetts, but I can't think of anyone else.'[45] Ann's husband Paul confirms, 'What happened at Pottery Cottage had a lasting effect on us, too – for years I kept a machete by the bed. The heart had gone out of the business, too. In 1980, Richard's friend Billy Martin bought Brett Plastics. We left Holymoorside for Sheffield after that and began our new life.'[46]

Following the sale of his shares to Billy Martin, David Brown went into property, then set up a chain of DIY shops before retraining to become a lawyer and establishing Wosskow Brown Solicitors, run today by his son and grandson. Twelve years after the murders at Pottery Cottage, a gunman broke into the Browns' home and took the couple hostage in a case of mistaken identity. They managed to escape unharmed. 'We were lucky,' David confirms. 'Very lucky indeed. But it just demonstrates again that no matter what happens, you have to keep moving forwards. Don't go under – stay positive and you can come through almost anything.'[47]

Gill was living proof of that adage, but in February 1988, her life once more became tabloid fodder. The *Daily Express* reported on 'a new nightmare' for 'tragic Gill Mulqueen [whose] family were slaughtered in the notorious Pottery Cottage massacre'.[48] Jim Mulqueen was due to be sentenced at Derby Crown Court, having 'cracked under the pressure' of dealing with the persistent, fabricated gossip about Gill's life immediately before and during Billy Hughes's escape.[49]

Jim's court appearance related to events that took place in January 1987, when he was barred from the Red Lion pub in Stone Edge by licensee John Gibling. Jim was then said to have threatened Mr Gibling in letters, one containing the body of a dead mouse, and in telephone calls, during which the Giblings heard gunshots that they suspected were tape recorded. On 31 July 1987, Jim arrived in an inebriated state at the Three Stags in Darley Bridge and pressed a local man, Timothy Bower, to join him for a drink. Bower refused, advising him to go home, where-upon Jim replied, 'If you want war, you've got one.'[50] He then drove home and loaded a pump-action shotgun – one of six weap-ons his solicitor later said Gill kept for security – and fired one round in the air, then waited for Bower to drive home past the cottage. Witnessing her husband's actions, Gill telephoned the Three Stags pub to warn Bower to travel home by a different route. The police were called and three officers arrived at Alden Cottage, where Jim pointed the gun at them but later threw it to the ground.

Following his arrest, Jim was held in custody for six months, a consequence his solicitor described as almost unendurable for the devoted couple: 'Living alone at night without her husband's company and comfort, the nightmare has been relived on many occasions. He has lived with her nightmare over the years. He has lived with the pressure of seeking to do everything to protect his wife and making sure everything goes right for their young daugh-ter. He has succumbed to pressure and taken to drink. He has shared her tears.'[51]

A jury convicted Jim Mulqueen of the firearms offence in December 1987, but an order was made preventing any publicity about the proceedings until after his trial on the charge of threat-ening to kill Gibling. As a result of the court hearing, Gill had been forced to tell their eight-year-old daughter about the events of January 1977, 'something she had hoped to put off until the child was older'.[52] Admitting the offence against Gibling, in March 1988 Jim was jailed for two years. The judge told him, 'I realise the distress the sentence will cause to your wife and also because you come before this court as a man of good character. But it is necessary to demonstrate to those who carry a loaded shotgun that this is something which the public will not tolerate because of the risks which will follow.'[53] The three police officers who confronted Jim at Alden Cottage were commended by the judge for their courage. Gill did not speak to reporters after the case and left the court by a back door.

It was to be her penultimate appearance in the press. After Jim's release from prison, the family of three emigrated to a small village in southern Ireland, where Jayne enjoyed a successful career as a jockey for several years. When an article appeared about the Pottery Cottage murders in 1999, Gill had only one statement for the journalist who called upon her, but it spoke volumes nonetheless: 'I've put everything behind me and my life is very happy.'[54]

Twenty years later, that remains so.

Acknowledgements

As co-authors, we would like to thank all those former Derbyshire CID officers who expanded upon the recorded facts of the case; their recollections proved invaluable. We are particularly grateful to Chris McCarthy, John Field, Ann Wain, Sean Murphy and Tony Pierce; also to Roger Bowler for his intuitive skills in helping to trace important figures including John Slater, who took the scene of crime photographs at Pottery Cottage and subsequent post-mortem examinations. John Keen, the inspector in charge of Force Control during the search and latter stages of the incident, was another valuable source of information, as was Fran Muldoon in his role as exhibits officer.

Detective Chief Inspector Sydney Thompson, who carried out the interviews with Gill Moran in the immediate aftermath of the murders, and Detective Sergeant Bill Miller, who was one of the first to enter Pottery Cottage on the night of 14 January 1977, are sadly no longer with us, but are remembered with gratitude. Two members of the redoubtable Firearms Team from Buxton, Alan

Nicholls and Peter Burgess, have also passed away in recent years, and we would like to remember them here. The swift actions of both men, together with those of their colleagues Frank Pell and Derek Beale, ensured that the life of the remaining hostage was saved. We thank all four men and extend further gratitude to those members of Cheshire Police who played an invaluable part in the pursuit and eventual roadblock in Rainow.

The current Chief Constable of Derbyshire, Peter Goodman, very kindly offered his full support to our research and writing the book, which we hope serves as testimony to the compassion and professionalism of all those officers and civilian staff involved in the case. We are also grateful to Simon Gough, Archives Officer at the Parliamentary Archives in the House of Lords, for his assistance in locating and obtaining a copy of Gordon Fowler's report on the escape of William Hughes; to Alex Habgood and Lara Reid of the Media Archive for Central England for television sources relating to the same, and to all those working at the National Archives, Chesterfield Library, Preston Harris Library and Blackpool Central Library who helped us in tracing files and original newspaper accounts relating to the case.

Our thanks, too, to Robert Smith, the literary agent who has provided us with such support throughout the research and writing of this book. We count ourselves fortunate indeed to be represented by him, and thanks, too, to Keith Skinner, for providing that initial introduction.

We are extremely grateful to the four friends of Richard and Gill Moran who talked to us in depth about their memories, some of which were extremely painful to recall. David and Glynis Brown, together with Paul and Ann Goldthorpe, spoke eloquently of and with deep affection for the Mintons and Morans. We owe a special debt of gratitude to Linda Browett for her assistance in contacting Gill Mulqueen (formerly Moran) and above all, to Gill herself, for holding no objections to our writing the book; we would not have proceeded otherwise, regardless of how necessary we felt it was to have a full and accurate account of the case. With that in mind, we hope above all else that the book stands as a memorial to those whose lives were so cruelly lost: Richard Moran, Arthur Minton, Amy Minton and Sarah Moran, whose future, especially, held such promise.

Finally, we would like to add our own individual acknowledgements.

Peter Howse: I am grateful to my family for supporting me in everything I have done over the years. This book is dedicated to them: my wife Beryl, son David and daughter Julia, our grand-children Leo and Aife Howse and Max and Harry Newby. I would like to give a special mention to our great-grandchildren, Lara and Eliza Newby, who bring great joy to everyone's lives.

Carol Ann Lee: the account of the Pottery Cottage murders as serialised in the *Daily Mail* during February 1977 was the first 'true crime' case I ever read. I was just eight years old at the time, and I cannot overstate what a deep impression it made upon me; I remember especially the detail of Billy Hughes helping Sarah Moran to thread her needle shortly after he had entered Pottery Cottage. In 2015, I began researching the case with a view to writing a book but abandoned it when I was unable to trace Gill Mulqueen. Two years later, on the fortieth anniversary of the murders, I read an interview with Peter Howse and contacted him immediately to ask if I could help in any way with the book he was reportedly writing. *The Pottery Cottage Murders* is the result, and so my first heartfelt thanks must go to Pete, for trusting me with the story we both so wanted to tell.

I also want to thank my son River, my mother Doreen Lee and my brother and sister-in-law John and Sally Lee, for their support as always. It means everything to me, along with the friendships of some very special women: Tina Barrott, Sarah Barnes, Kirsty Koch, Ali Dunnell, Tricia Room, Angela Handley, Jo Jacques and Janet Walker.

Finally, I would like to remember my father, who is no longer with us but who fostered my desire to be a writer from a very early age. I remember him writing a short story based on the Pottery Cottage case a few months after it occurred, called 'X Marks the Spot'. I dedicate this book to him, Raymond Lee, with love.

Endnotes

Prologue

1 *Derbyshire Times*, 'Pottery Cottage for Sale', 4 November 1977.
2 *Star*, 'What Will Happen to the Cottage of Death?', 30 September 1977.
3 *Daily Mail*, 'Haunted by a House of Real Horrors', Lynda Lee-Potter, 26 November 2003.

Chapter 1

1 Charles Dickens, *Hard Times* (London: Penguin Classics, 2003). Preston acquired city status in 2002.
2 *New York Daily Tribune*, 'The Troubles at Preston', Karl Marx, 31 March 1854.
3 *Daily Express*, 'He's Left Me Nothing', John Burns, Peggie Robinson, Paul Berra and Frank Welsby, 7 January 1977.
4 Ibid.
5 HM Chief of the Prison Service, *Report of an Inquiry by the Chief Inspector into the Security at HM Prison Leicester, and the Arrangements for Conducting Prisoners to Court (Escape of William Thomas Hughes on*

12 January 1977) (London: HMSO, 1977), Appendix G: William Thomas Hughes – History as Known to the Prison Authorities. Unless otherwise stated, details of his criminal offences are taken from this source.

6 *Lancashire Evening Post*, 'Boy (15) Was Mad, So Smashed Windows', 28 December 1961. Hughes's first accomplice was given a conditional discharge on payment of costs, and the second was put on probation for twelve months.

7 *Daily Express*, 'He's Left Me Nothing'.

8 Michael Wolff, *Prison: The Prison System in Britain, How it Works, and What Life is Like in Prisons, Borstals and Other Penal Institutions* (London: Eyre & Spottiswoode, 1967), p. 114.

9 Gloria K. Laycock, *Absconding from Borstals: Home Office Research Study No. 41* (London: HMSO, 1977), p. 3. Approved schools were merged into a system of community homes as a result of the Children and Young Persons Act 1969.

10 Criminal record of William Thomas Hughes, CRO 37921/61.

11 Michael Wolff, *Prison*, p. 64.

12 HM Chief of the Prison Service, *Report of an Inquiry by the Chief Inspector*.

13 Ibid.

14 Sports writer Frank O'Malley, online quote.

15 HM Chief of the Prison Service, *Report of an Inquiry by the Chief Inspector*.

16 Michael Wolff, *Prison*, p. 95.

17 CRO 37921/61.

18 HM Chief of the Prison Service, *Report of an Inquiry by the Chief Inspector*.

19 Ibid.

20 Ibid.

21 Ibid.

22 'He lived off . . .' *Daily Express*, 'He's Left Me Nothing'; 'He never did . . .' *Daily Mirror*, 'New Ordeal for Wife who Survived', Stanley Vaughan and Harry King, 19 January 1977.

23 *Daily Mirror*, 'New Ordeal for Wife who Survived'.

Chapter 2

1 HM Chief of the Prison Service, *Report of an Inquiry by the Chief Inspector into the Security at HM Prison Leicester, and the Arrangements for Conducting Prisoners to Court (Escape of William Thomas Hughes on 12 January 1977)* (London: HMSO, 1977).

2 Ibid.

3 Ibid.

4 Ibid.

5 Ibid.

6 Ibid.

7 *Lancashire Evening Post*, 'He Butts PC After "Surrender"', 28 January 1969.

8 Ibid.

9 *Lancashire Evening Post*, 'Escaper Jailed on Drink Charge', 6 August 1969.

10 HM Chief of the Prison Service, *Report of an Inquiry by the Chief Inspector*.

11 Ibid.

12 Ibid.

13 Ibid.

14 Ibid.

15 *Daily Mirror*, 'New Ordeal for Wife who Survived', Stanley Vaughan and Harry King, 19 January 1977.

16 *Derbyshire Times*, 'Hughes' Wife Led Life of Terror', 21 January 1977. The date when Jean met Billy Hughes is wrongly given as 1972.

17 *Daily Mail*, 'The Murders at Pottery Cottage', Day Two, 15 February 1977.

18 *Derbyshire Times*, 'Hughes' Wife Led Life of Terror'.

19 *Lancashire Evening Post*, 'My Violent Marriage to Mad, Bullying Billy', 17 January 1977.

20 Criminal record of William Thomas Hughes, CRO 37921/61.

21 *Lancashire Evening Post*, 'Man Has Sentence Suspended', 8 July 1972.

22 *Lancashire Evening Post*, 'My Violent Marriage to Mad, Bullying Billy'.

23 Dr Joseph Cox, witness statement, 17 January 1977.

24 *Lancashire Evening Post*, 'Man Has Sentence Suspended'.

25 *Derbyshire Times*, 'Hughes' Wife Led Life of Terror'.

26 Ibid.

27 Ibid.

28 *Sunday Mirror*, 'Baby Drama of the Knife Maniac', 23 January 1977.

29 Ibid.

30 *Derbyshire Times*, 'I Kicked Billy in Head But He Bounced Back Up', 21 January 1977. All Bob Ashworth quotes derive from this source.

31 *Lancashire Evening Post*, 'Jail Chiefs Blamed in Massacre Sequel', 10 March 1977.

32 Ibid.

33 Dr Joseph Cox, witness statement, 17 January 1977.

34 HM Chief of the Prison Service, *Report of an Inquiry by the Chief Inspector*.

35 *West Lancashire Evening Gazette*, 'Five Policemen Injured', 13 November 1972.

36 *Lancashire Evening News*, '"Violent" Assault on Policemen', 12 November 1972.

37 *West Lancashire Evening Gazette*, 'Resort's Public Enemy No.1', 17 January 1977.

38 *Daily Mail*, 'The Murders at Pottery Cottage', Day Two.

Chapter 3

1 *Derbyshire Times*, 'Hughes' Wife Led Life of Terror', 21 January 1977.

2 'I thought ...' *News of the World*, 'Our Lives with the Massacre Monster', Keith Beaby, 16 January 1977; 'I paid ...' *Derbyshire Times*, 'Hughes' Wife Led Life of Terror'.

3 *Derbyshire Times*, 'Hughes' Wife Led Life of Terror'.

4 *Daily Express*, 'He's Left Me Nothing', John Burns, Peggie Robinson, Paul Berra and Frank Welsby, 7 January 1977.

5 HM Chief of the Prison Service, *Report of an Inquiry by the Chief Inspector into the Security at HM Prison Leicester, and the Arrangements for Conducting Prisoners to Court (Escape of William Thomas Hughes on 12 January 1977)* (London: HMSO, 1977).

6 Ibid.

7 Ibid.

8 *Daily Mail*, 'The Savage Murderer with an Artist's Gentle Touch', 17 January 1977.

9 Ibid.

10 Ibid.

11 Ibid.

12 Ibid.

13 Ibid.

14 *Daily Mail*, 'The Murders at Pottery Cottage', Day Two, 15 February 1977.

15 *Derbyshire Times*, 'Hughes' Wife Led Life of Terror'.

16 *Derbyshire Times*, 'He was Like a Son to Me', 21 January 1977. All quotes from Margaret Blatch derive from this source.

17 *Derbyshire Times*, 'Hughes' Wife Led Life of Terror'.

18 Ibid.

19 Ibid.

20 Jean Hughes, witness statement, 15 January 1977.

21 *Daily Express*, 'He's Left Me Nothing'.

22 *Derbyshire Times*, 'My Ten Months with the Mad Knifeman', 21 January 1977.

23 Ibid.

24 *Morning Telegraph*, 'The Monster Who Refused to be Shackled', January 1977.

25 *Lancashire Evening Post*, 'My Violent Marriage to Mad, Bullying Billy', 17 January 1977.

26 *Daily Mail*, 'The Pottery Cottage Murders', 28 August 1999.

27 Ibid.

28 *Derbyshire Times*, 'I Kicked Billy in Head But He Bounced Back Up', 21 January 1977.

29 *Sunday Mirror*, 'Baby Drama of the Knife Maniac', 23 January 1977.

30 Ibid.

31 *Derbyshire Times*, 'Hughes' Wife Led Life of Terror'.

32 *Sunday Mirror*, 'Baby Drama of the Knife Maniac'.

33 *Morning Telegraph*, 'The Monster Who Refused to be Shackled'.

34 Ibid.

35 *Morning Telegraph*, 'Jekyll and Hyde Mass Murderer', 17 January 1977.

36 Ibid.

37 Teresa O'Doherty, televised interview, 21 January 1977, for ATV.

38 *Derbyshire Times*, 'My Ten Months with the Mad Knifeman'.

39 Criminal record of William Thomas Hughes, CRO 37921/61.

40 Chris McCarthy, Personal Account, August 2017.

41 *Derbyshire Times*, 'Massive Hunt for Vicious Rapist', 27 August 1976.

42 *Morning Telegraph*, 'Jekyll and Hyde Mass Murderer'.

43 Ibid.

44 *Derbyshire Times*, 'Massive Hunt for Vicious Rapist'.

45 John Field, interview with authors, Chesterfield, 2017.

46 Ann Wain, interview with authors, Chesterfield, 2017.

47 CRO 37921/61.

48 John Slater, interview with authors, Chesterfield, 2017.

Chapter 4

1 HM Chief of the Prison Service, *Report of an Inquiry by the Chief Inspector into the Security at HM Prison Leicester, and the Arrangements for Conducting Prisoners to Court (Escape of William Thomas Hughes on 12 January 1977)* (London: HMSO, 1977). Unless otherwise specified, all quotes within this chapter are taken from the same source.

2 *Morning Telegraph*, 'The Monster Who Refused to be Shackled', January 1977.

3 Criminal record of William Thomas Hughes, CRO 37921/61.

4 *Guardian*, 'Jail Protest Puts Extra Burden on Police', Clive Borrell, 19 January 1977.

5 *Morning Telegraph*, 'Killer Delayed Court Date', 19 January 1977.

Chapter 5

1 *Daily Mirror*, 'We Were Kept in the Dark', Frank Palmer, 17 January 1977.

2 Donald Sprintall, witness statement, 13 January 1977.

3 *Daily Mail*, 'The Murders at Pottery Cottage', Day Three, 16 February 1977.

4 Donald Sprintall, televised interview, 17 January 1977, for ATV.

5 HM Chief of the Prison Service, *Report of an Inquiry by the Chief*

Inspector into the Security at HM Prison Leicester, and the Arrangements for Conducting Prisoners to Court (Escape of William Thomas Hughes on 12 January 1977) (London: HMSO, 1977).

6 Ibid.

7 Ibid.

8 David Reynolds, witness statement, 12 January 1977.

9 Ibid.

10 Kenneth Simmonds, witness statement, 12 January 1977.

11 David Reynolds, witness statement, 12 January 1977.

12 Donald Sprintall, witness statement, 13 January 1977.

13 Ibid.

14 *Derbyshire Times*, 'Dangerous Hijacker Still Free Despite Moorland Hunt: Hostage Fear Among Police Theories', 14 January 1977.

15 Kenneth Simmonds, witness statement, 12 January 1977.

16 Ibid.

17 HM Chief of the Prison Service, *Report of an Inquiry by the Chief Inspector*.

18 Donald Sprintall, witness statement, 13 January 1977.

19 Ibid.

20 David Reynolds, witness statement, 12 January 1977.

21 Ibid.

22 Ibid.

23 Donald Sprintall, witness statement, 13 January 1977.

24 Kenneth Simmonds, witness statement, 12 January 1977.

25 David Reynolds, witness statement, 12 January 1977.

26 Ibid.

27 Mark Fisher, witness statement, 12 January 1977.

28 Edward Miles, witness statement, 13 January 1977.

29 Derbyshire Constabulary, *Escape of William Thomas Hughes (Deceased) from Prison Officers: General Report of Police Search*, Alfred Mitchell, Assistant Chief Constable, 14 February 1977.

30 HM Chief of the Prison Service, *Report of an Inquiry by the Chief Inspector*.

31 Ibid.

32 Peter Howse, author reflections, 2019.

33 Ibid.

34 Derbyshire Constabulary, *Escape of William Thomas Hughes (Deceased) from Prison Officers: General Report of Police Search.*

35 Peter Howse, author reflections, 2019.

36 Ibid.

37 Ibid.

38 Ibid.

39 Ibid.

40 *Lancashire Evening Post*, 'Knifeman Prisoner Hijacks Taxi', 12 January 1977.

41 *West Lancashire Evening Gazette*, 'Blackpool Danger Alert for Fugitive', 12 January 1977.

42 *Daily Mail*, 'The Pottery Cottage Murders', 28 August 1999.

43 *Lancashire Evening Post*, 'My Violent Marriage to Mad, Bullying Billy', 17 January 1977.

44 Peter Howse, author reflections, 2019.

45 Ibid.

Chapter 6

1 Detective Sergeant William Miller recorded in his witness statement of 15 January 1977 that according to his calculations, the shortest possible route between the crash point on Beeley Moor and Pottery Cottage was exactly four miles. The account of Hughes's journey on foot is based on the one he gave Amy Minton, who passed it on to her daughter Gill.

2 *Daily Mail*, 'The Murders at Pottery Cottage', Day One, 14 February 1977. Unless otherwise specified, all quotes in this chapter are taken from Gill Moran's witness statement, dated 15/16 January 1977, and the serialisation of her story in the *Daily Mail*.

3 *Derbyshire Times*, 'Terror House Survivor a Woman of Courage', 21 January 1977.

4 Joyce Newman, witness statement, 14 January 1977.

5 *Derbyshire Times*, 'Terror House Survivor a Woman of Courage'.

6 David Brown, interview with authors, Chesterfield, October 2018.

7 Ann and Paul Goldthorpe, interview with authors, Sheffield, October 2018.

8 Ibid.
9 Ibid.
10 *Daily Mail*, 'The Murders at Pottery Cottage', Day One.

Chapter 7

1 *Daily Mail*, 'The Murders at Pottery Cottage', Day One, 14 February 1977. Unless otherwise specified, all quotes in this chapter are taken from Gill Moran's witness statement, dated 15/16 January 1977, and the serialisation of her story in the *Daily Mail*.
2 Ann and Paul Goldthorpe, author interview, Sheffield, October 2018.
3 Ibid.

Chapter 8

1 *Daily Mail*, 'The Murders at Pottery Cottage', Day Three, 16 February 1977. Unless otherwise specified, all quotes in this chapter are taken from Gill Moran's witness statement, dated 15/16 January 1977, and the serialisation of her story in the *Daily Mail*.
2 *Derbyshire Times*, 'Terror House Survivor a Woman of Courage', 21 January 1977.
3 Joyce Newman, witness statement, 14 January 1977.
4 Alan Buckley, witness statement, 17 January 1977.
5 Ibid.
6 Ibid.
7 Len Newman, witness statement, 15 January 1977.

Chapter 9

1 Derbyshire Constabulary, *Escape of William Thomas Hughes (Deceased) from Prison Officers: General Report of Police Search*, Alfred Mitchell, Assistant Chief Constable, 14 February 1977.
2 Ibid.
3 Peter Howse, author reflections, 2019.
4 Ibid.
5 Ibid.
6 Gillian Moran, witness statement, 15/16 January 1977. Unless

otherwise specified, all quotes in this chapter are taken from Gill Moran's witness statement, dated 15/16 January 1977, and the serialisation of her story in the *Daily Mail*.

7   Ernest Jones, witness statement, 17 January 1977.

8   *Derbyshire Times*, 'Couple's Silence Failed to Prevent Slaughter', Alex Leys, Tony Whiting and Barrie Farnsworth, 21 January 1977.

9   Robert Coles, witness statement, 17 January 1977.

10 Ibid.

11 Ann Burnage, witness statement, 15 January 1977.

12 Margaret Goodall, witness statement, 16 January 1977.

13 *Daily Mail*, 'The Murders at Pottery Cottage', Day Four, 17 February 1977.

14 David Brown, interview with authors, Chesterfield, 2018.

15 Susan Silkstone, witness statement, 15 January 1977.

16 *Derbyshire Times*, 'Dangerous Hijacker Still Free Despite Moorland Hunt: Hostage Fear Among Police Theories', 14 January 1977.

17 Keith Bradshaw, witness statement, 15 January 1977.

Chapter 10

1   Alfred Horobin, televised interview, 13 January 1977, for ATV.

2   *West Lancashire Evening Gazette*, 'Fugitive Aiming for Resort', 13 January 1977.

3   Gillian Moran, witness statement, 15/16 January 1977. Unless otherwise specified, all quotes in this chapter are taken from Gill Moran's witness statement, dated 15/16 January 1977, and the serialisation of her story in the *Daily Mail*.

4   Joyce Newman, witness statement, 14 January 1977.

5   *Daily Mail*, 'The Murders at Pottery Cottage', Day Five, 18 February 1977.

Chapter 11

1   Joyce Newman, witness statement, 14 January 1977.

2   *Daily Mail*, 'The Murders at Pottery Cottage', Day Six, 19 February 1977. Unless otherwise specified, all quotes in this chapter are taken from Gill Moran's witness statement, dated 15/16 January 1977, and the serialisation of her story in the *Daily Mail*.

3 Ellen Parsons, witness statement, 17 January 1977.

4 Peter Howse, author reflections, 2019.

5 John Grosvenor, witness statement, 15 January 1977.

6 Phillip Bagshaw, witness statement, 15 January 1977.

Chapter 12

1 Gillian Moran, witness statement, 15/16 January 1977. Unless otherwise specified, all quotes in this chapter are taken from Gill Moran's
witness statement, dated 15/16 January 1977, and the serialisation of
her story in the *Daily Mail*.

2 *Daily Mail*, 'The Murders at Pottery Cottage', Day Seven, 21 February
1977.

3 Joyce Newman, witness statement, 14 January 1977.

4 Ibid.

5 *Daily Mail*, 'The Murders at Pottery Cottage', Day Seven.

6 Len Newman, witness statement, 15 January 1977.

7 Ibid.

8 ibid.

9 Ibid.

10 Ibid.

11 Ibid.

12 Ibid.

13 Ibid.

14 Joyce Newman, witness statement, 14 January 1977.

15 Len Newman, witness statement, 15 January 1977.

16 Ibid.

17 Ibid.

18 Ibid.

19 Gillian Moran, witness statement, 15/16 January 1977.

20 Madge Frost, witness statement, 14 January 1977.

21 Ibid.

22 Ibid.

23 Ibid.

24 Ibid.

25 Ibid.

26 Ronald Frost, witness statement, 15 January 1977.

27 Ibid.

28 Ibid.

29 Ibid.

30 Ibid.

31 Ibid.

32 Ibid.

33 Ibid.

Chapter 13

1 *Derbyshire Times*, 'Knifeman Kept Family Apart', 21 January 1977.

2 Ibid.

3 Charles Smart, witness statement, 16 January 1977.

4 Derbyshire Constabulary, *Escape of William Thomas Hughes (Deceased) from Prison Officers: General Report of Police Search*, Alfred Mitchell, Assistant Chief Constable, 14 February 1977.

5 Madge Frost, witness statement, 14 January 1977.

6 Ibid.

7 Jeffrey Edwards, witness statement, 15 January 1977.

8 Ibid.

9 Ibid.

10 Ibid.

11 Detective Constable Fran Muldoon, witness statement, 24 January 1977.

12 Detective Sergeant William Miller, witness statement, 15 January 1977.

13 Ibid.

14 Chris McCarthy, Personal Account, August 2017.

15 Ibid.

16 Gillian Moran, witness statement, 15/16 January 1977. Unless otherwise specified, all quotes in this chapter are taken from Gill Moran's witness statement, dated 15/16 January 1977, and the serialisation of her story in the *Daily Mail*.

17 Chris McCarthy, Personal Account, August 2017.

18 Ibid.

19 Police Constable Chris McCarthy, witness statement, 15 January 1977.

20 Derbyshire Constabulary, *Escape of William Thomas Hughes (Deceased) from Prison Officers: General Report of Police Search*.

21 Police Constable Chris McCarthy, witness statement, 15 January 1977.

22 Ibid.

23 Ibid.

24 Ibid.

25 Ibid.

26 Police Constable Paul Gardner, witness statement, 15 January 1977.

27 Ibid.

Chapter 14

1 *Daily Mail*, 'Police Shoot Kidnapper', 15 January 1977.

2 Gillian Moran, witness statement, 15/16 January 1977. Unless otherwise specified, all quotes in this chapter are taken from Gill Moran's witness statement, dated 15/16 January 1977, the serialisation of her story in the *Daily Mail* and Peter Howse's own memories of that night.

3 Peter Howse, internal report, January 1977.

4 Peter Howse, internal report, January 1977.

5 Ibid.

6 Police Constable Eric Harris, witness statement, 15 January 1977.

7 Chris McCarthy, Personal Account, August 2017.

8 Peter Howse, internal report, January 1977.

9 Detective Sergeant Frank Pell, witness statement, 18 January 1977.

10 Detective Inspector Peter Burgess, witness statement, 18 January 1977.

11 Police Constable Eric Harris, witness statement, 15 January 1977.

Chapter 15

1 Peter Howse, author reflections, 2019.

2 *Daily Mail*, 'The Murders at Pottery Cottage', Day Eight, 22 February 1977. Unless otherwise specified, all quotes in this chapter are taken from Gill Moran's witness statement, dated 15/16 January 1977, and the serialisation of her story in the *Daily Mail*.

3 John Slater, interview with authors, Chesterfield, 2017.

4 Anthony Pearce, interview with authors, Chesterfield, 2017.

5 Ibid.

6 A theory was later put forward in the press that the open window in Sarah's room was due to Amy climbing out and breaking a flower pot as she fell before alerting Len Newman and then crawling round to the front of the house where she was spotted by her daughter and the killer. However, Amy had already been severely wounded before she arrived at the car on the driveway, and it seems highly doubtful, if not impossible, that she could have survived the fall in her weakened and injured state, then made it round to the front. Gill remembered seeing her mother emerge from the front door, and there appears to have been no reason for her to jump from the window when she could move through the house.

7 Ann and Paul Goldthorpe, interview with authors, Sheffield, October 2018.

8 David Brown, interview with authors, Chesterfield, 2018.

9 Peter Howse, author reflections, 2019.

10 Jean Hughes, witness statement, 15 January 1977.

11 *Daily Mail*, 'The Pottery Cottage Murders', 28 August 1999.

12 Ibid.

13 *Observer*, 'Police: We Had to Shoot Killer', Michael Nally and Nigel Hawkes, 16 January 1977.

14 Anthony Pearce, witness statement.

15 Anthony Pierce, interview with authors, Chesterfield, 2017.

16 Peter Howse, author reflections, 2019.

17 *Daily Mail*, ' "My God, She's a Brave Woman" ', 17 January 1977.

18 Ibid.

19 Ibid.

20 *Daily Express*, 'He's Left Me Nothing', John Burns, Peggie Robinson, Paul Berra and Frank Welsby, 7 January 1977.

21 Ann and Paul Goldthorpe, interview with authors, Sheffield, October 2018.

22 David and Glynis Brown, interview with authors, Chesterfield, August 2018.

23 *Star*, 'Death Cottage Not Checked, Police Reveal', 18 January 1977.

24 Teresa O'Doherty, televised interview, 21 January 1977, for ATV.

25 Ibid.

26 *Lancashire Evening Post*, 'My Violent Marriage to Mad, Bullying Billy', 17 January 1977.

27 Ibid.

28 *Derbyshire Times*, 'Hughes' Wife Led Life of Terror', 21 January 1977.

29 *West Lancashire Evening Gazette*, 'I Want Billy Buried in Blackpool', 17 January 1977.

30 *West Lancashire Evening Gazette*, 'Psychopath to Get Roman Catholic Burial,' 18 January 1977.

31 *Lancashire Evening Post*, ' "Torment" of Mass Murderer', 19 January 1977.

32 *Daily Express*, 'Brave and Alone', Peggie Robinson, 22 January 1977.

33 Ibid.

Chapter 16

1 *Star*, 'Mass Murderer Cremated After 11th Hour Switch', 25 January 1977.

2 Ibid.

3 *Daily Mirror*, 'The Funeral of Mad Billy', Stanley Vaughan, 26 January 1977.

4 *Star*, 'Mass Murderer Cremated After 11th Hour Switch'.

5 *Daily Mirror*, 'The Funeral of Mad Billy'.

6 *West Lancashire Evening Gazette*, 'Give My Billy a Blackpool Mass', 26 January 1977.

7 Ibid.

8 *Sunday Mirror*, 'Baby Drama of the Knife Maniac', 23 January 1977.

9 *West Lancashire Evening Gazette*, 'Ashes Won't Be Kept Here', 27 January 1977.

10 *Daily Mail*, 'For Gill Moran, the Lonely Road Back', Lynda Lee-Potter, 24 February 1977.

11 Ibid.

12 Ibid.

13 Ibid.

14 Derbyshire Constabulary, *Escape of William Thomas Hughes (Deceased) from Prison Officers: General Report of Police Search*, Alfred Mitchell, Assistant Chief Constable, 14 February 1977.

15 *Daily Express*, 'He's Left Me Nothing', John Burns, Peggie Robinson, Paul Berra and Frank Welsby, 7 January 1977.

16 Peter Howse, author reflections, 2019.

17 *The Times*, 'Prison Officers' Threat after Inquiry Order', Clive Borrell, 18 January 1977.

18 Derbyshire Constabulary, *Escape of William Thomas Hughes (Deceased) from Prison Officers: General Report of Police Search*.

19 HM Chief of the Prison Service, *Report of an Inquiry by the Chief Inspector into the Security at HM Prison Leicester, and the Arrangements for Conducting Prisoners to Court (Escape of William Thomas Hughes on 12 January 1977)* (London: HMSO, 1977).

20 Ibid.

21 Ibid.

22 *Guardian*, 'The Blunders that Led to Tragedy', Malcolm Pithers, 11 March 1977.

23 Ibid.

24 Ibid.

25 Ibid.

26 Ibid.

27 *The Times*, 'Errors of Judgement led to Man's Escape from Leicester Prison', 11 March 1977.

28 *Daily Mail*, 'How Gill Moran Lost Her Family', Anthony Bevins, 11 March 1977.

29 *Guardian*, 'Warning on "Violent Hughes"', 27 April 1977.

30 *Derbyshire Times*, 'Police Hero Relives Fifty Minutes with Killer', Alex Leys and Barrie Farnsworth, 29 April 1977.

31 Ibid.

32 *The Times*, 'Police Shot Hughes to Save Woman Hostage', Arthur Osman, 28 April 1977.

33 Ibid.

34 Ibid.

35 Ibid.

36 Ibid.

37 *Daily Mail*, 'The Hero Who Rescued Gill Moran', Robert Turner and Alan Rees, 28 April 1977.

Epilogue

1 *The Times*, 'Stabbed Officers' Award Raised', Malcolm Stuart, June 1979.
2 Ibid.
3 *Leicester Mercury*, 'Knife Attack "Shaped the Life" of Hero Donald, 82', 16 July 2012.
4 *The Times*, 'Police Chief Awarded £4,000 for Paper's Libel', undated.
5 Ibid.
6 Chris McCarthy, Personal Account, August 2017.
7 Peter Howse, author reflections, 2019.
8 *Derby Telegraph*, 'The Hero Cop Who Brought Mass Murderer's Rampage to an End', Isaac Crowson, 22 November 2017.
9 Peter Howse, author reflections, 2019.
10 *London Gazette*, 4 June 1954.
11 Peter Howse, author reflections, 2019.
12 John Slater, interview with authors, Chesterfield, 2018.
13 *West Lancashire Evening Gazette*, 'Give My Billy a Blackpool Mass', 26 January 1977.
14 *West Lancashire Evening Gazette,* 'The Department of Health and Social Security "appeared to be choosy" who they prosecute in Blackpool', 29 September 1977.
15 Ibid.
16 Ibid.
17 Ibid.
18 Ibid.
19 *Glasgow Herald*, 'Killer's Widow Charge "Farce" ', 30 September 1977.
20 Ibid.
21 *Daily Mail*, 'The Pottery Cottage Murders', 28 August 1999.
22 Ibid.
23 Ibid.
24 Ibid.
25 Ibid.
26 Ibid.

27 Ibid.

28 *Daily Mail*, 'For Gill Moran, the Lonely Road Back', Lynda Lee-Potter, 24 February 1977.

29 Ibid.

30 Ibid.

31 *Star*, 'What Will Happen to the Cottage of Death?', 30 September 1977.

32 *Derbyshire Times*, 'Rumours of Film Company Buying Pottery Cottage', 14 October 1977.

33 Ibid.

34 *Derbyshire Times*, 'Pottery Cottage for Sale', 4 November 1977.

35 *Derbyshire Times*, 'Gill Moran Ordered to Keep Dog Under Control', 2 June 1978.

36 Ibid.

37 *Derbyshire Times*, 'Pottery Cottage Sold', 22 September 1978.

38 Ibid.

39 Ibid.

40 Ibid.

41 Ibid.

42 Ann and Paul Goldthorpe, interview with authors, Sheffield, October 2018.

43 *Daily Mirror*, 'Murder Wife's New Love', Margaret Hall, 24 November 1978.

44 Ibid.

45 Ann and Paul Goldthorpe, interview with authors, Sheffield, October 2018.

46 Ibid.

47 David Brown, interview with authors, Chesterfield, August 2018.

48 *Daily Express*, 'Pottery Cottage Survivor Gill's New Heartbreak', Declan Cunningham, 1 March 1988.

49 Ibid.

50 *Derbyshire Times*, 'Tragic Gill's Fresh Torment', 4 March 1988.

51 Ibid.

52 Ibid.

53 Ibid.

54 *Daily Mail*, 'The Pottery Cottage Murders', 28 August 1999.

Bibliography

Dickens, Charles, *Hard Times* (London: Penguin Classics, 2003).

Fowler, Gordon, HM Chief of the Prison Service, *Report of an Inquiry by the Chief Inspector into the Security at HM Prison Leicester, and the Arrangements for Conducting Prisoners to Court (Escape of William Thomas Hughes on 12 January 1977)* (London: HMSO, 1977). Internal report.

Laycock, Gloria K., *Absconding from Borstals: Home Office Research Study No. 41*, Her Majesty's Stationery Office, 1977.

Mitchell, Arthur, Assistant Chief Constable, Derbyshire Constabulary, *Escape of William Thomas Hughes (Deceased) from Prison Officers: General Report of Police Search*, 14 February 1977. Internal report.

Wolff, Michael, *Prison: The Prison System in Britain, How it Works, and What Life is Like in Prisons, Borstals and Other Penal Institutions* (London: Eyre & Spottiswoode, 1967).

Picture Credits

The Pottery Cottage Murders: Photo Insert

Photo 1: Source: PA Archive/PA Images.
Photo 2: Source: Solo Syndication.
Photo 3: Source: Ann Goldthorpe, private collection.
Photo 4: Source: *Derby Evening Telegraph*, 1977.
Photo 5: Source: Solo Syndication.
Photo 6: Source: Solo Syndication.
Photo 7: Source: Derbyshire Police.
Photo 8: Source: Derbyshire Police.
Photo 9: Source: Solo Syndication.
Photo 10: Source: John Winston Slater, private collection.
Photo 11: Source: John Winston Slater, private collection.
Photo 12: Source: John Winston Slater, private collection.
Photo 13: Source: John Winston Slater, private collection.
Photo 14: Source: PA Archive/PA Images.
Photo 15: Source: Derbyshire Police, author collection.
Photo 16: Source: John Winston Slater, private collection.
Photo 17: Source: Solo Syndication.

Photo 18: Source: *Derbyshire Times*, 1977.
Photo 19: Source: Solo Syndication.
Photo 20: Source: Brian Bould/ANL/Shutterstock.

Index